AF575395

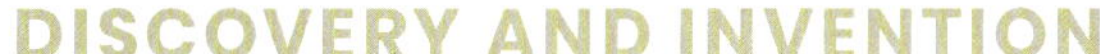

DISCOVERY AND INVENTION

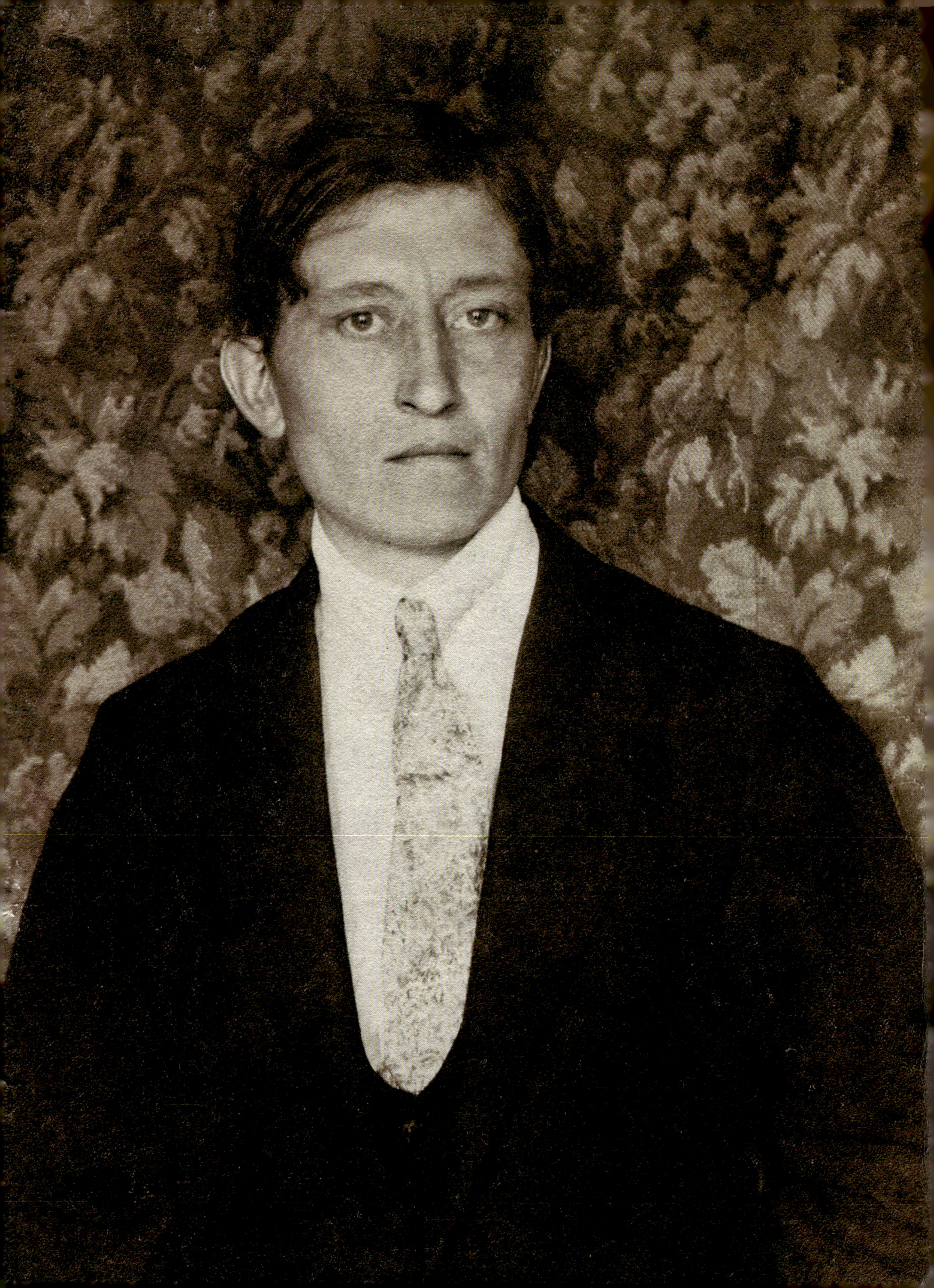

JOSEF ALBERS
DISCOVERY AND INVENTION
The Early Graphic Works

with texts by
David Cleaton-Roberts
Brenda Danilowitz
Jeannette Redensek

ART/BOOKS

In association with the
Josef and Anni Albers Foundation
and Cristea Roberts Gallery

PUBLISHER'S NOTE In keeping with the naming conventions of the Josef Albers catalogue raisonné, titles of works given by the artist are typeset in italic in the original language and translated if necessary: *Aufwärts* (Upward), *c.* 1926. Descriptive titles of works not given by the artist himself are set in roman and appear in English: Self-portrait, *c.* 1919; Vase with anemones, *c.* 1914.

TITLE PAGE Josef Albers, Bottrop, Germany, 1919

Published on the occasion of the exhibition
Josef Albers: Discovery and Invention,
Cristea Roberts Gallery, London

First published in the United Kingdom in 2021
by Art Books Publishing Ltd in association with
the Josef and Anni Albers Foundation and
Cristea Roberts Gallery

Art Books Publishing Ltd
77 Oriel Road
London E9 5SG
Tel: +44 (0)20 8533 5835
info@artbookspublishing.co.uk
www.artbookspublishing.co.uk

British Library Cataloguing-in-Publication Data
A catalogue record for this book is available from the British Library

ISBN 978-1-908970-57-2

Editorial, design, reprographics, and production
by Art Books Publishing Ltd

Printed and bound in Italy by EBS

Distributed outside North America by
Thames & Hudson
181a High Holborn
London WC1V 7QX
United Kingdom
Tel: +44 (0)20 7845 5000
Fax: +44 (0)20 7845 5055
sales@thameshudson.co.uk

Available in North America through
ARTBOOK | D.A.P.
75 Broad Street, Suite 630
New York, N.Y. 10004
www.artbook.com

Contents

‘Art as a creative process is discovery and invention. We consider it a creative rather than productive process, as creation leads to spiritual effect, and production to practical result.’

Josef Albers, 1946

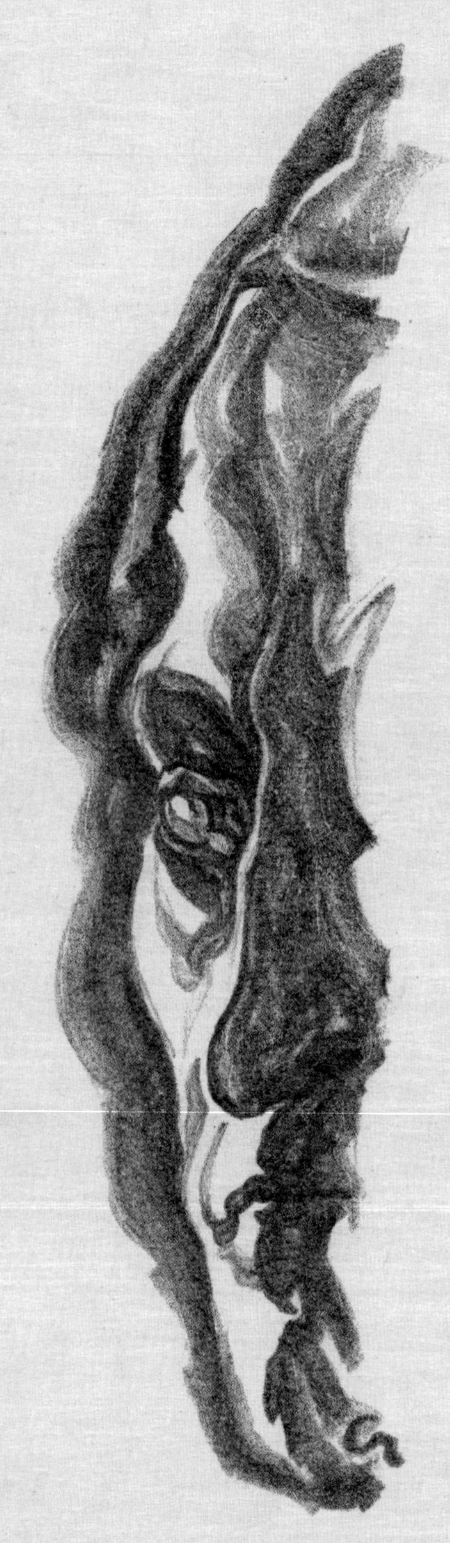

David Cleaton-Roberts

Foreword

OPPOSITE *Self-Portrait 'Mephisto'*, 1916, lithograph, paper 34.9 × 26.7 cm, image 21.3 × 5.1 cm. Josef and Anni Albers Foundation, 1976.4.20

OVERLEAF *Sandgrube II* (Sandmine II), state II, 1916 (detail)

Josef Albers painted his first *Homage to the Square* in 1950 at the age of sixty-two, and he made the first silkscreen version eleven years later in 1961. While it is true that this series preoccupied him for the remainder of his life, the great myth of Albers is that it was only through this one geometric form that he articulated his panoply of theories on colour and composition. Instead, this relatively late body of work represented a distillation and a clarity born from years of development, revision and, experimentation. It was the culmination of a lifetime of complex artistic investigation, an evolution revealed through the historical arc of his printmaking practice.

Albers was a naturally gifted printmaker who pushed techniques and materials to new limits. The progression from his first print – a small linoleum cut made in 1915 – to the final portfolios of *Variants* and *Squares* is neither straightforward nor predictable, and straddles the key movements of twentieth-century art. From his powerful early Expressionist compositions – which he later disavowed – to the graphics he made at the Bauhaus, at Black Mountain College, and, finally, during his tenure at Yale, it is in his prints that Albers honed the abstract aesthetic for which he is now celebrated.

In this book, Jeannette Redensek and Brenda Danilowitz focus on the development of his graphic art, providing fascinating new insights into the works and highlighting the personal and historical context in which they were created. Both in their essays and through their unrivalled access to archive material at the Josef and Anni Albers Foundation, they show how for Albers printmaking lay at the heart of his practice, his teachings, and his beliefs.

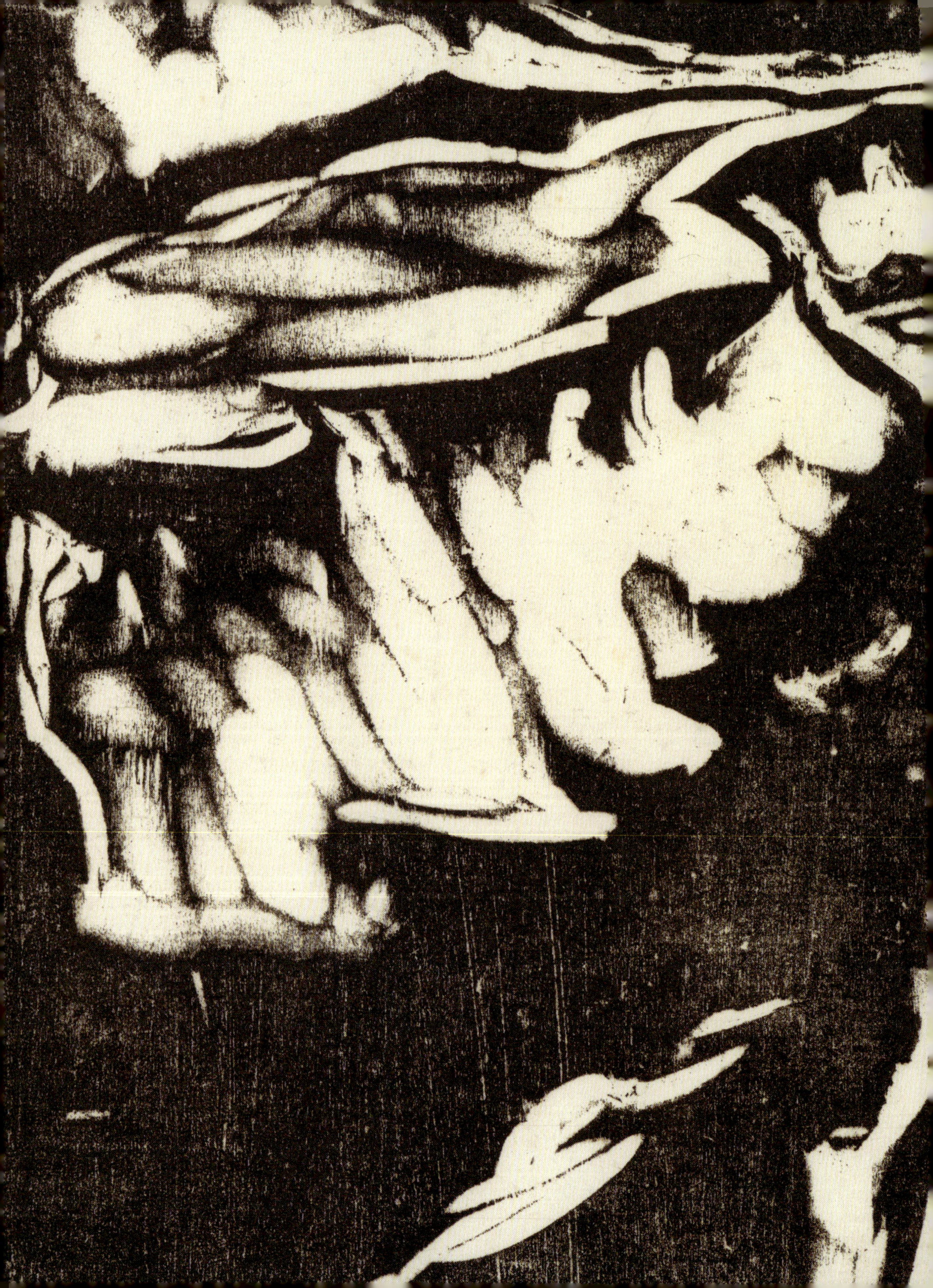

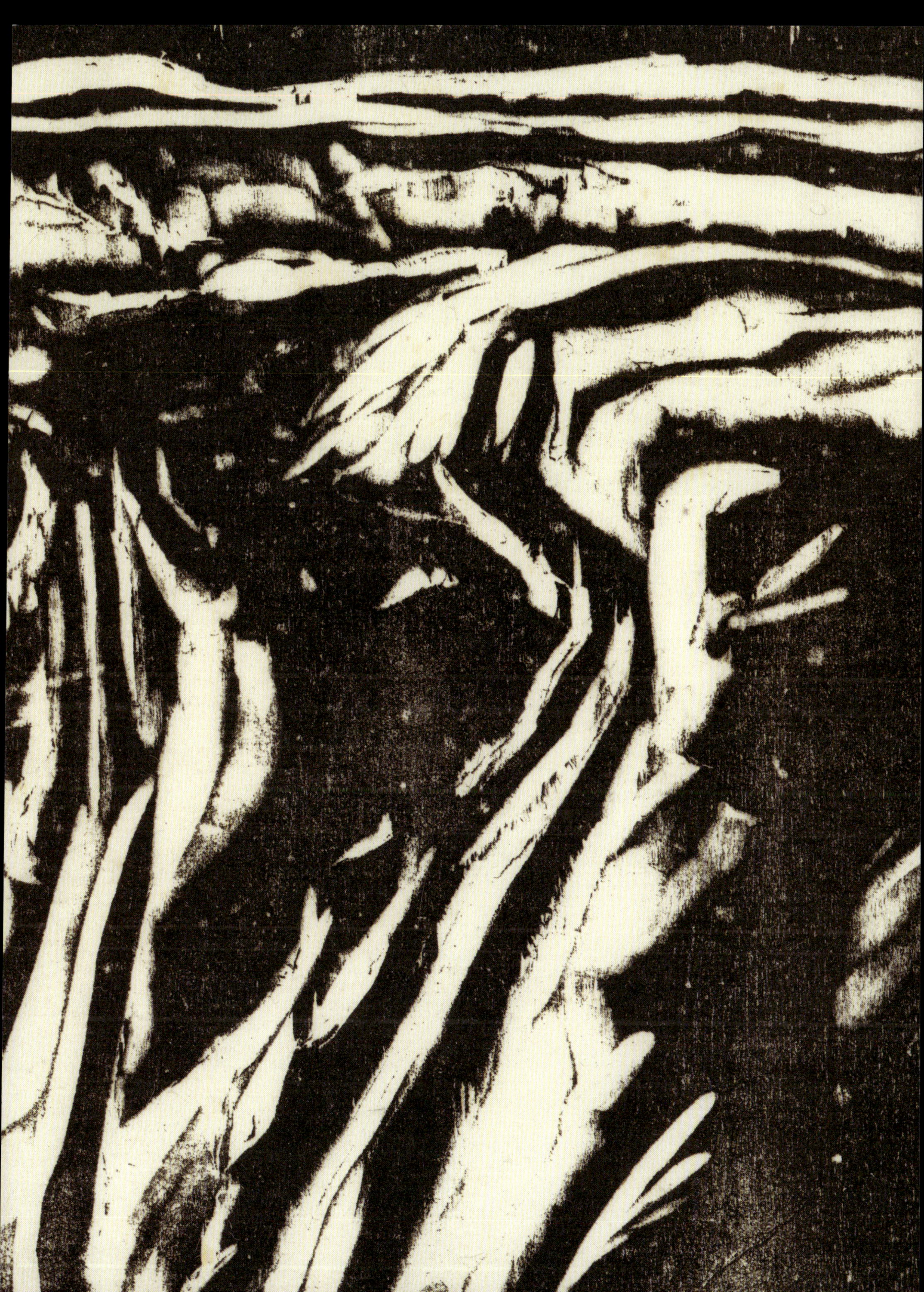

Frau Amtsvogt Nehemb. — An diese wiederum reihten sich die Verwandten und Freunde des Hauses: die Ratsherrn Grave und von Lengerke mit ihren Gattinnen, die greise Frau Modemann mit ihrem Sohne, dem regierenden Bürgermeister, der Kaufmann Rutger Vortkamp und manche andere in ihren Festtagskleidern. — Die Tafel war mit dem feinsten, weißen Damastlaken belegt, in welches eine ganze Jagd eingewirkt war. Das Tafeltuch war mit prächtigen, selbstgeklöppelten Spitzen besetzt, und das längs darüber gelegte, in bunten Farben gestickte Zwehl, welches ebenfalls mit breiten Spitzen umrändert und durchsetzt war, war ein Triumpf der feinen Nadelarbeit. Kunstvolle Pokale und Becher in Glas, Zinn und Silber zierten den Tisch, dazwischen waren blaue Delfter Vasen mit Herbstblumen aufgestellt. Man speiste von zinnernen Tellern, deren Rand in Rosenform gehalten war, mit silbernem Gerät. Die Becher klangen, verbindliche Redensarten wurden herüber und hinüber gewechselt, und so war man allmählich beim Nachtisch angekommen, der aus mancherlei seltsam geformtem Backwerk und köstlichen eingesottenen Früchten bestand. — Da trat durch die Tür von der Küche her ein junges Weib, welches den Täufling in seinen Armen hielt, ins Steinwerk ein. Es war Marie Mejer, die Amme des Kindes. Stolze Mutterfreude leuchtete auf dem feinen, regelmäßigen Gesichte Frau Anna's auf und strahlte aus ihren seelenvollen, großen Augen. Marie Mejer war ebenfalls in ihrem Sonntagsstaat. Die silberne Haube und das buntgestickte weiße Schultertuch, sowie das Filigrankreuz, welches sie an reicher Verkettung um den Hals trug, kennzeichneten sie als Ehefrau, wenn sie auch keinen Ring am Finger getragen hätte. Der Täufling war im Steckkissen, Puck genannt. Er trug ein kleines gesticktes Häubchen. Das seidene Taufzeug war reich mit Kanten benäht. Marie Mejer reichte jedem der Gäste den Täufling hin, und jeder, der ihn in seine Arme schloß, ließ ein Geldstück in der Amme Hand gleiten. So wollte es die Sitte. Auch Marie's Gesicht leuchtete; besonders, als sie den Kleinen aus seines Vaters Armen zurücknahm; die Gabe mußte keine geringe gewesen sein. Nachdem alle das Kind nach Gebühr bewundert hatten, verließ die Amme mit ihm die Steinkammer. „Der kleine Hans hat ganz seines Vaters Augen," sagte die alte Frau Modemann. „Ich meine, er ist der lieben Frau Anna wie aus dem Gesichte geschnitten," entgegnete Rutger Vortkamp. „Hoffentlich bekommt er der Mutter Schönheit und des Vaters Verstand", sprach Herr Caspar Mönnich. „Und wächst heran zu seiner Eltern und unser aller Freude," fügte der Junker von Böselager hinzu. „Glück und Segen, Heil und Friede soll er diesem Hause bringen," sagte der Ratsherr Grave, „und wolkenlos wie der heutige Tag möge ihm und seinen verehrlichen Eltern das Leben dahinfließen.

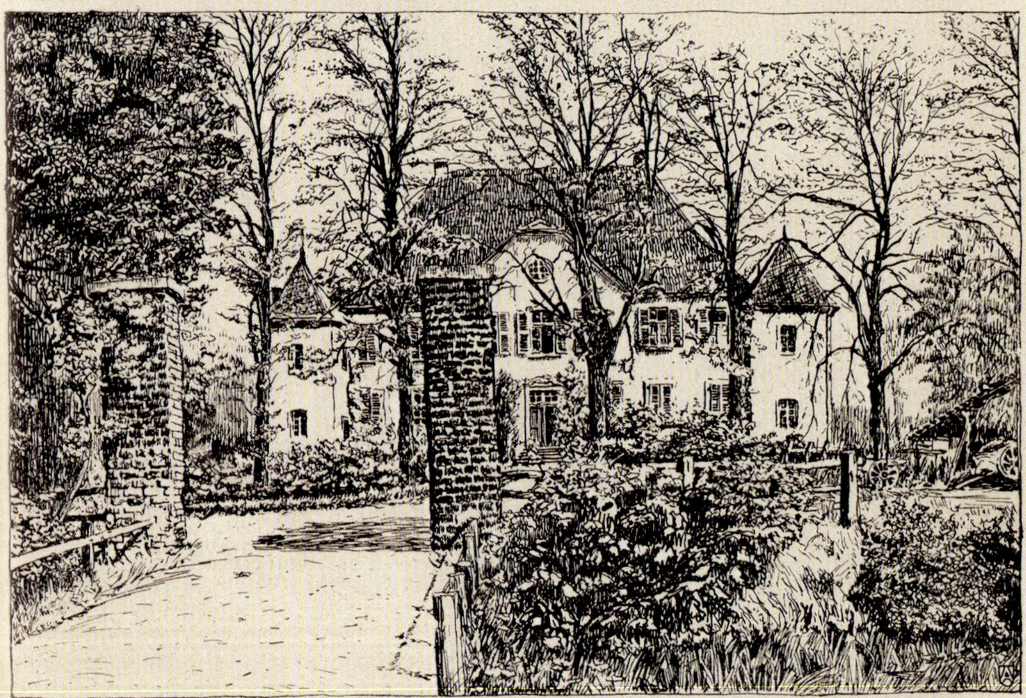

Kommende Welheim bei Bottrop. Jos. Albers, Bottrop.

Jeannette Redensek

Josef Albers: *Heimatkünstler*

Kommende Welheim bei Bottrop, from *De Kiepenkerl*, no. 4 (1913)

Some time in or around 1913 the world learned that Josef Albers was an artist. On page 33 of that year's *De Kiepenkerl: Westfälischer Volkskalender*[1] appeared a pen-and-ink sketch of Kommende Welheim, an eighteenth-century manor house near Bottrop, Albers's home town in Westphalia.[2] The artist's identity was quietly trumpeted by a monogrammed 'A' inscribed lower right and captioned in Fraktur type beneath: 'Jos. Albers, Bottrop'. The drawing was one among many by several artists scattered through the issue – bucolic vistas of cottages amidst cultivated fields and distant hills, birds soaring against the cumulus clouds of midsummer.

In 1913, there was nothing more typically German than a small-town school teacher having his sketches published in a local *Heimatkalender*. In the years before the First World War, nearly every region in the country had such a publication, and teachers were among the most frequent contributors. The genre of the popular *Volkskalender* first appeared in the early nineteenth century and flourished thereafter throughout Europe. The journals took many forms, presented as almanacs, yearbooks, farmers' calendars, all dedicated to the experiences, memories, and aspirations of the local population.[3] *De Kiepenkerl* is considered the first of the Westphalian *Heimat* journals. It was founded and edited by Dr Augustin Wibbelt (1862–1947), a historian and Catholic priest from the Münsterland in north-west Germany near the Dutch border, as well as a leading advocate for the preservation of Plattdeutsch, a dialect of the region.[4] In Westphalia and the Münsterland, the name 'Kiepenkerl' is almost as familiar as Santa Claus. The figure of the wandering

1. *De Kiepenkerl: Westfälischer Volkskalender*, nos. 1–7 (Essen: Verlag von Fredebeul & Koenen, 1909–15).

2. The author and the Josef and Anni Albers Foundation are grateful to Herr Ulrich Söbbing of the Stadtarchiv Stadtlohn, who in 2008 and 2010 first drew our attention to these early drawings by Josef Albers in the *De Kiepenkerl*, along with two drawings reproduced on postcards.

3. See Thomas Ostendorf, 'Westfälische Heimatkalender. Eine Bibliographie', in Alfred Brun (ed.), *Kalender in Westfalen: Dokumentation* (Münster: Landschafttsverband Westfalen-Lippe, Westfälisches Archivamt, 1984), p. 114; and Karl Ditt, 'Vom Heimatschutz zur Heimatbewegung: Westfalen 1875–1915', *Westfälische Forschungen*, no. 39 (1989):, pp. 232–55.

4. See 'Augustin Wibbelt' in *Lexikon Westfälischer Autorinnen und Autoren 1750 bis 1950*, https://www.lwl.org, accessed 13 June 2019; and Robert Peters, 'Augustin Wibbelt (1862_1947): Dichter des Münsterlandes', *Heimatpflege in Westfalen*, vol. 26, no. 1 (2013), pp. 1–8.

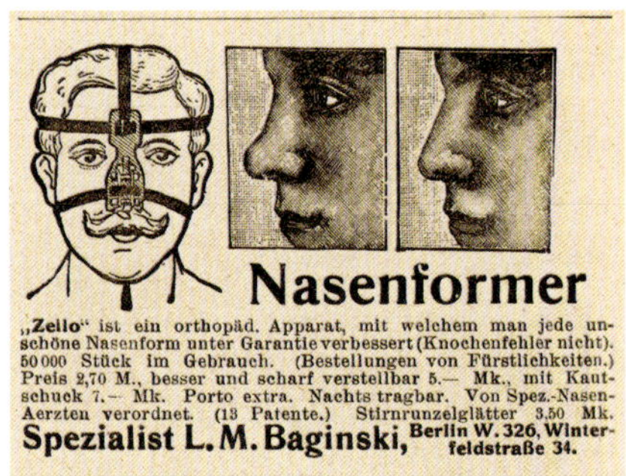

Advertisement for a 'nose former', created by Berlin 'specialist' L. M. Baginski, from *De Kiepenkerl*, no. 5 (1914). The caption reads: '"Zello" is an orthopaedist. An apparatus with which every unsightly nose shape can be improved, under guarantee (not bone defects). 50,000 pieces in use (orders from princes). Price 2.70 marks; better and more sharply adjustable, 5 marks; with rubber, 7 marks. Postage extra. Wearable at night. Prescribed by specialist nose doctors (13 patents). Frown straightener, 3.50 marks.'

peddler – the '*Kerl*' with his '*Kiep*', the basket of goods he carries on his back, while he travels with a walking stick in hand, smoking a pipe – was memorialized in an 1896 statue by August Schmiemann (1846–1927) in Münster's Spiekerhof, and has appeared for more than a century on beer steins, tobacco boxes, and seed packets.

In all of its nostalgic and pedantic glories, *De Kiepenkerl* serves as a document of the times. It is like the deep, narrow trenches that archaeologists dig through certain sites, especially where an area's modest historical importance does not merit a full excavation, but where the recovery of simple artefacts can reveal so much about everyday habits. The pages of *De Kiepenkerl* offer something of a narrow excavation through the milieux of Albers's life in the first decade and a half of the twentieth century. Especially in the advertisements tucked into the back of each issue, one senses the habits, hopes, and needs of the readers. There are the expected agricultural implements and aids, fertilizers, weedkillers, seeds, and announcements for new varieties of potato and rutabaga. Tobacco and the pipes in which to smoke it. Pocket knives and safety razors from Solingen. Musical instruments, notably accordions and zithers. Miracle cures that offer hope to all sufferers of pain, broken bones, cancer, skin ailments, stuttering, rheumatism, alcoholism, nervousness, headaches, constipation, jitters, and muscle cramps. Hair dye and rouge, for men. Remarkable technologies of the physical self: braces, trusses, and corsets, contraptions that promise to correct the posture and to make the nose more shapely. And here and there are small inserts that speak to the changing times of Westphalia. A ship travelling twice weekly between Bremen and New York, also twice a month to Brazil. A country school offering courses in management, bookkeeping, and secretarial skills for the sons of farmers and other young men with good handwriting.

Between 1913 and 1915, eleven drawings by Albers were published in *De Kiepenkerl*. In the 1913 issue alone, there were five: views of churches in Coesfeld, the spires of Vreden – historical and

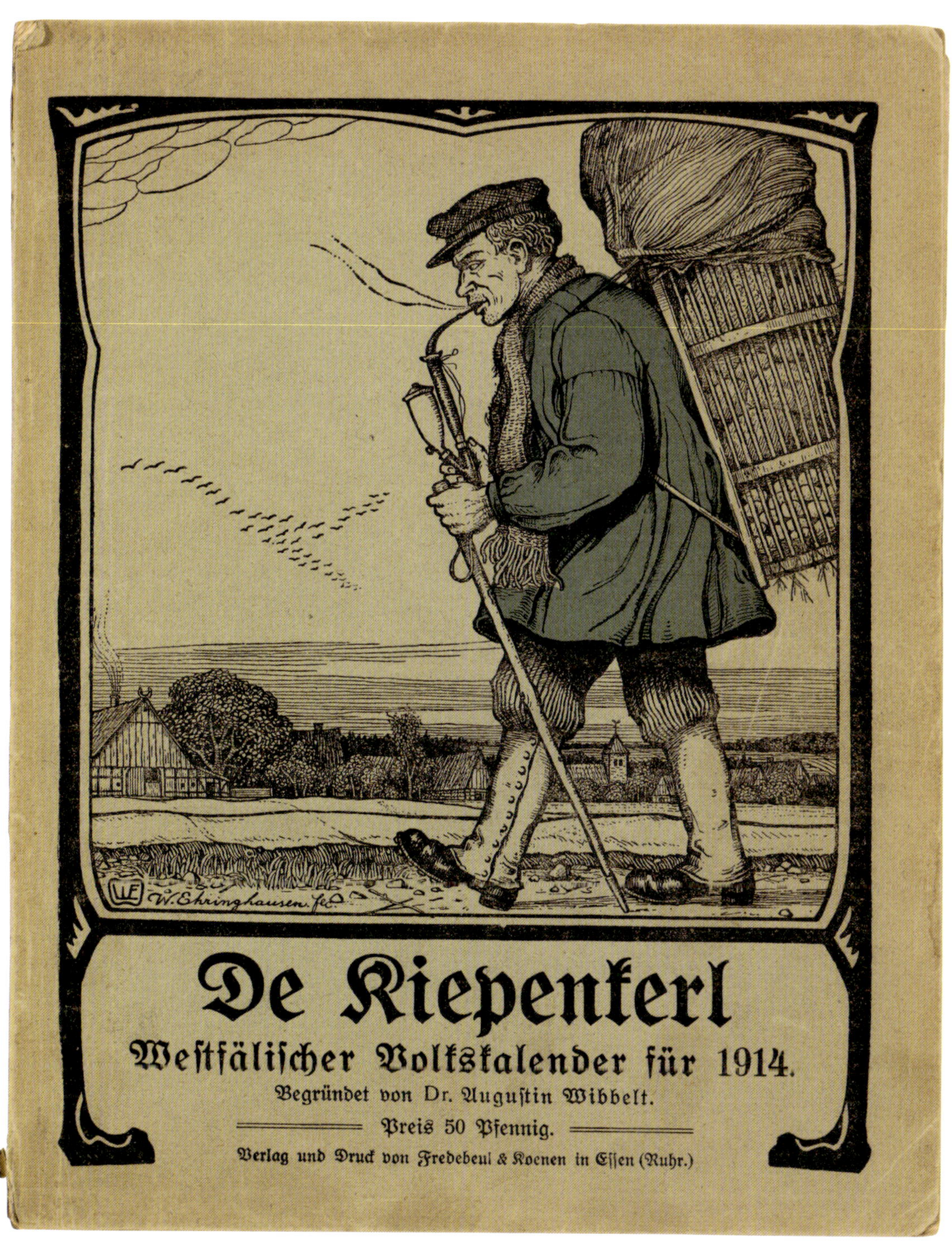

The cover of *De Kiepenkerl: Westfälischer Volkskalender für 1914*, edited by Dr Augustin Wibbelt and printed by Verlag von Fredebeul & Koenen, Essen

vernacular monuments of the Münsterland. In the 1915 issue, six more drawings by Albers were reproduced: a village street, a wayside chapel, an old city wall, a mill, a dark church crypt. The subjects are in keeping with the homey, regional character of the magazine. Across its seven-year run, *De Kiepenkerl* published many drawings, all of which were by any measure of artistic judgment competently drafted according to the traditions of landscape composition. A few of the drawings made by Albers follow these conventions: idealized, lyrical, romantic. But the other drawings by him are different. They are different in composition, different in choice of subject matter, different in the manner in which they are delineated. These sketches are, firstly, not sentimentalized views of pastoral landscapes. No well-ploughed fields or tidy cottages; no birds wheeling against summer clouds. Instead, Albers sought a kind of *realism* – which is not to say that the drawings were not at the same time completely confected. Realism is also an abstraction of the perceived world. This was Josef Albers as a young artist as he learned to manage the coefficient between what is seen and how it is portrayed, between what the eye perceives and how the hand depicts those perceptions on the paper. It was not just a matter of representing the visible world: it was about making an interesting picture. In the way that he chose his subjects, framed those subjects, and rendered those subjects, Albers sought an alternative artistic economy of the pastoral.

In the best of these early drawings, Albers superimposed compositional elements and compressed space in a manner associated with photography, indeed, with snapshots. There is an understated, almost theatrical aspect to the views wherein the putative or titular subject of the drawing is largely masked in favour of what otherwise would be considered secondary elements of a composition. For instance, the grand country house in Welheim is glimpsed through its entry gate, the facade visible behind an enfilade of just-leafing trees. The largest part of the drawing is

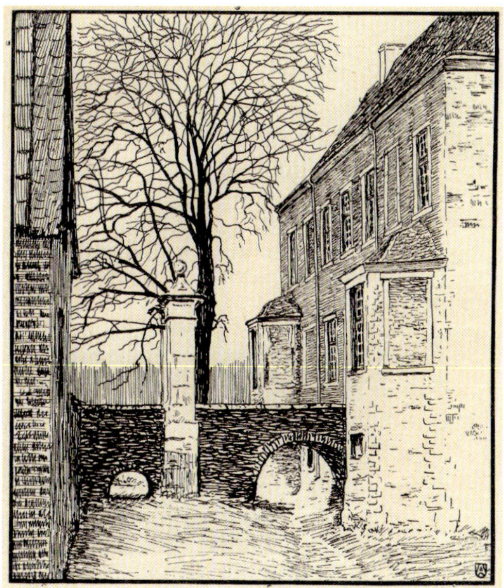

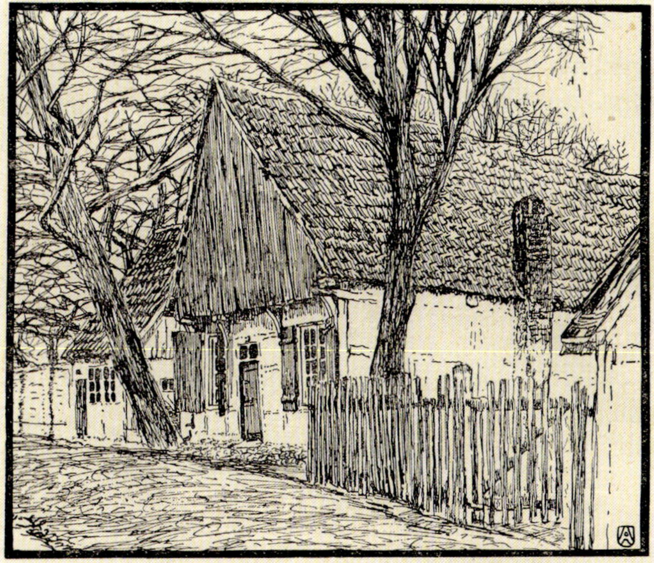

ABOVE *Haus Vondern bei Osterfeld*, from *De Kiepenkerl*, no. 6 (1915). Stadtarchiv, Stadtlohn

ABOVE RIGHT *Altes Haus in Telgte*, from *De Kiepenkerl*, no. 6 (1915). Stadtarchiv, Stadtlohn

devoted to the foliage, stone, and brick of the house's front gardens and border walls. Two years later, the manor house of Burg Vondern near Osterfeld is presented not as a stately elevation, but as a foreshortened and shadowed plane pressed tight to the right side of the picture while the just-visible strip of a brick outbuilding frames the left. In between stands what seems to be the true subject of the drawing: a dark and looming, bare-branched tree silhouetted against the sky.

Albers had a feeling for the materiality of things, the way the depicted world could be built up out of textures rendered in strokes of pen and ink. He could imply the aged state of surfaces: the vertical grain of the old wooden slatted fence and gable of an old house in Telgte, the rounded flow of the worn cobblestone street, the stippled rhythm of the tiled roof. In using such a range of rendering marks, he demonstrated his awareness of the kinds of materials and techniques that might best translate into printed reproduction: cross-hatching parallel lines such as would also be used in etchings or woodcuts (although he had not yet worked in those media).

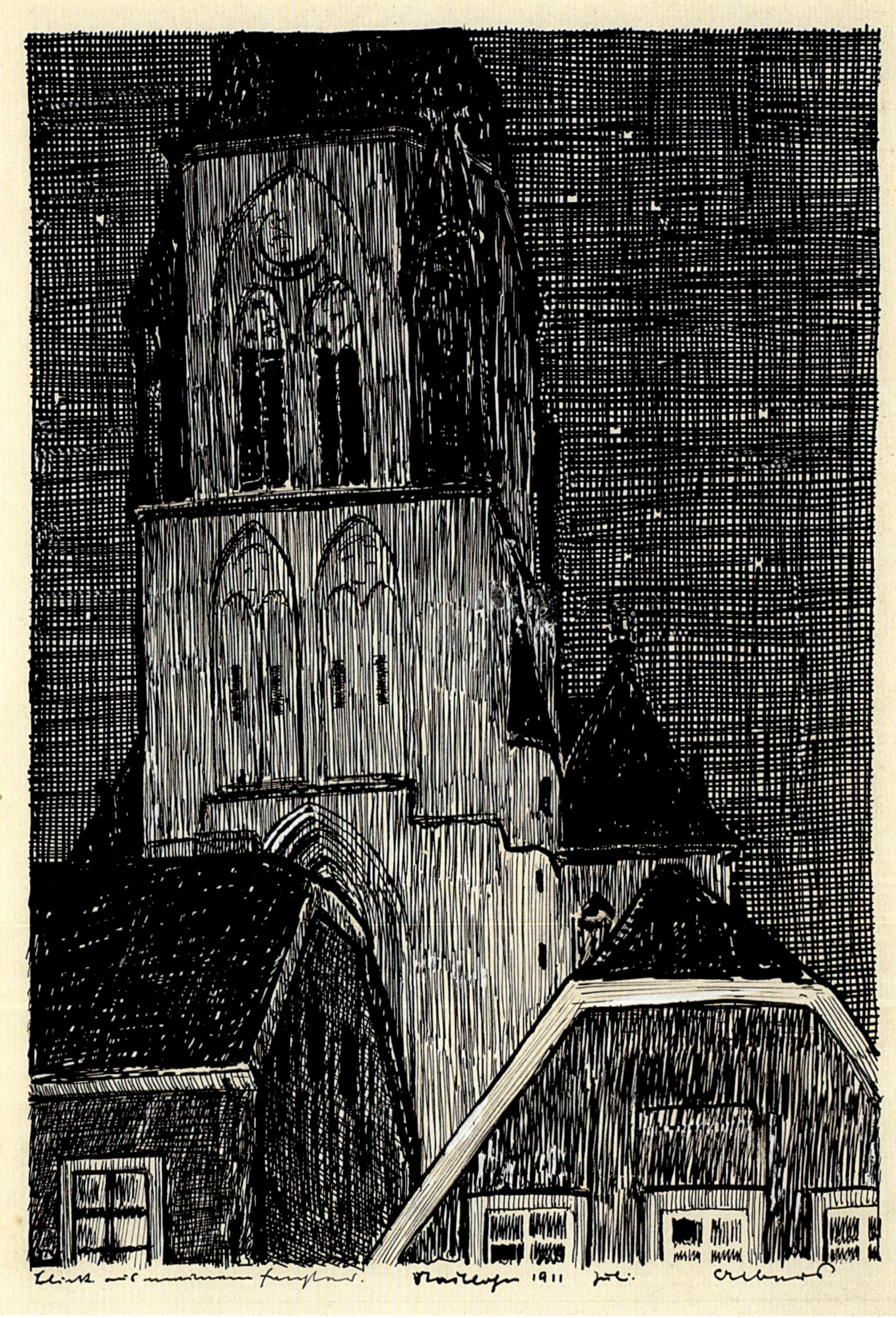

OPPOSITE *Blick aus meinem Fenster Stadtlohn 1911 Juli*, 1911, ink on paper with white gouache, 28.8 × 20.3 cm. Josef and Anni Albers Foundation, 1976.3.1

RIGHT *View of St Otger, Stadtlohn*, c. 1911, postcard. Stadtarchiv Stadtlohn

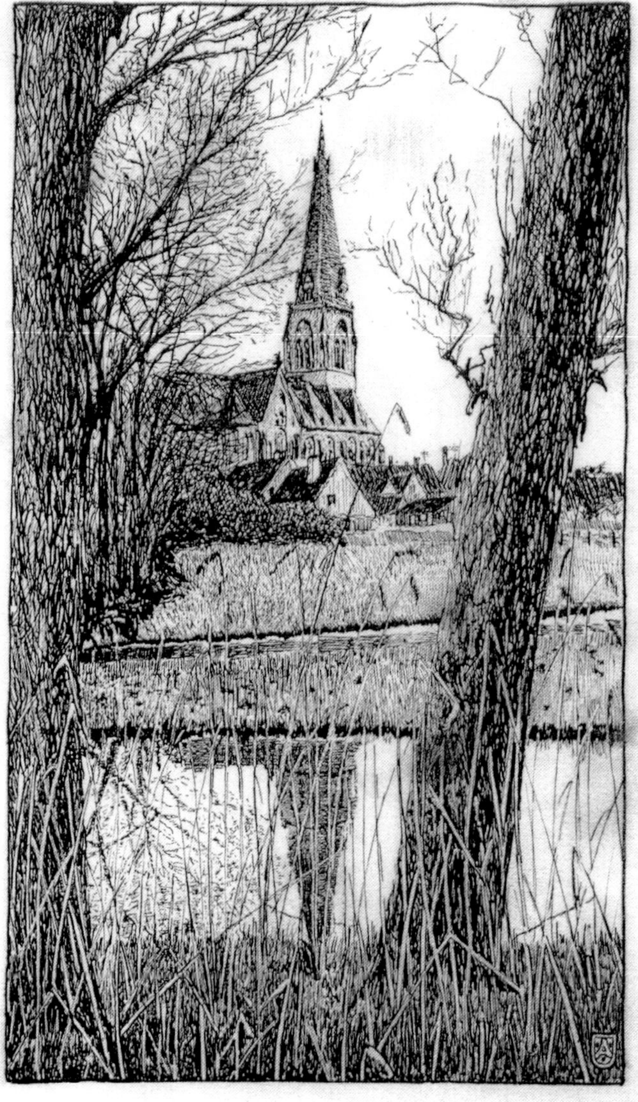

Albers's original drawings for the *De Kiepenkerl* illustrations are now lost. Only a very few works from this early period still exist. An ink drawing, *Blick aus meinem Fenster Stadtlohn 1911 Juli* (View from my window in Stadtlohn July 1911), made while Albers was a school teacher in that small market town, depicts a moonlit scene of the Catholic church of St Otger.[5] The Stadtarchiv Stadtlohn has postcards with reproductions of drawings of a wayside pilgrimage chapel and another view of St Otger, published around 1911 by

5. This drawing was also published in an early *Heimat* journal, *Westmünsterland: Zeitschrift für Heimatpflege*, no. 2 (1915), p. 53. The foundations of St Otger dated from the sixteenth century; the church drawn by Albers was completed in 1892.

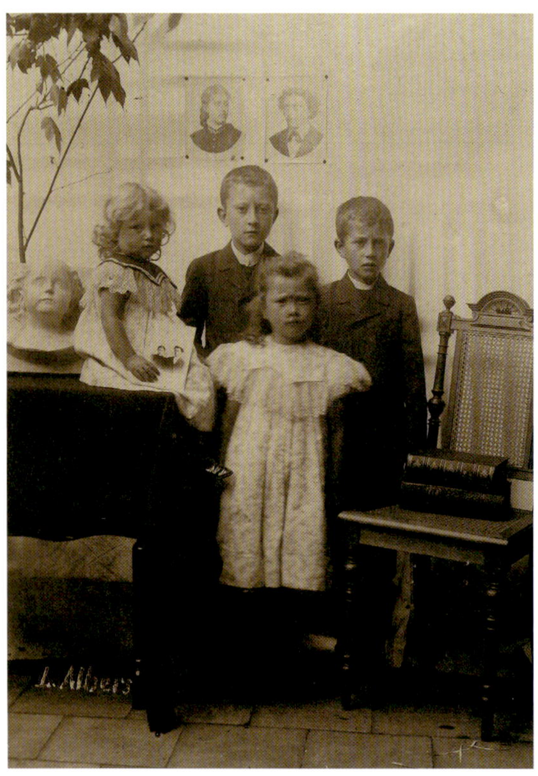

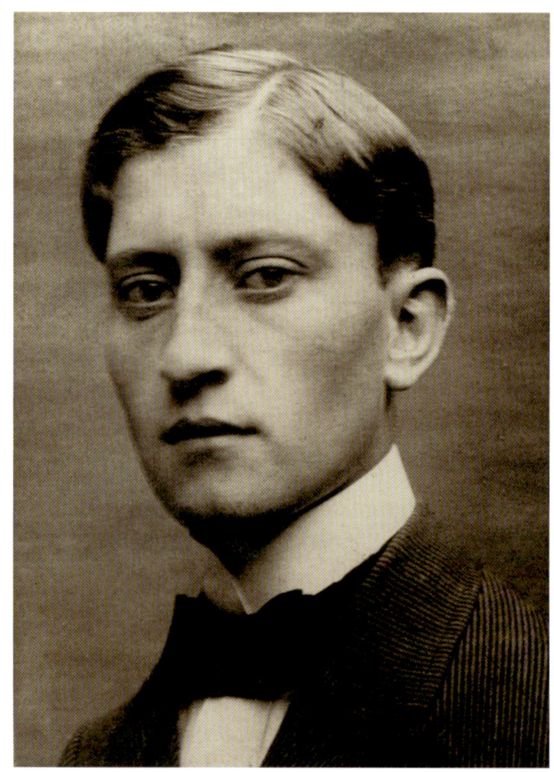

ABOVE LEFT Josef Albers (centre) and his siblings, 1899

ABOVE RIGHT Josef Albers, 1908

Verlag Caspar Wüllner Stadtlohn. A drawing of a farmer's cottage in Bottrop-Boy from the same period was given by Albers to a friend, and it remains in that family to the present day.

Josef Albers was born in 1888 into the family of a skilled craftsman. His father Lorenz Albers was a *Anstreichermeister* and a leading member of the guild of *Malerinnung*, the master painters of interiors, including such features as decorative mouldings and borders, faux surfaces, as well as walls, doors, and woodwork.[6] Even by the turn of the twentieth century, it was evident that the demand for the craft speciality was fading. As the clever, oldest son of four children, Albers did not follow in his father's footsteps, but was rather sent in 1902 at the age of fourteen to begin training as an elementary-school teacher at the Präparandenschule in Langenhorst, north of Bottrop. Three years later, he moved on to the

6. See Johannes Geurts (ed.), *Fünfzig Jahre Malerinnung Bottrop* (Bottrop: Buch- und Verlagsdruckerei W. Postberg, 1955).

7. For more on Albers's early life and education, see Brenda Danilowitz, 'Teaching Design: A Short History of Josef Albers', in Frederick A. Horowitz and Brenda Danilowitz, *Josef Albers: To Open Eyes. The Bauhaus, Black Mountain, and Yale* (London: Phaidon, 2006).

8. Fritz Bause papers, Josef and Anni Albers Foundation Archive.

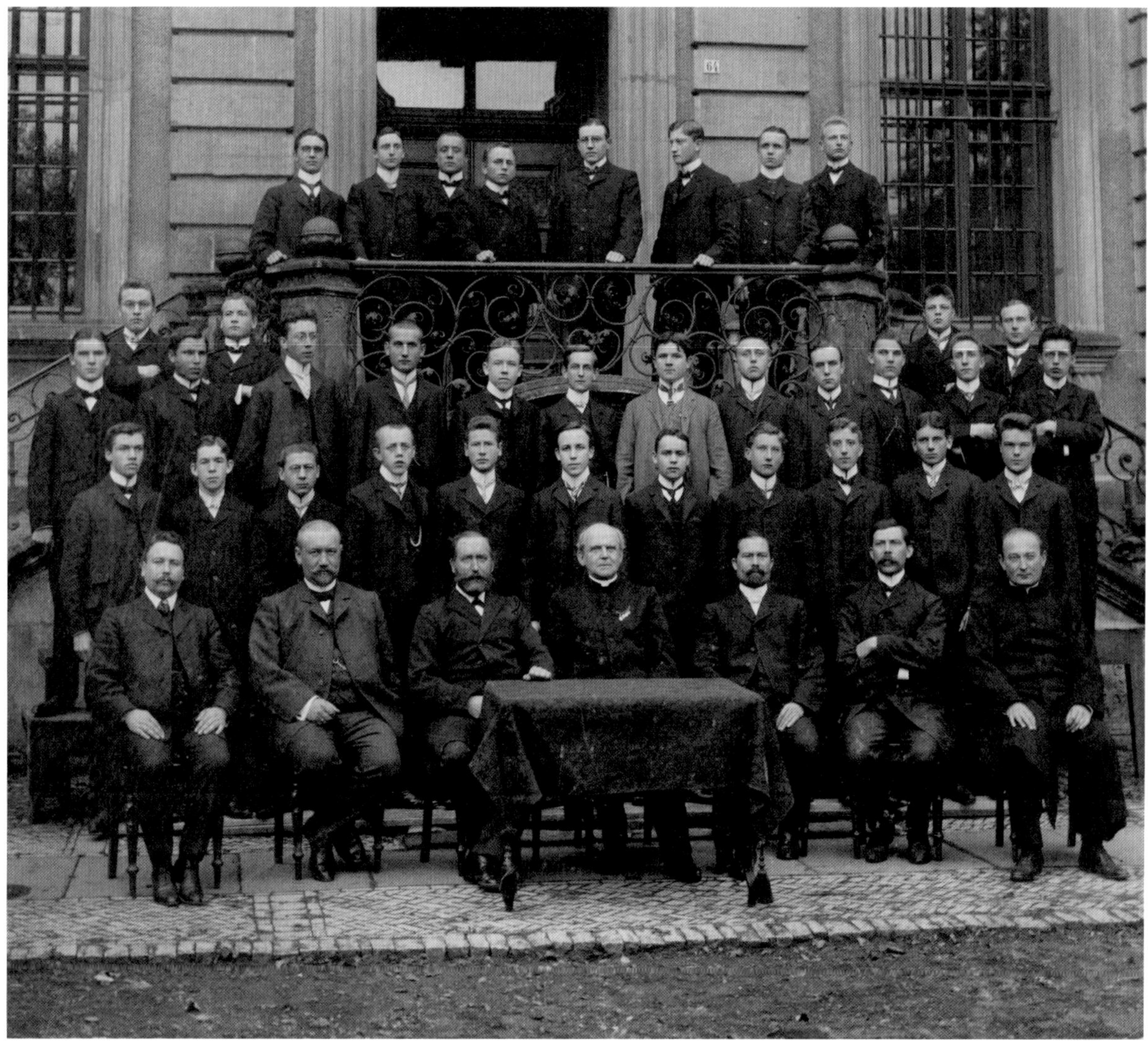

Graduating class of the Lehrerseminar Büren in 1908. Josef Albers is in the back row, third from right.

Lehrerseminar in Büren. Upon his graduation, he taught from 1908 to 1913 in rural and town schools throughout the region.[7]

A fellow student-teacher at Büren recalled that young Jupp Albers was always drawing while a student there.[8] In the years immediately after his graduation, he continued to draw portraits and to make plein-air sketches in the streets and fields. But more than just making drawings, by 1911, just three years out of teachers' seminary, he was having his sketches printed on postcards by the

Self-portrait, *c.* 1914–15, pencil on paper, 43.5 × 33.3 cm. Josef and Anni Albers Foundation, 1976.3.5

town's book press, and sending off drawings for publication in the local history almanac. Josef Albers wanted to be an artist, and within the confines of his rural and small-town world, he made the most of every opportunity he encountered to become an artist.[9]

By 1911, he was as well-acquainted with the flat fields and watery meadows of the Münsterland – of Vreden, Coesfeld, Stadtlohn, Nottuln, and Telgte – as he was with the farms and villages around Bottrop. When looking at his drawings from these early years, one is struck that, as with any young and curious artist, Albers was someone who learned and changed with every fresh sheet of paper torn from the sketchpad.

His choices of subject matter during these years trace the economic and demographic changes affecting the entire region of Westphalia. At the time of Albers's birth in Bottrop in 1888, the town had a population of around 13,000; when he returned to teach in the town's Josefsschule in September 1911, there were 50,000 people. Bottrop was being transformed by industry. Mineyards and sandpits were consuming the farms and fields; new housing for workers lined the roads that spidered southwards toward Essen and north towards Gladbeck. Two-hundred-year-old, half-timbered cottages were felled to make way for factories; baroque-era country houses, levelled to make way for headframes. What this meant was that many of the landscapes that Albers drew were scenes that were practically disappearing as he limned them. The farmer's cottage at Bottrop-Boy that he sketched around 1911 was likely demolished by 1915; the manor house at Burg Vondern was nearly swallowed by the tailings from neighbouring mines.

In 1913, Albers took a two-year leave of absence from teaching to study for a certificate in art education at the Königliche Kunstschule (Royal School of Art) in Berlin. The curriculum, shaped by artist-educator Philipp Franck, emphasized drawing.[10] While in Berlin, Albers had ample opportunities to see original works of modern as well as historical art.

9. For an in-depth discussion of Albers's early years as an artist and art student, see the catalogue edited by Ulrike Growe for her exhibition at the Josef Albers Museum Quadrat Bottrop, *Der junge Albers: Aufbruch in die Moderne* (Munich: Hirmer Verlag, 2019).

10. See Jeannette Brabenetz, 'Von der Natur sehen lernen. Philipp Francks Wirken als Zeichenlehrer und Reformer', in *Der junge Josef Albers. Aufbruch in die Moderne*, pp. 59–66.

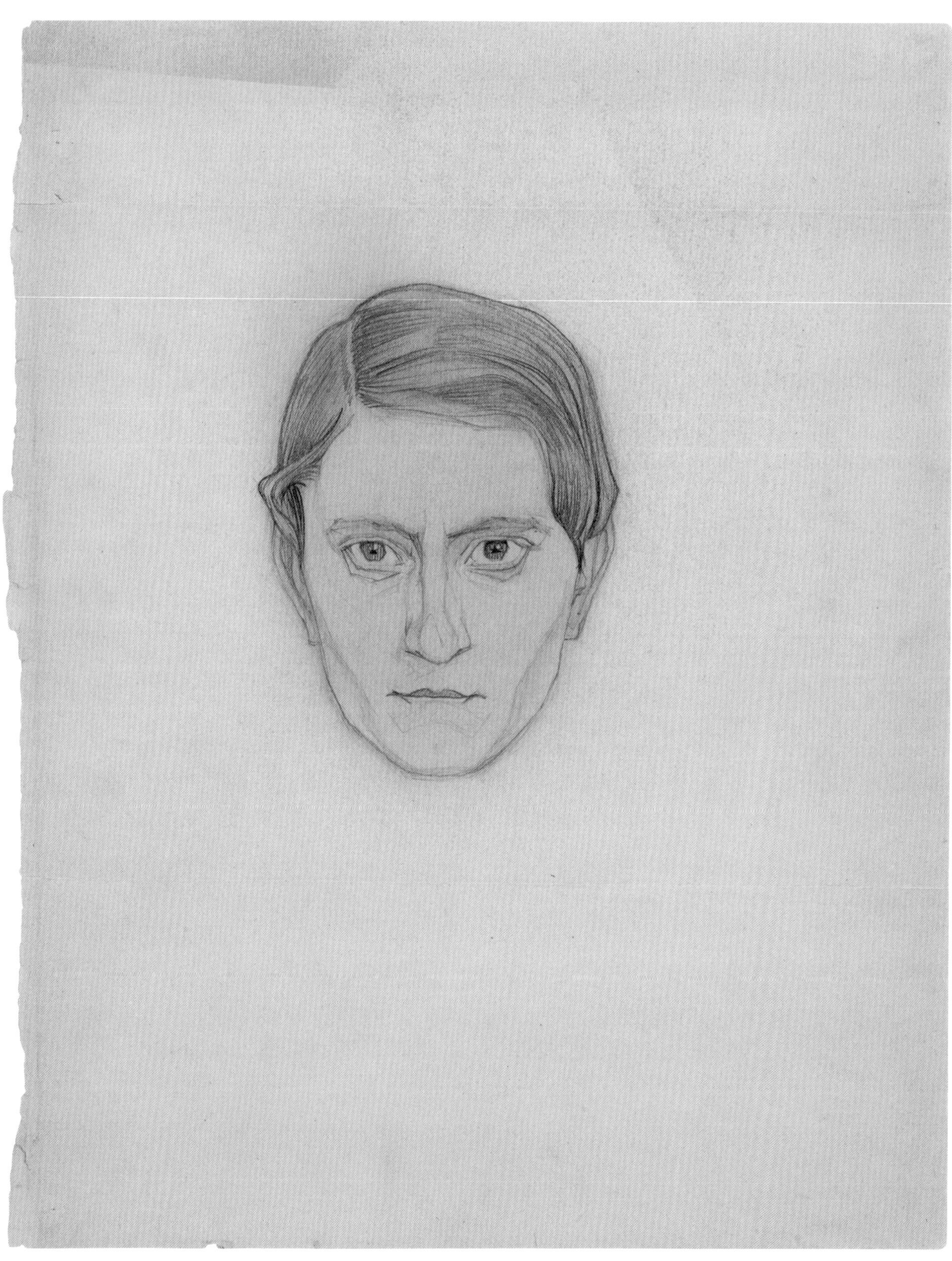

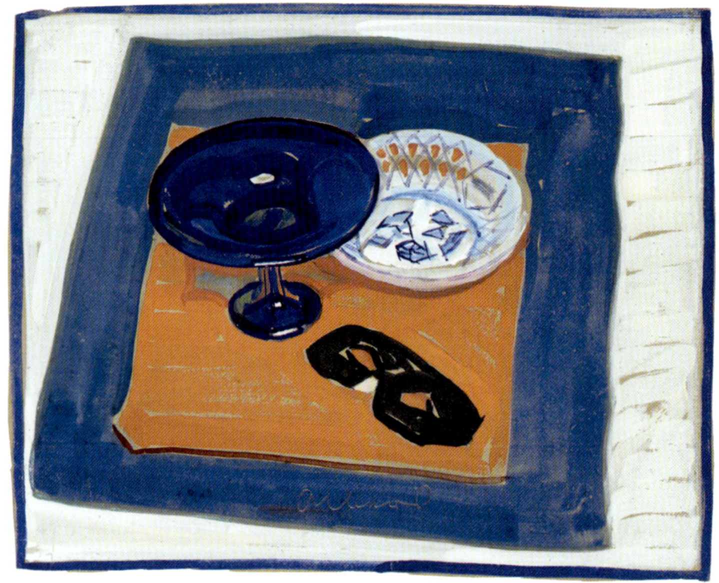

Still life with small black mask, *c.* 1914, watercolour and tempera on paper, 26.4 × 33.5 cm. Private collection, Germany

Still life with ranunculus and violet vase, *c.* 1914, watercolour on paper, 38 × 29.5 cm. Private collection, Germany

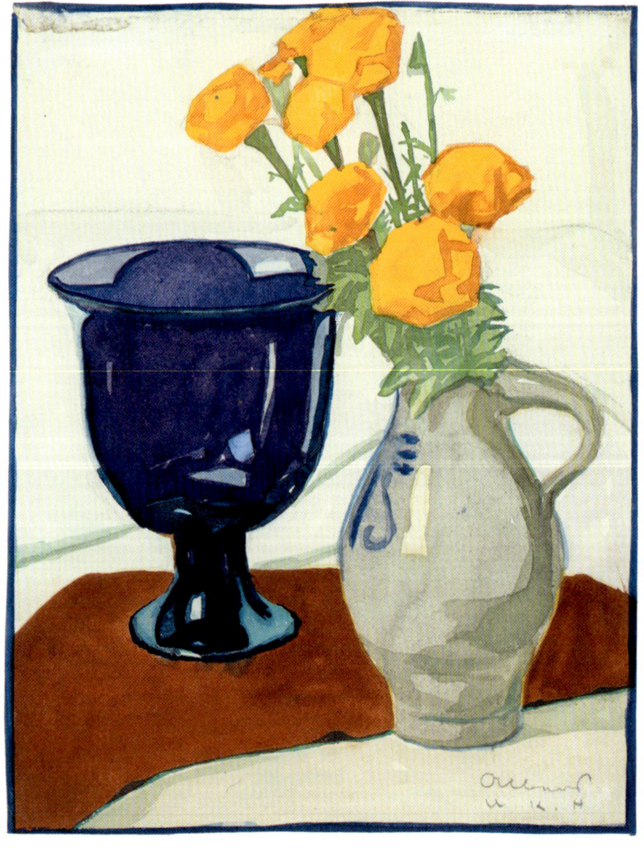

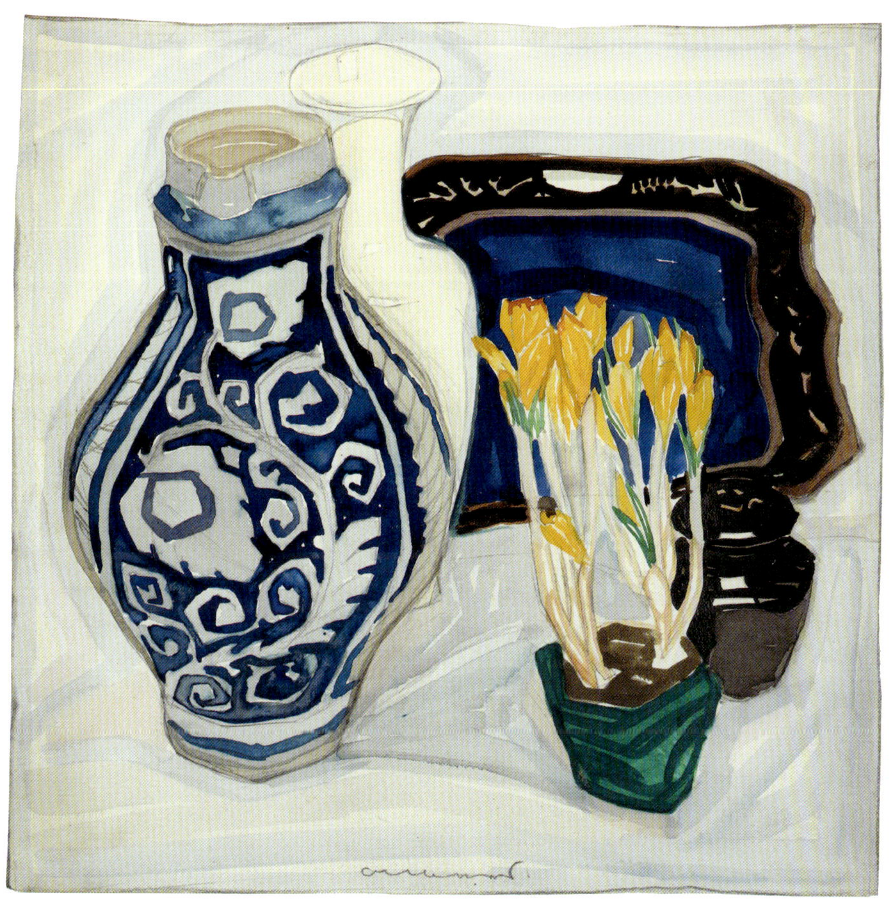

Still life with crocuses, *c*. 1914, watercolour on paper, 42 × 41.4 cm. Private collection, Germany

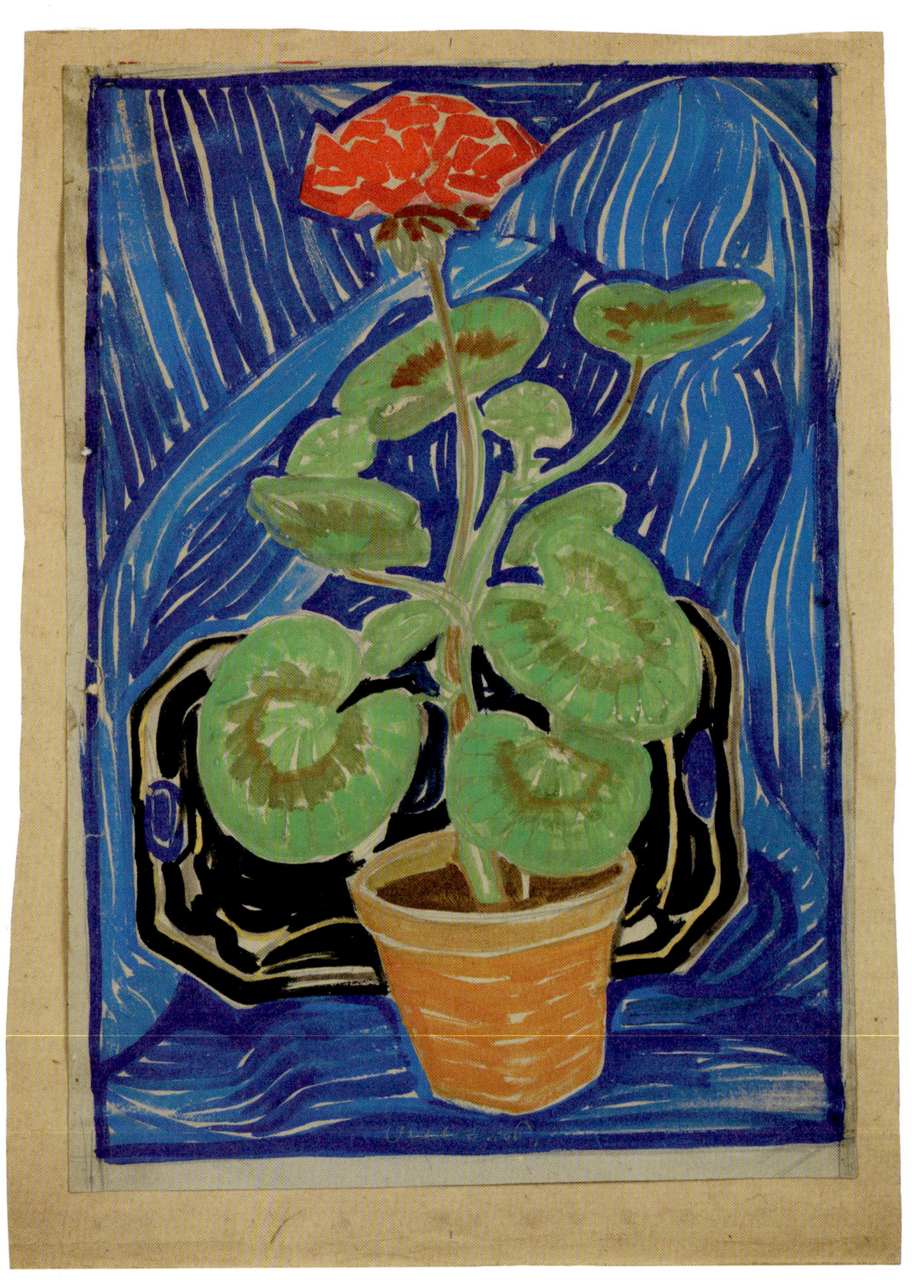

Still life with geranium, *c.* 1914,
gouache on paper, 47.5 × 37 cm.
Private collection, Germany

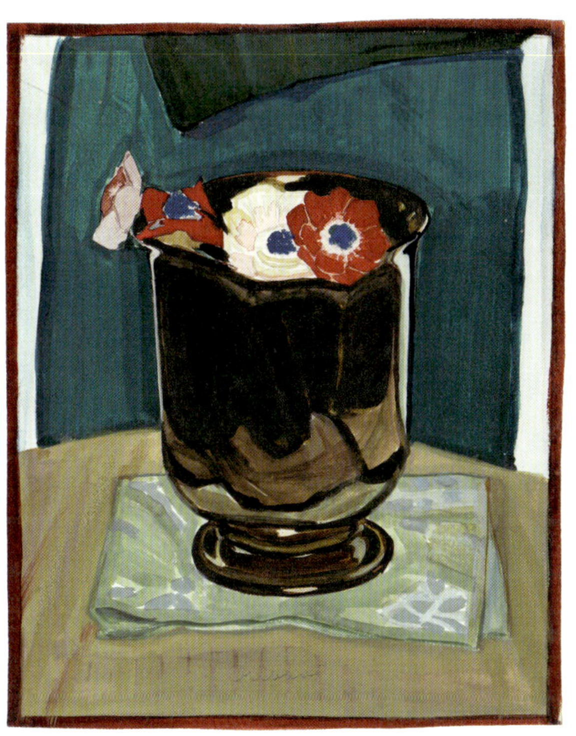

Vase with anemones, *c.* 1914,
watercolour on paper, 39.8 × 32.2 cm.
Private collection, Germany

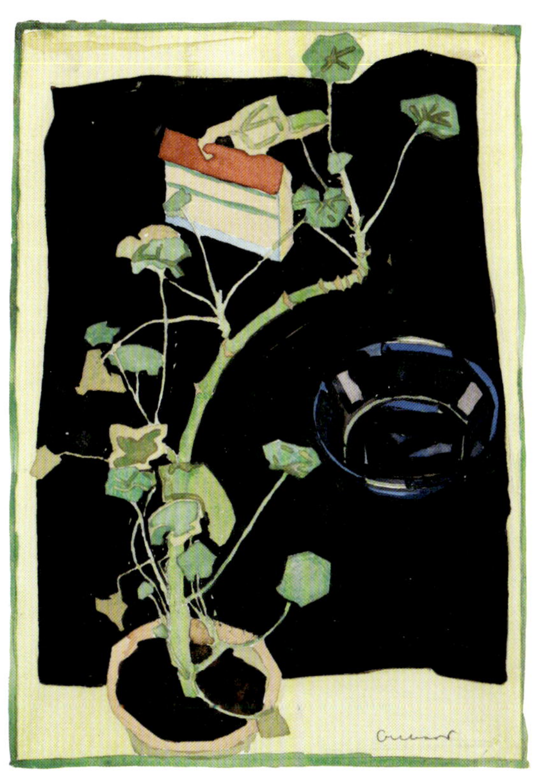

Still life with geranium and blue bowl, *c.* 1914,
watercolour on paper, 43.4 × 31.9 cm.
Private collection, Germany

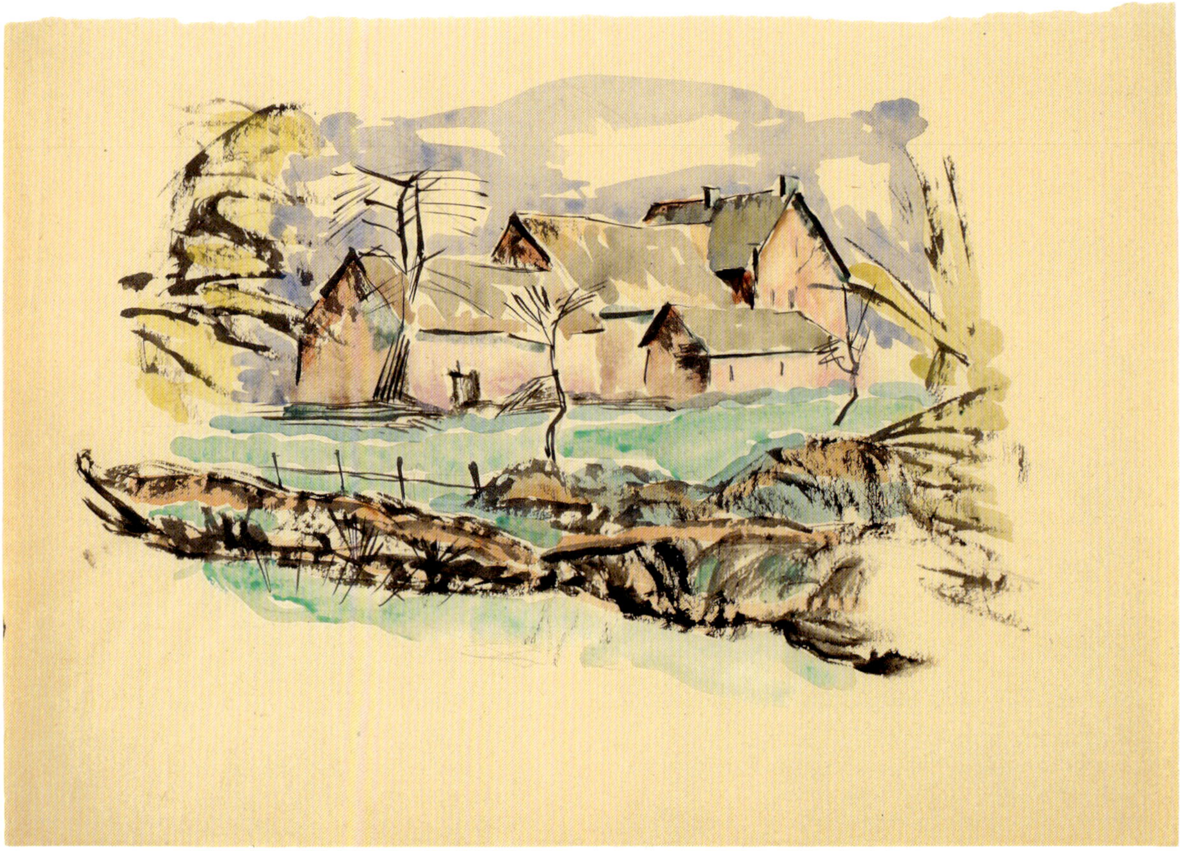

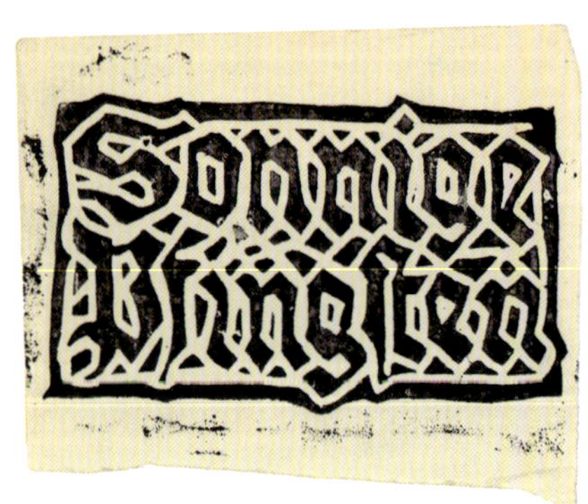

TOP Farm, *c.* 1914, watercolour on wove paper with pencil underdrawing, 24.1 × 34.9 cm. Josef and Anni Albers Foundation, 1976.2.345

ABOVE One of the earliest known prints by Josef Albers, a greetings card wishing the recipient a 'Sonnige Pfingsten' (Happy Pentecost), *c.* 1915. Josef and Anni Albers Foundation, 1976.17.25

When he returned to Bottrop from Berlin with art-teaching certificate in hand, he continued to sketch and draw from life – but 'life' had changed. Inside and out. He resumed teaching elementary school in Bottrop. He began taking evening classes at the Handwerker und Kunstgewerbeschule (School of Crafts and Applied Arts) in nearby Essen, likely studying printmaking with Dr Wilhelm Pötter and certainly passing within the umbra of painter and glass artist Johan Thorn Prikker.

On his return, Albers still worked in a pictorial mode, but he took as his subject the landscapes of industrial development – the burgeoning sandpits, rows of workers' houses, railroad bridges, and electricity lines. And his style changed, too. Loose sweeps of brush and ink, and broad, faceted chops with the lithographer's crayon took the place of fastidious hatchings of pen and ink.

Barge in canal harbour, *c.* 1914,
watercolour on paper, 31.8 × 34.8 cm.
Private collection, Germany

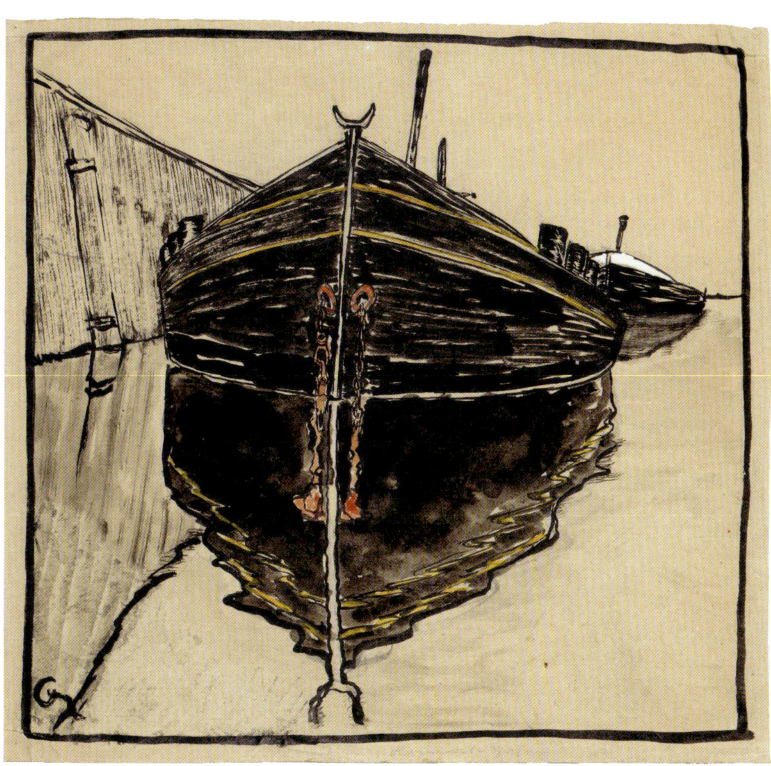

Construction of railroad overpass
on the road from Essen to Bottrop, 1915,
ink and brush on paper, 34.9 × 40 cm.
Private collection, Germany

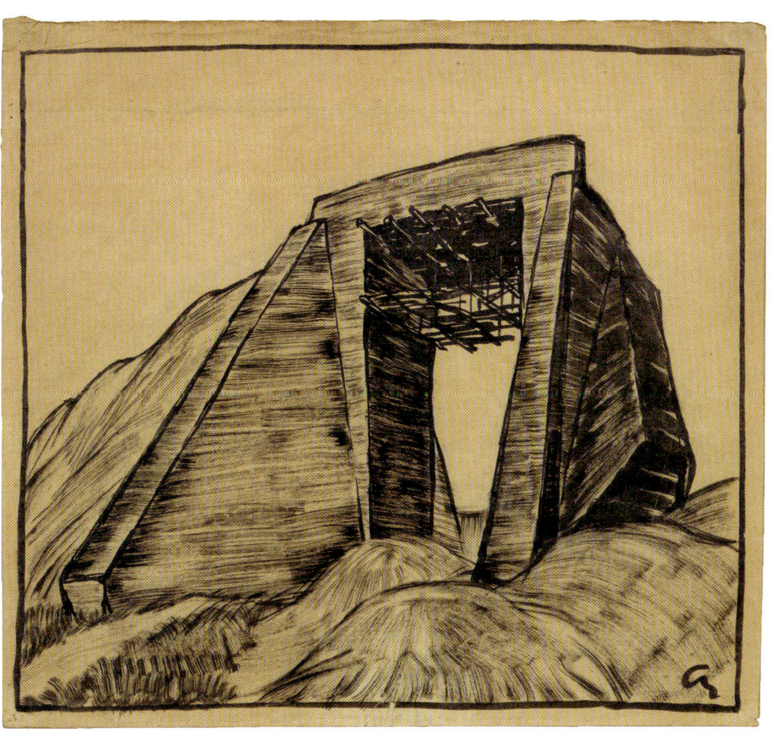

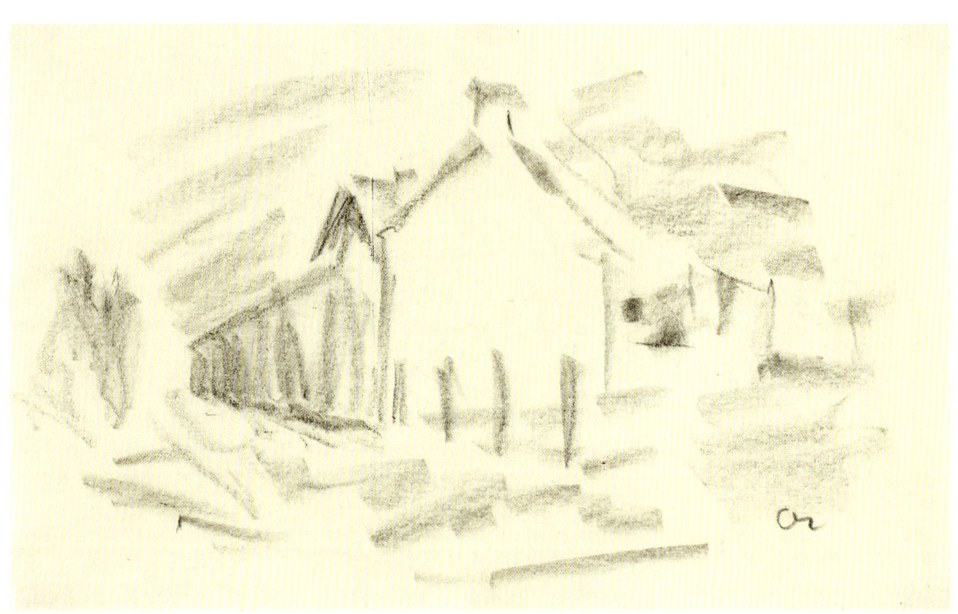

Empty End, c. 1917,
lithographic crayon
on paper, 20 × 34.7 cm.
Josef and Anni Albers
Foundation, 1976.3.415

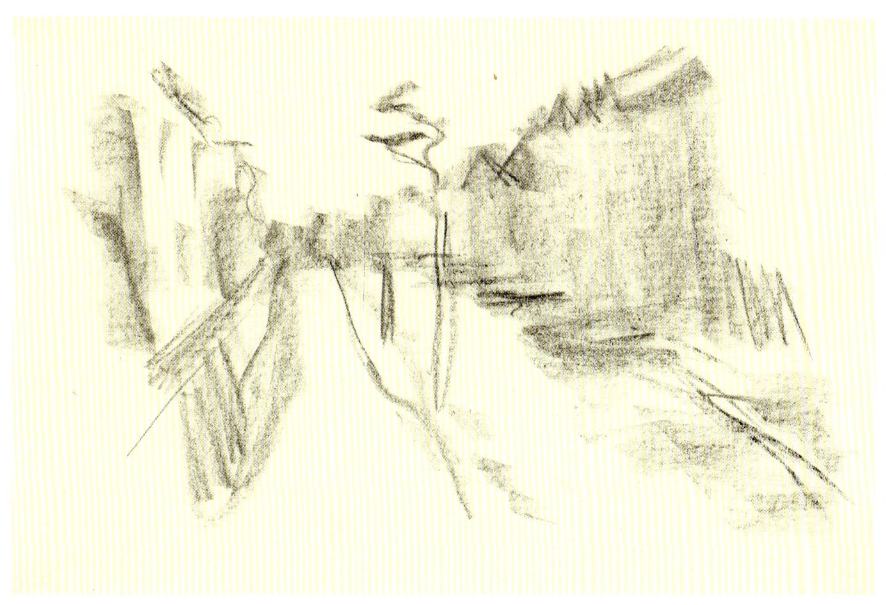

Ostring I, *c.* 1917,
lithographic crayon
on paper, 20.5 × 32.7 cm.
Josef and Anni Albers
Foundation, 1976.3.414

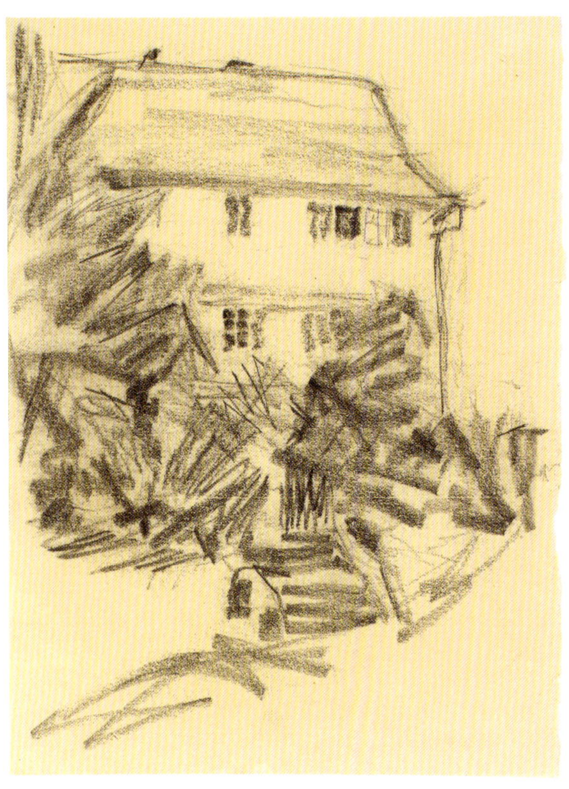

LEFT House in Nottuln, *c.* 1918, lithographic crayon on paper, 30.3 × 22.8 cm. Josef and Anni Albers Foundation, 1976.3.60

BELOW Apartment houses, *c.* 1918, pencil on paper torn from a tablet, 25.4 × 33.3 cm. Josef and Anni Albers Foundation, 1976.3.41

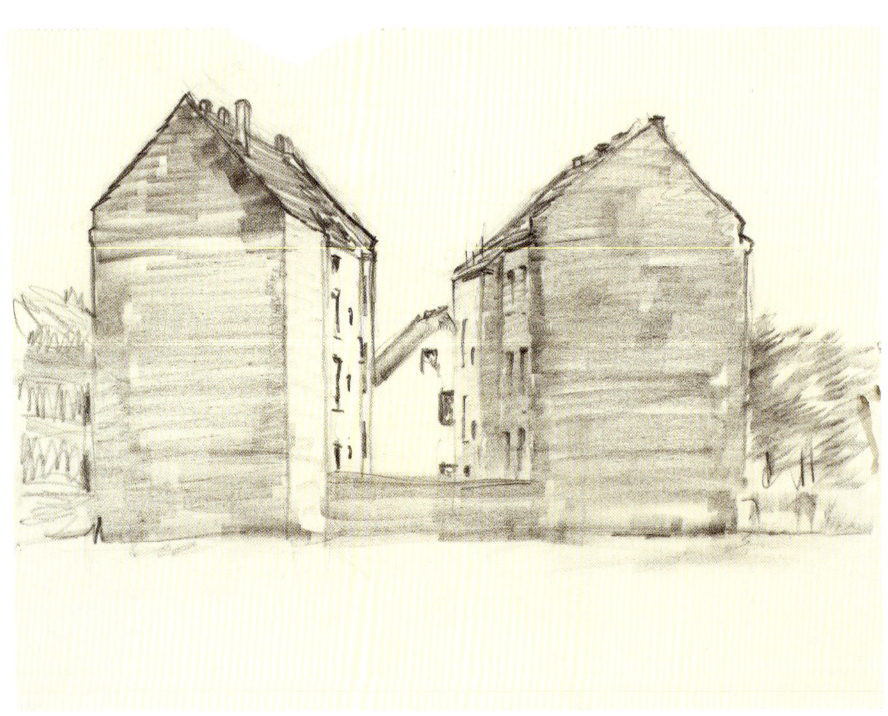

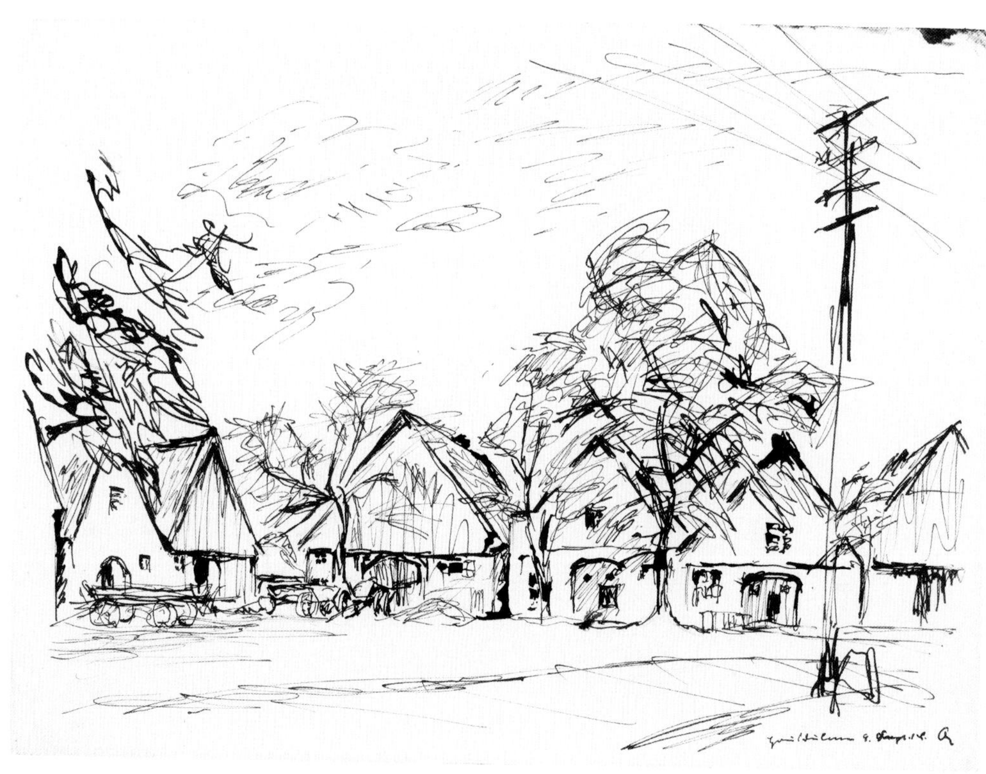

ABOVE *Hausdülmen 8. Sept. 18*, 1918,
pencil, pen, and ink on paper, 26.3 × 35.2 cm.
Josef and Anni Albers Foundation, 1976.3.62

RIGHT Electrical repairmen, *c.* 1918,
pencil on paper, 28.2 × 20.0 cm.
Josef and Anni Albers Foundation, 1976.3.449

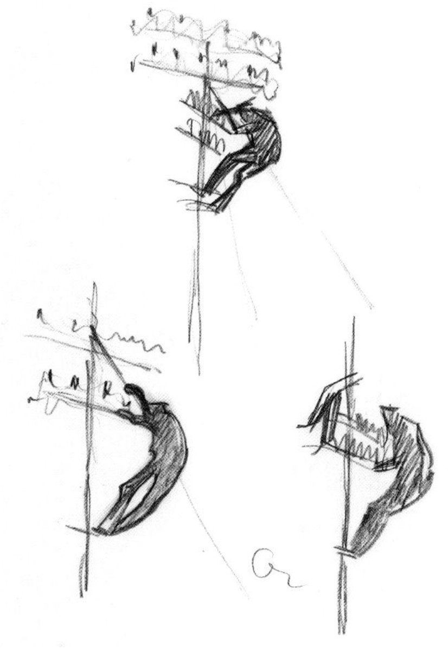

RIGHT Self-portrait, *c.* 1918, tempera on canvas, 27.9 × 22.9 cm. Josef and Anni Albers Foundation, 1984.1.1

FOLLOWING PAGES *Adjusted*, 1944 (detail)

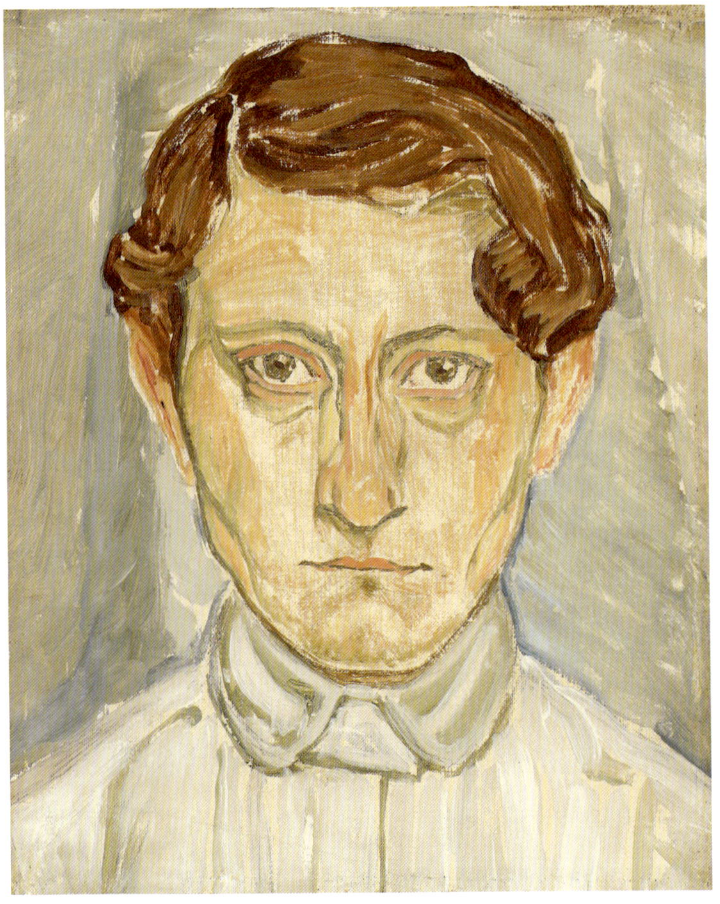

Josef Albers was, of course, never a true *Heimatkünstler*. He just walked in that world for a short time. And although he was no stranger to rural life – his relatives had farmed in the forested hills of the Sauerland in eastern Westphalia for a century or more – he was in many ways an accidental visitor to the Westphalian hinterlands, as a child, an elementary-school teacher, a wanderer with pencils and sketchbook. A restless and ambitious soul.[11]

It is the character of art-historical writing to want to wind together the incidents of an artist's life into a unified narrative, to create a developmental history. Every act leads ineluctably to the next. Art history cannot resist entelechy: the belief that the seed of what is yet to come is contained in every moment of the artist's

11. From the sparse documentation available in archives and letters, Charles Darwent has sketched a brief but indelible picture of the life of the young artist and teacher in these years, hemmed in as it was by the tedium of classroom routine, see *Josef Albers: Life and Work* (London: Thames & Hudson, 2018), pp. 65–75.

life, every mark, every picture. The art historian becomes the sibyl, uniquely able to read the tea leaves and ashes, the paint strokes and ink scratches – uniquely able to say, 'Look! See. He was already himself. Even then.'

In this view, the past makes sense only when it produces our present. But there are other ways of looking at the past. The course of any life contains a multitude of alternative futures, points of chance or decision after which events might have transpired quite differently. What if Albers's drawings had never been published in *De Kiepenkerl*? What if he had not gone to study in Berlin? Or Essen? Or Munich? He would never had encountered that prospectus from the new design school in Weimar called the Bauhaus. He would never had met Anneliese Fleischmann. But instead he might have enjoyed a long and full life as a teacher and Sunday painter. He might have written a book. Or two.

So we can imagine 'Jos. Albers, Bottrop, Lehrer', a name read glancingly on a page in a musty book found in the deep reaches of a library, and for a moment imagine that this young man made other choices. His life took other turns. We can imagine that he became one of Eliot's 'number who lived faithfully a hidden life, and rest in unvisited tombs'. A dedicated teacher, lover of nature. A man with a keen eye and skilled hands, enamoured of the pastoral landscapes and townscapes of his homeland, which, of course, he was and remained thereafter.

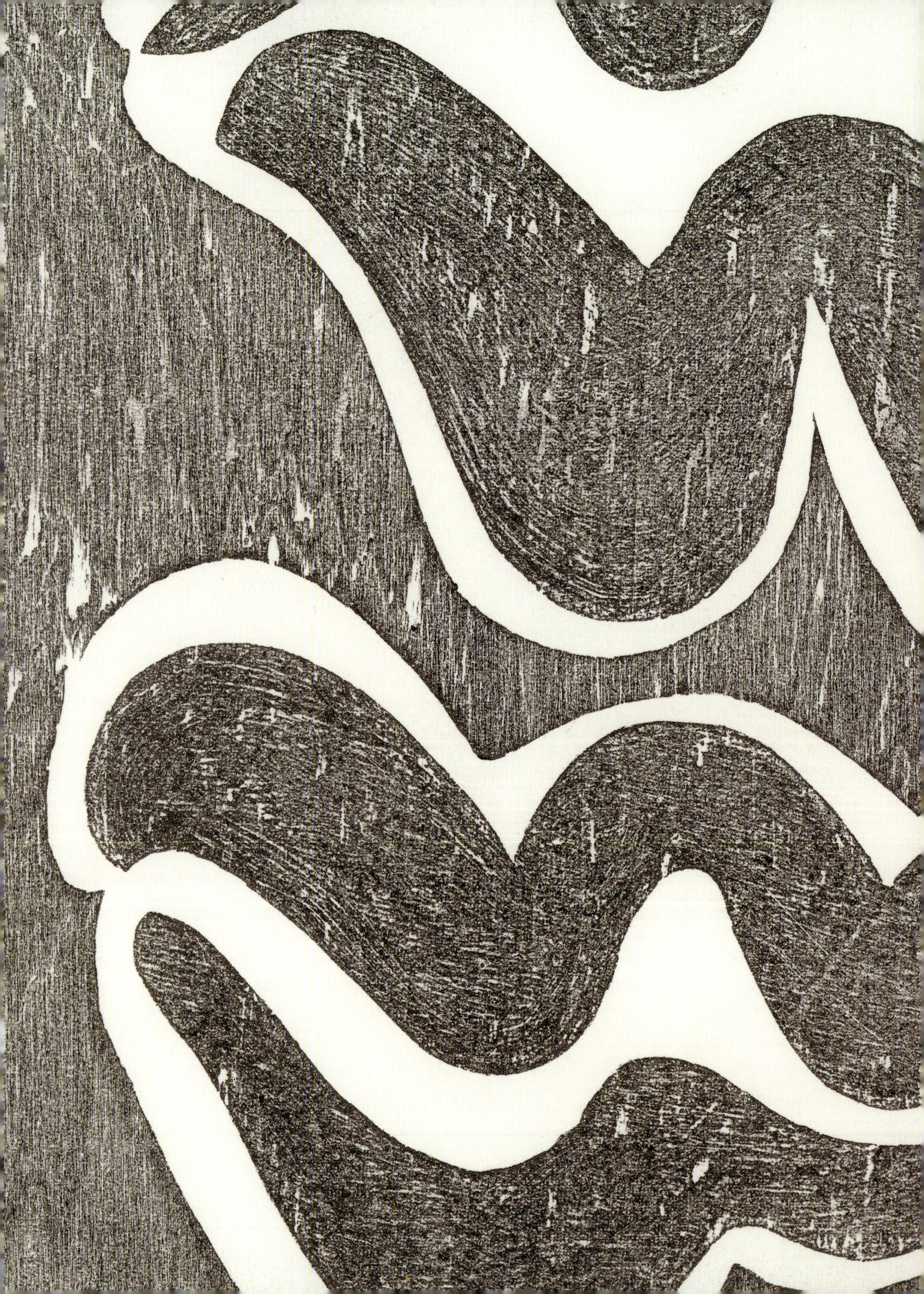

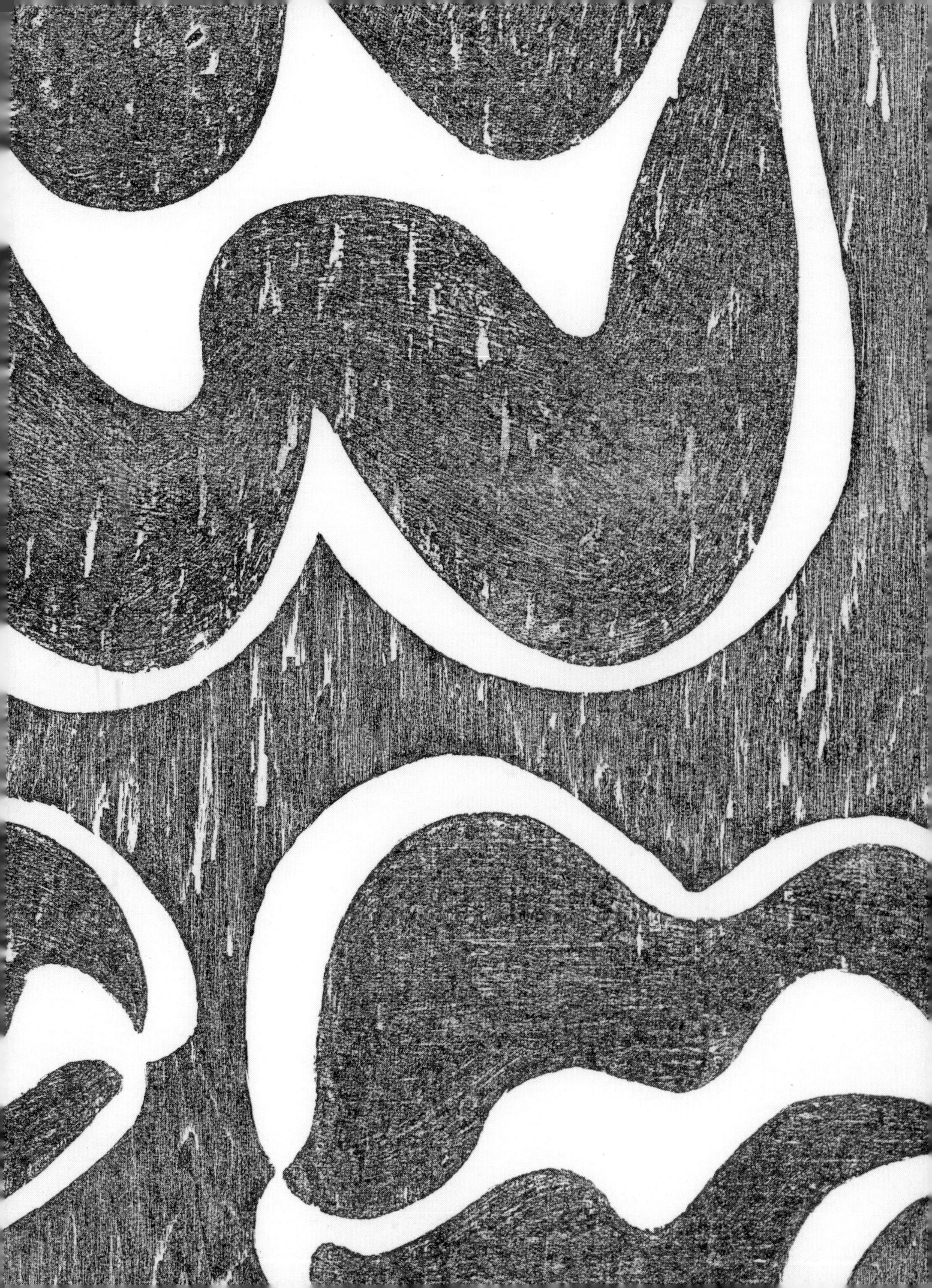

‘Art is concerned with the HOW, not the WHAT; not with literal content, but its performance of the content. The performance – how it is done – that is the content of Art.’

Josef Albers, ‘The Meaning of Art’, 1940

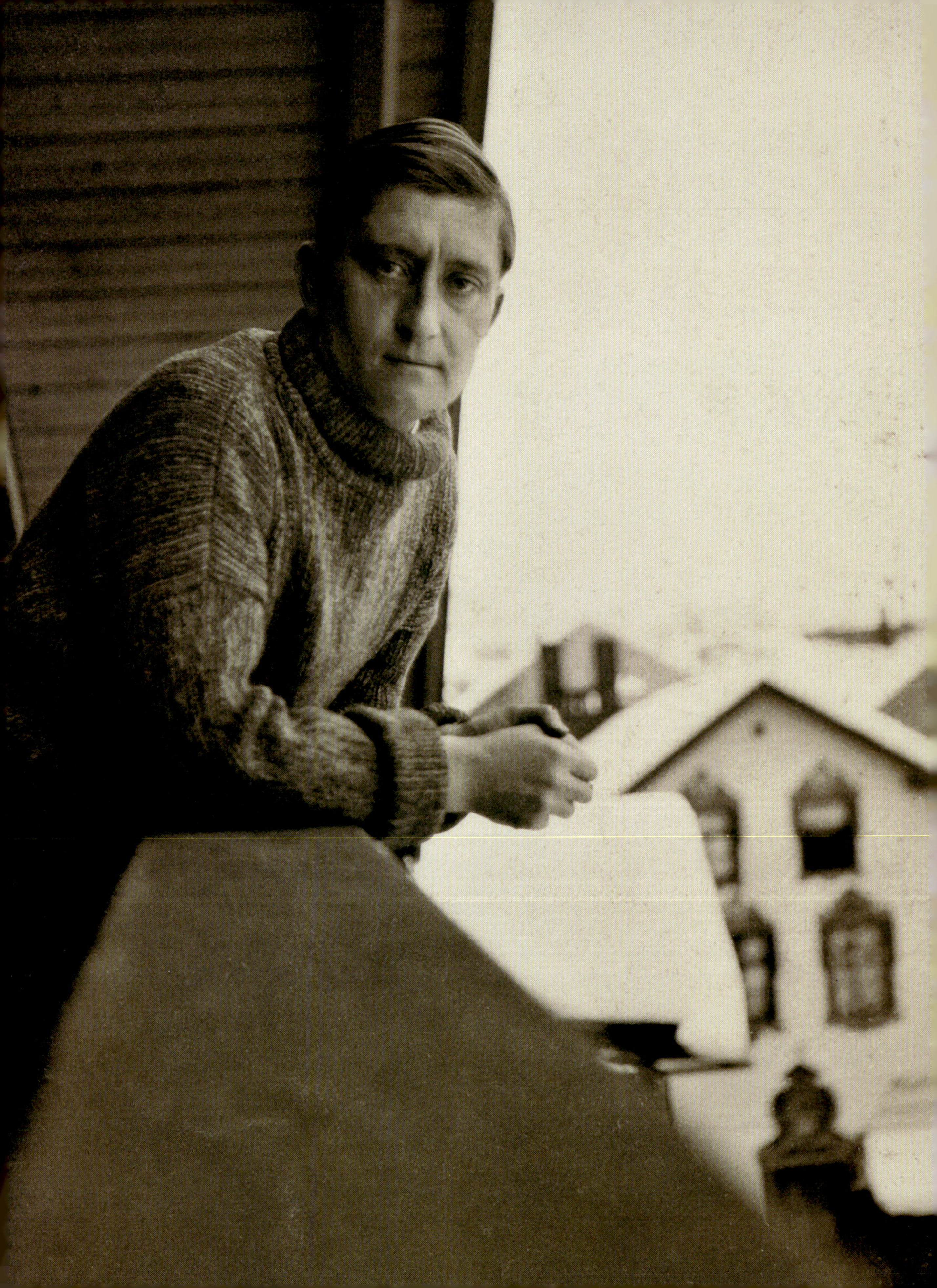

Brenda Danilowitz

The HOW of Art

Josef Albers, *c.* 1920, photographer unknown. The J. Paul Getty Museum, Los Angeles

Josef Albers was a prolific artist and designer. His production runs the gamut from photography and graphic design to furniture design and, most famously, the *Homage to the Square* paintings. When it comes to his printmaking, the wide range of subject matter, style, method, and process makes generalizations impossible. What is consistent is an enduring curiosity about the medium of print, and a willingness to explore new methods and processes. There is also frequently a sense of adventure and a whimsicality, a surprise at what the process yields.

The purpose of art for Albers was 'the revelation and evocation of vision', his formulation of Paul Klee's 'making the invisible visible'. Art had a transformative power, and it was up to the artist to make this manifest. From his earliest known works, which drew inspiration from the visible world, Albers developed his own personal visual language to translate this known world into 'vision'. How this was achieved, the 'HOW' of art, its performance, was paramount. Nowhere do we see this more clearly than in his graphic work, which began around 1914, when, in his mid-twenties, he started to realize seriously his ambition to become an artist – although he himself would most likely not have put it that way. One thing he did know was that he would not be a follower, one of those who look around to see which way the wind is blowing and then move in the most expedient direction.

Greetings card, 'Frohe Ostern' (Happy Easter), *c.* 1915, linoleum cut on paper, 7.3 × 12.4 cm. Josef and Anni Albers Foundation, 1976.17.26

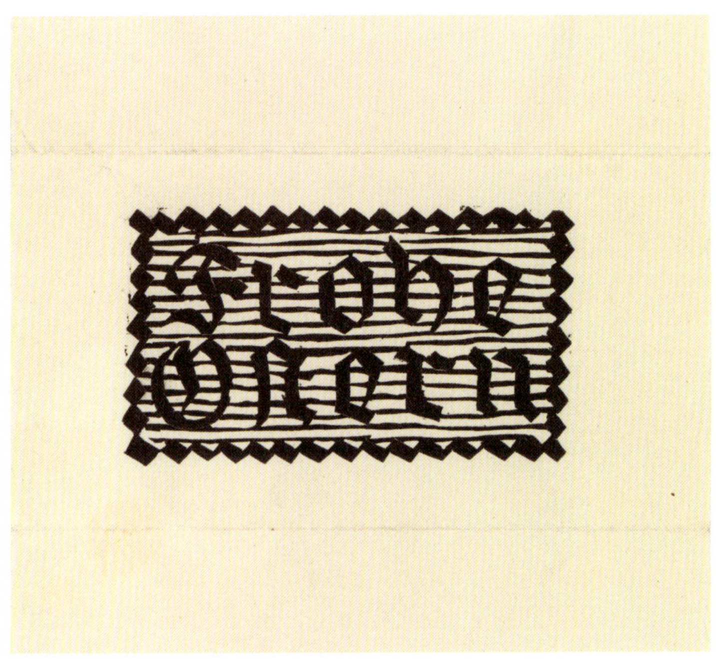

Albers's printmaking falls into three broad periods. First are the years between 1915 and 1918 in Germany, when he studied printmaking in Essen while also teaching in an elementary school. The second period began with the closing of the Bauhaus in Berlin in 1933 and continued through his years at Black Mountain College in the United States from 1934 to mid-1949. Finally, towards the end of his tenure at Yale University in 1958 until his death in 1976, Albers embarked on a new burst of printmaking and particularly the production of a large number of colour lithographs and *Homage to the Square* screenprints. The present book and associated exhibition focus on the first two of these periods. The works have been selected from the more than three hundred prints and the thousands of drawings and studies that preceded them – some almost finished works, other mere jottings on scraps of paper – that Albers made, in a range of graphic mediums, until the end of his life.

Albers set his sights on becoming an artist early, even though his education at a *Volksschul* (elementary school) predestined him

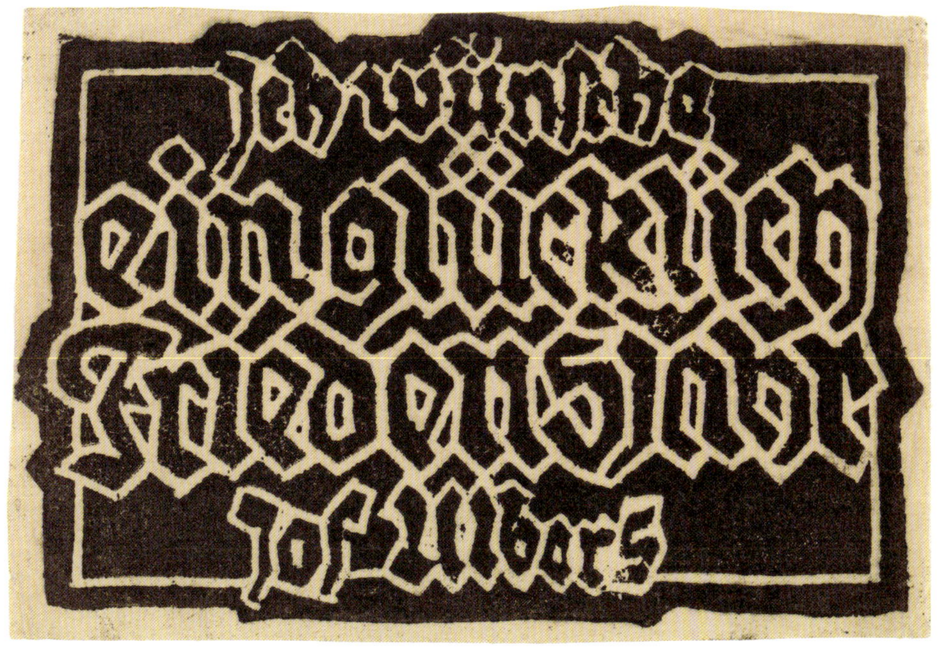

Greetings card, 'Ich wünsche ein glücklich friedensjahr. Jos. Albers' (I wish you a happy and peaceful year. Jos Albers), *c.* 1915, linoleum cut on paper, 10.2 × 14.7 cm. Josef and Anni Albers Foundation, 1976.17.27

to be ineligible for admission into Germany's fine-arts academies, which were reserved for those who had graduated from the elite high schools, or *Gymnasia*. Instead, Albers became a teacher in those same *Volksschule*, where drawing was taught alongside arithmetic and religious studies. He began his teaching career in 1908 in Bottrop in the Ruhr Valley, Germany's industrial heartland. Five years later, taking advantage of an opportunity for advanced study for teachers, he moved to Berlin, where, he received his certification as an art teacher at the Königliche Kunstschule in June 1915. He then returned to Bottrop, probably towards the end of that year, to resume his teaching position, while studying printmaking in the evenings at the Handwerker und Kunstgewerbeschule in Essen.

Because the prints that Albers produced between 1915 and 1917 are undocumented, little is known of his working method, the precise dates of these works, or whether and in what numbers they were editioned.[1] Although his first forays into printmaking – a series of greeting cards – appear amateurish, in a short time he was

1. Albers assigned few dates to works made before he entered the Bauhaus in the fall of 1920. Dates have been attributed either on grounds of works made in known locations or on stylistic grounds.

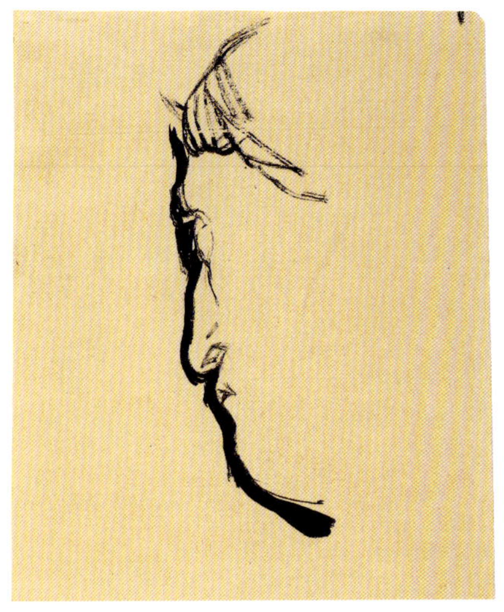

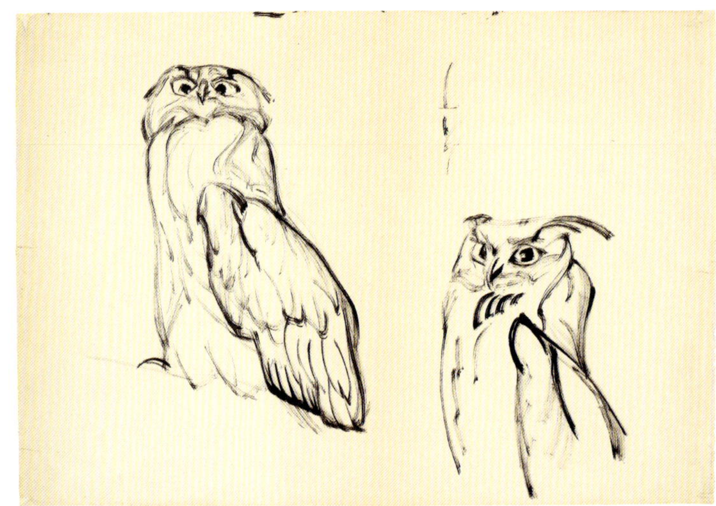

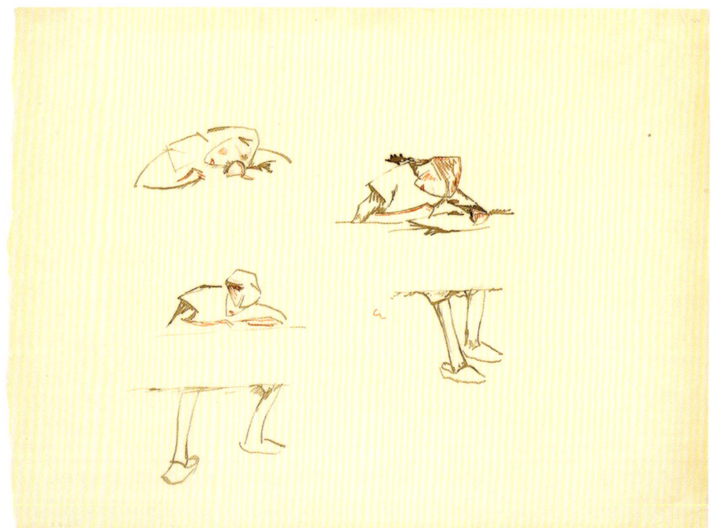

ABOVE Self-portrait, *c.* 1919, ink on paper, 29.2 × 19.7 cm. Josef and Anni Albers Foundation, 1976.3.133

ABOVE RIGHT Two owls, *c.* 1917, ink on paper, 50.5 × 72.4 cm. Josef and Anni Albers Foundation, 1976.3.39

RIGHT Three schoolgirls, *c.* 1917, ink on paper, 26 × 35.6 cm. Josef and Anni Albers Foundation, 1976.3.433

producing accomplished linocut and lithographic prints. The subjects were his surroundings, landscapes and interiors, domestic animals, portraits, and self-portraits – a range narrower than, but closely related to, his contemporaneous drawings.[2] The self-portrait prints and drawings typically show the young artist using his own features as a model.[3] Albers's striking profile served him as a particularly good example.

2. See Nicholas Fox Weber, *The Drawings of Josef Albers* (New Haven and London: Yale University Press, 1984).

3. Ibid., plates 15–20.

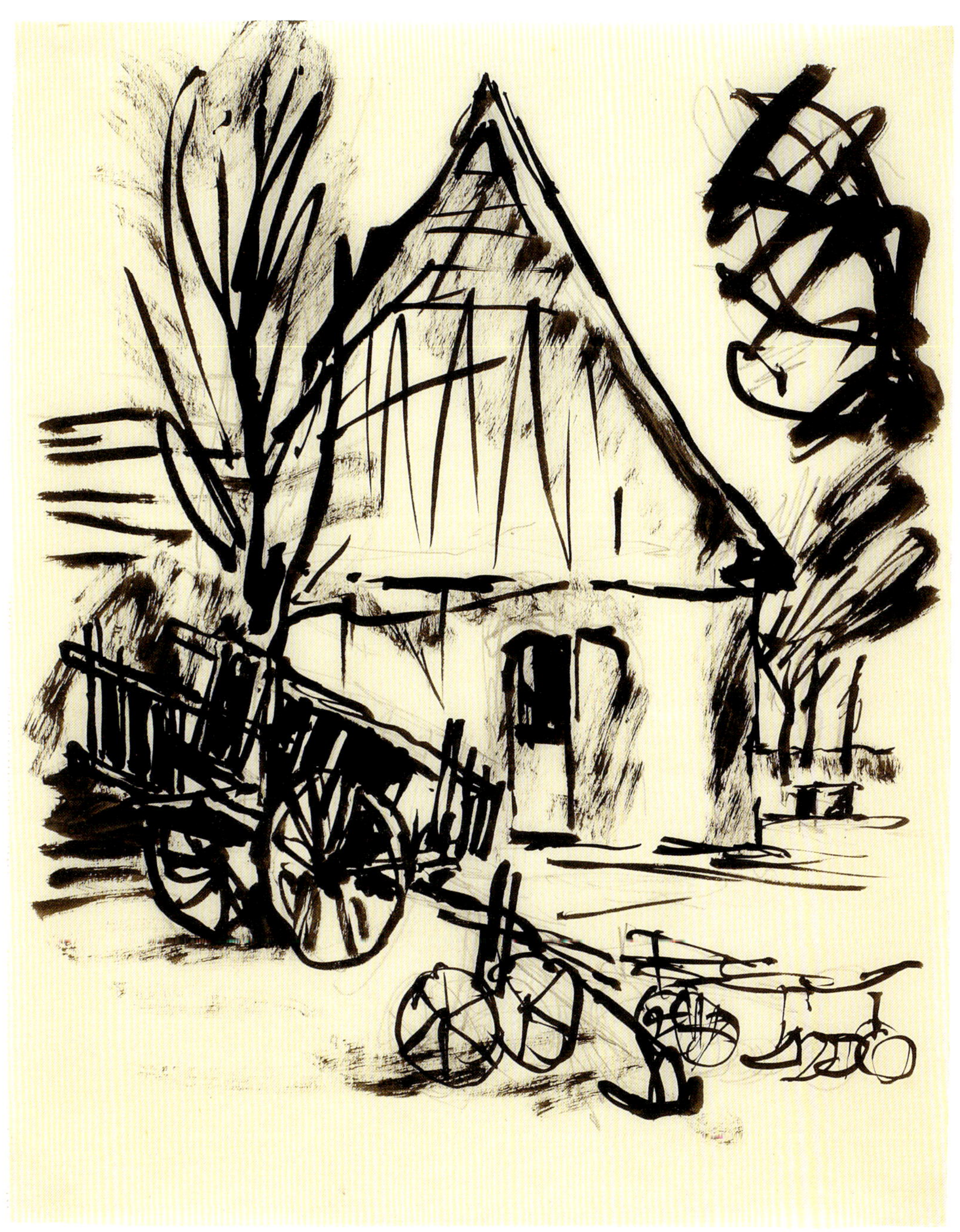

Farmhouse, *c.* 1918, pencil, brush, and india ink on transparent wove paper, 32 × 25.7 cm. Josef and Anni Albers Foundation, 1976.3.63

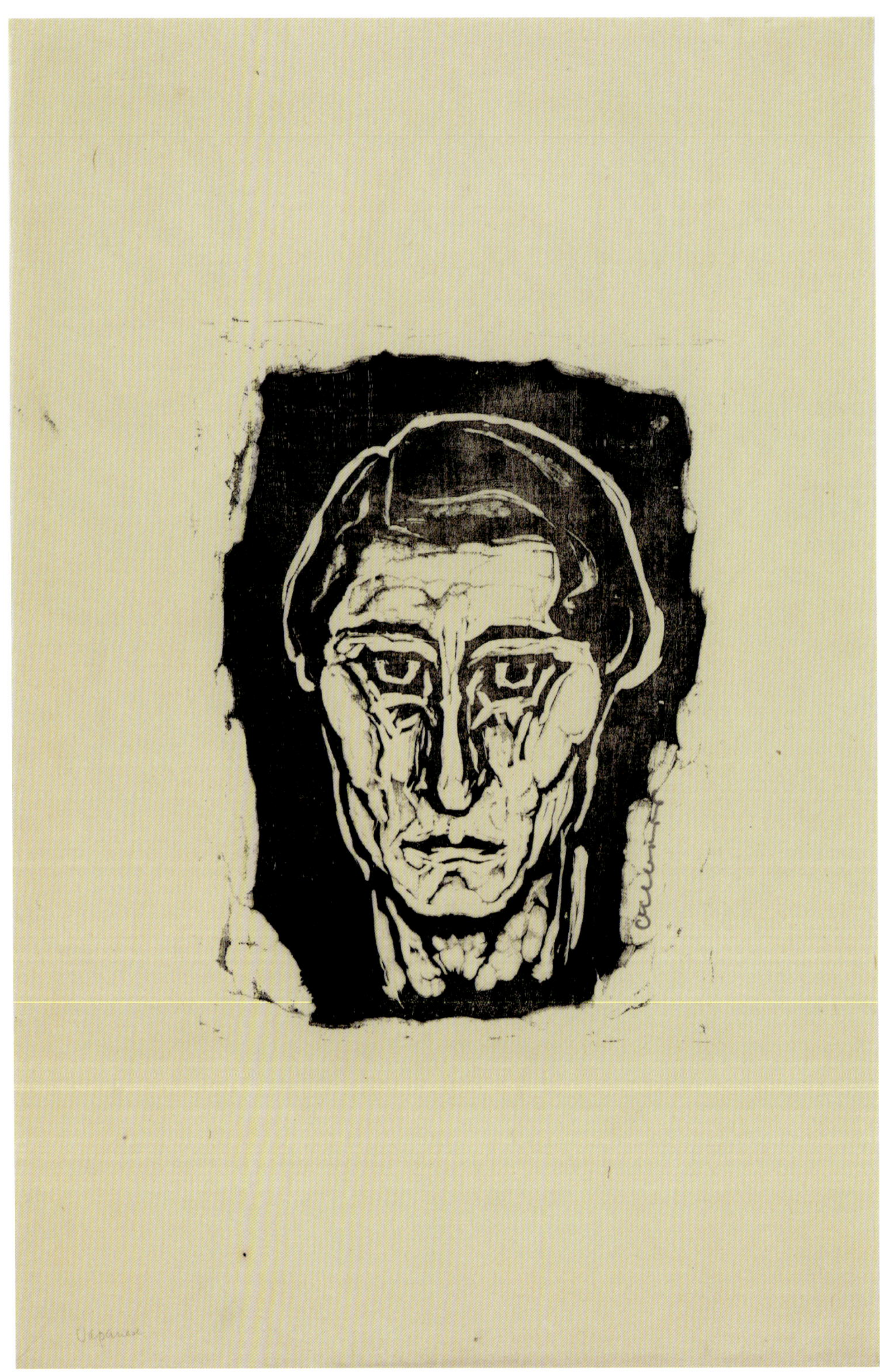

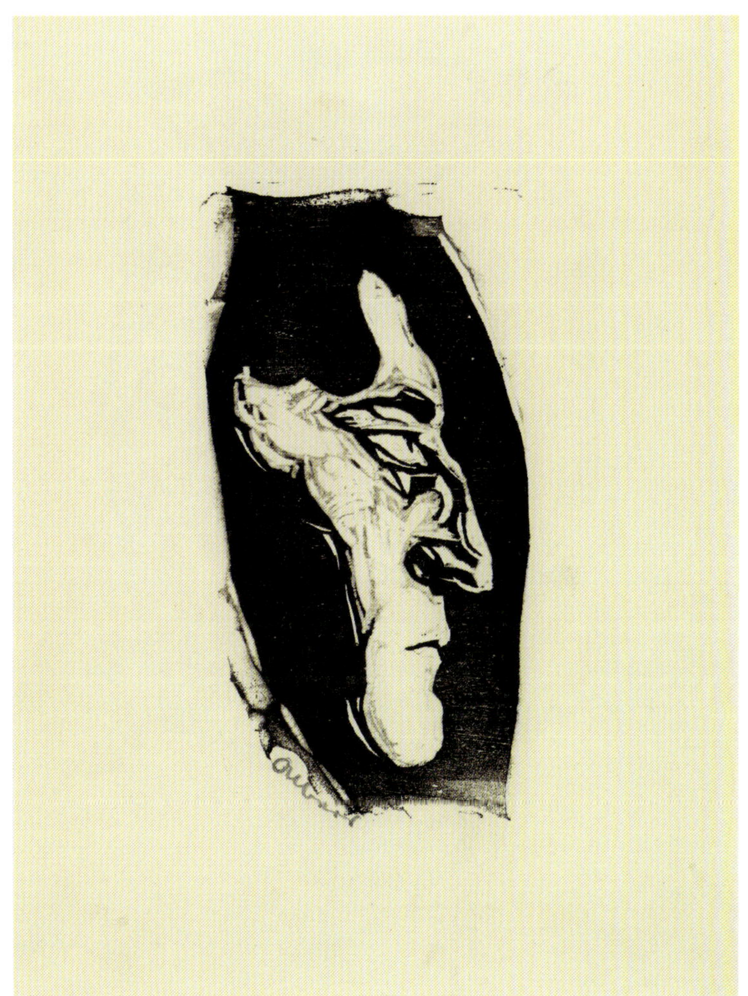

ABOVE Self-portrait, 1916, linoleum cut, paper 32.4 × 25.1 cm, image 18.4 × 10.8 cm. Josef and Anni Albers Foundation, 1976.4.17b

OPPOSITE Self-portrait, 1916, linoleum cut, paper 46 × 29.5 cm, image 21.6 × 16.5 cm. Josef and Anni Albers Foundation, 1976.4.13a

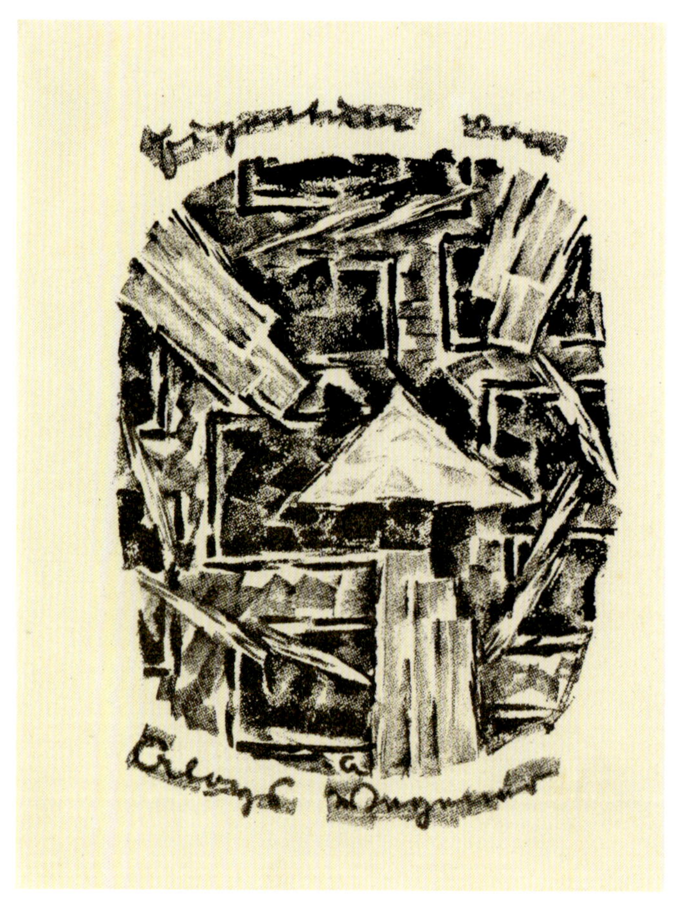

ABOVE *Eigentum von Aloys Wegener* (Property of Aloys Wegener), 1916, lithograph on stone on various wove and laid sheets, paper 20 × 14 cm, image 13.3 × 9.5 cm. Josef and Anni Albers Foundation, 1976.4.2

OPPOSITE In the Cathedral: Small Middle Nave, 1916, linoleum cut, paper 47 × 29.5 cm, image 16.8 × 14.3 cm. Josef and Anni Albers Foundation, 1976.4.9b

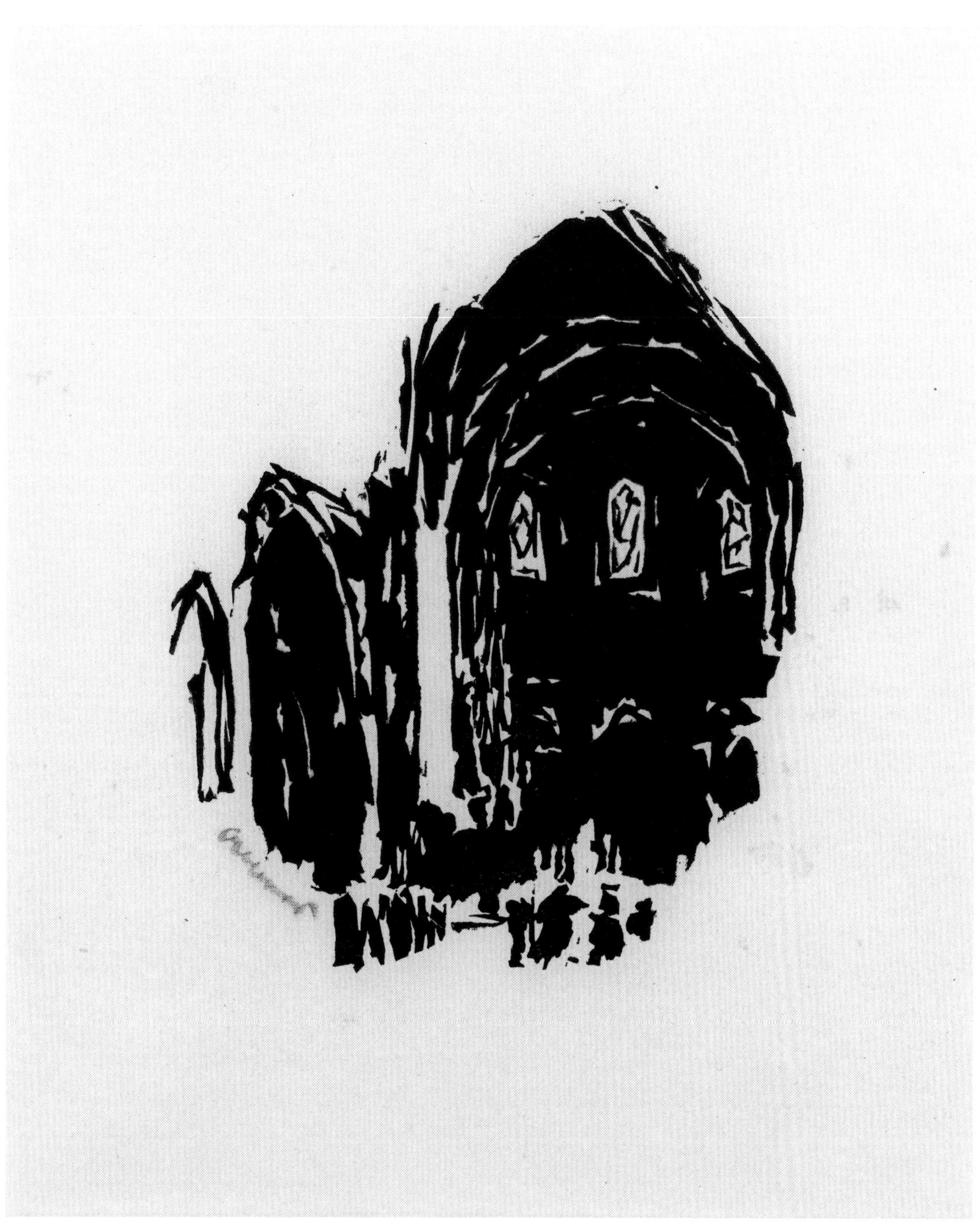

Two soldiers from behind, *c.* 1917, transfer lithograph, 28 × 21.3 cm. Josef and Anni Albers Foundation, 1999.4.6

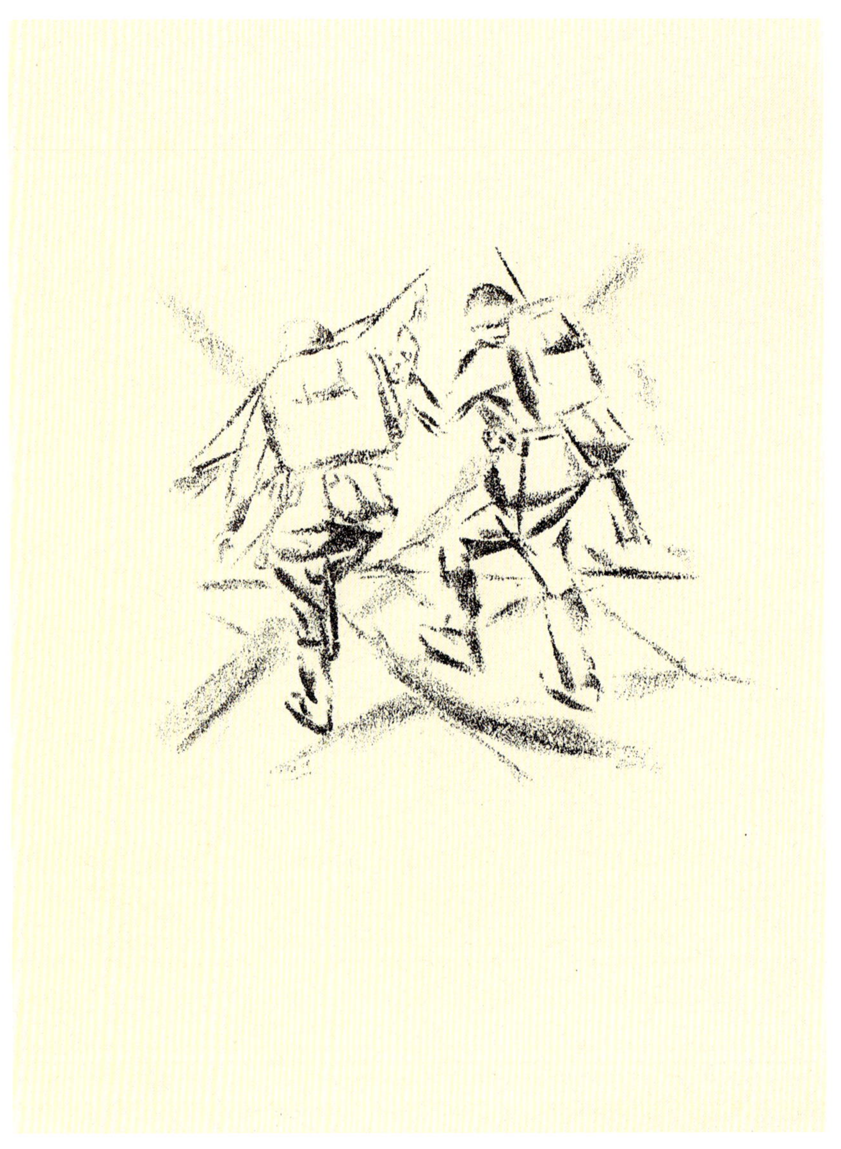

These early lithographs and linocuts were printed on a variety of papers and on sheets of different sizes, probably whatever was available at the art school in Essen, since Germany was at war and materials were hard to come by. As a school teacher, Albers was exempt from military service. The only hint in his work that the drama and carnage of the First World War were raging close to home can be found in four lithographs of soldiers in uniform.[4]

4. These lithographs, previously unknown, came to light at auction in 1999. Their provenance was the estate of a Dr Wilhelm Pötter of Essen (see catalogue Sotheby's London, *Old Master, Modern, and Contemporary Prints*, Sale, L09121. 29–30 June 1999, Lot 657).

TOP Soldier in motion, *c.* 1917, transfer lithograph, 28.6 × 43.5 cm, Josef and Anni Albers Foundation, 1999.4.7

MIDDLE Two men pulling off their boots, *c.* 1917, transfer lithograph, 21.5 × 28.3 cm. Josef and Anni Albers Foundation, 1999.4.5

BOTTOM Kneeling soldier with weapon, 1917, transfer lithograph, 28.4 × 41.9 cm. Josef and Anni Albers Foundation, 1999.4.8

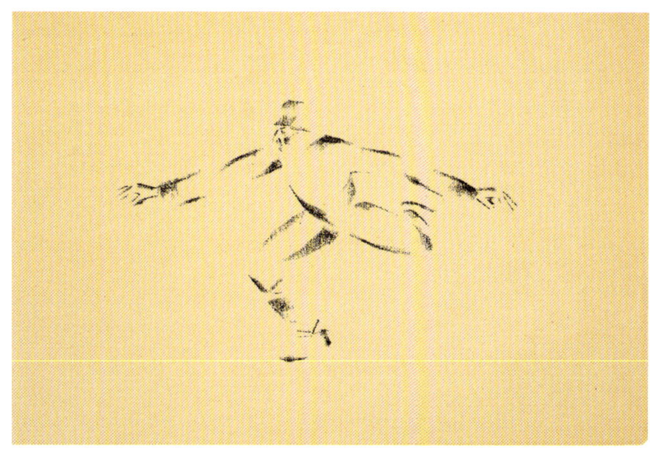

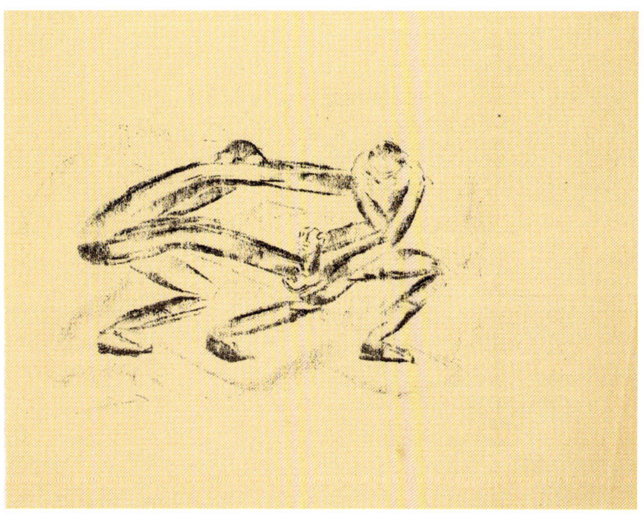

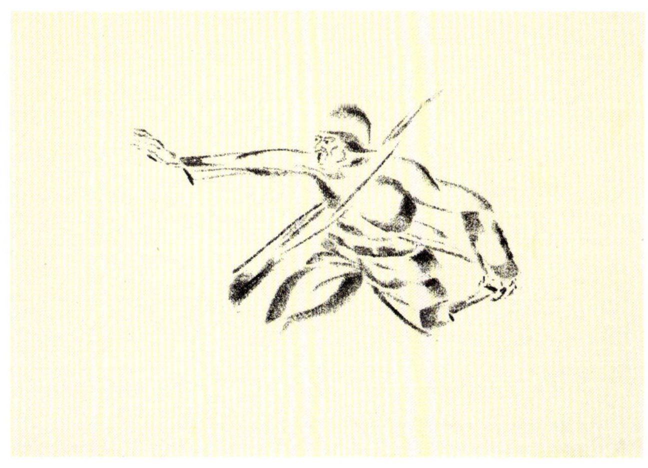

Sandmine, Bottrop, *c.* 1930, photographer unknown. Bottrop Museum für Ur- und Ortsgeschichte

Josef Albers made numerous sketches, a painting, and at least five prints of the sandmines near Bottrop. The town and its surrounding farms and villages sat atop an ancient seabed, whose fine sand was ideal for making iron- and steel-casting moulds. Albers's linoleum cuts are at once documents of the industrial landscape of the Ruhr Valley and richly abstract images that prefigure his later pedagogical matière studies. [J.R.]

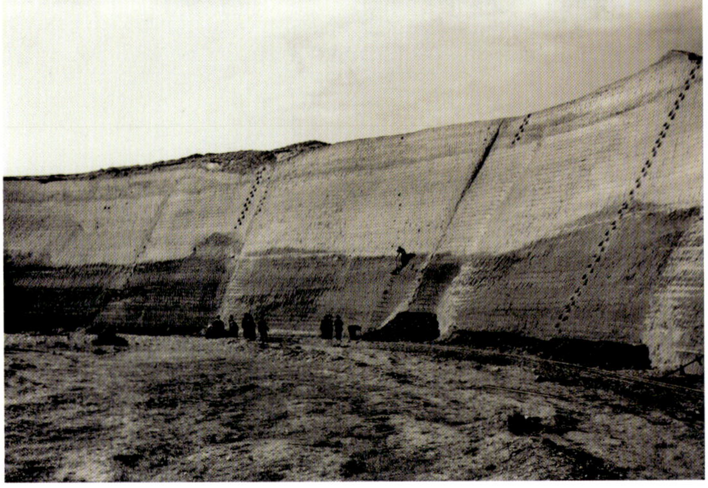

The environs of Bottrop, a small but rapidly developing coal- and sand-mining centre, are unbucolic.[5] Their character is best described as 'gritty', the predominant colour, shades of northern grey. From this unpromising subject, Albers conjured an ink sketch of a sandmine that is a lyrical study of blacks and greys, lifted and brightened by generous expanses of white paper. Using this single drawing, in 1916 he created a series of linoleum cut prints, each one a study of dark and light. The four *Sandmine* linocuts (pp. 54–7) are early evidence of Albers's proclivity for working in series. With their shifting viewpoints and versatile cutting, they show him simultaneously exploring ways of translating the world into pictorial form and testing the possibilities of his medium. *Sandmine II* zooms in on the scene of *Sandmine I* and diminishes the spatial effect of the receding lines of the tracks. In its first state, the relief surface of *Sandmine II* is quite shallow, so that a tracery of fine lines divides the gouged area into irregular 'cells' that pick up traces of the ink. This introduces shades of grey into the printed landscape. In the second state, the relief is deeper, its surfaces smoother, and thus the greys are eliminated. The bold brushstrokes of the ink drawing that informs this print suggest that Albers was seeking a painterly effect.

5. Sand mining was second only to coal mining in Bottrop's industrial history.

RIGHT Sandmine, *c.* 1916, brush and ink on two sheets of paper, 21.3 × 26.1 cm overall. Josef and Anni Albers Foundation, 1976.3.25

BELOW Sandmine, *c.* 1916–17, tempera on canvas, 64.5 × 68 cm. Private collection, Germany

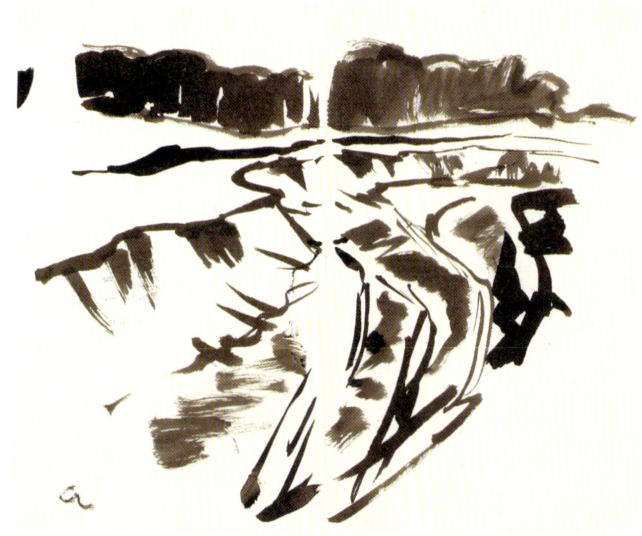

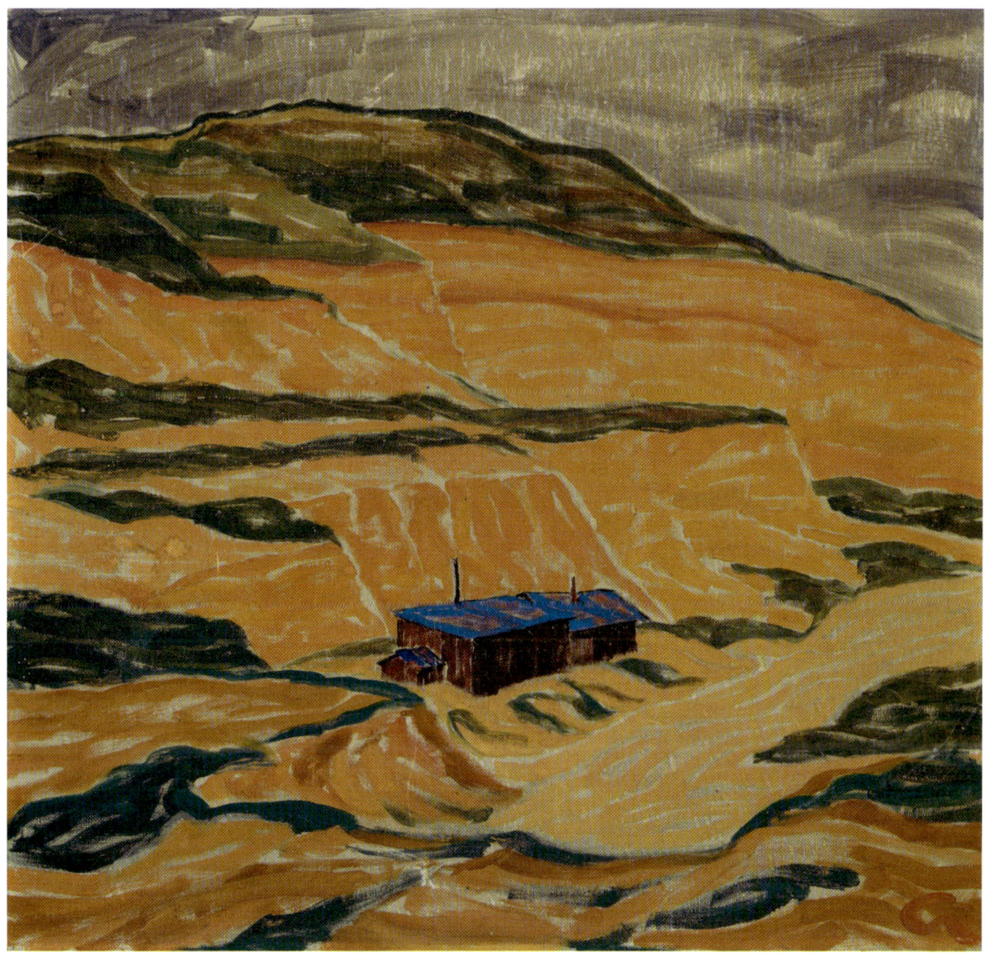

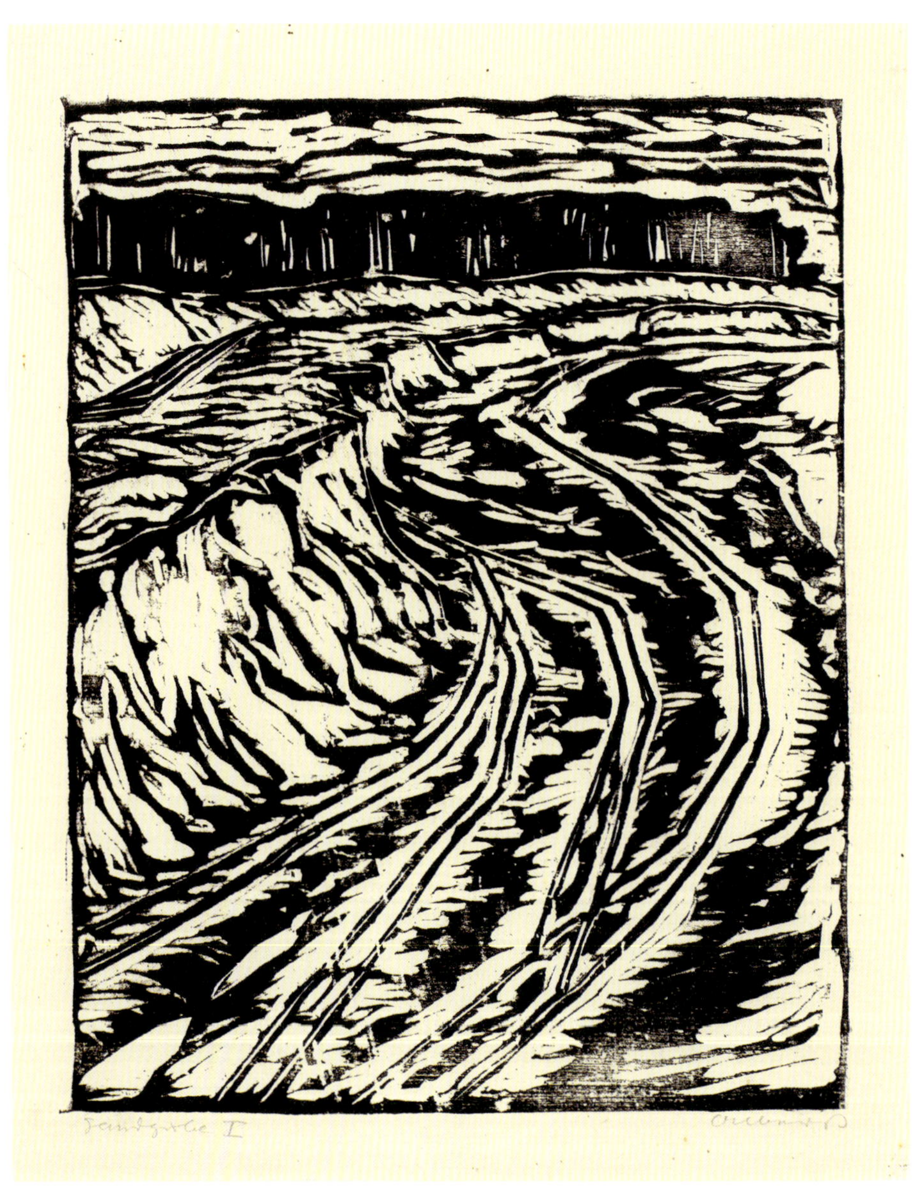

Sandgrube I (Sandmine I), 1916,
linoleum cut, paper 35.2 × 30.2 cm,
image 30.2 × 23.8 cm. Josef and Anni Albers
Foundation, 1976.4.4

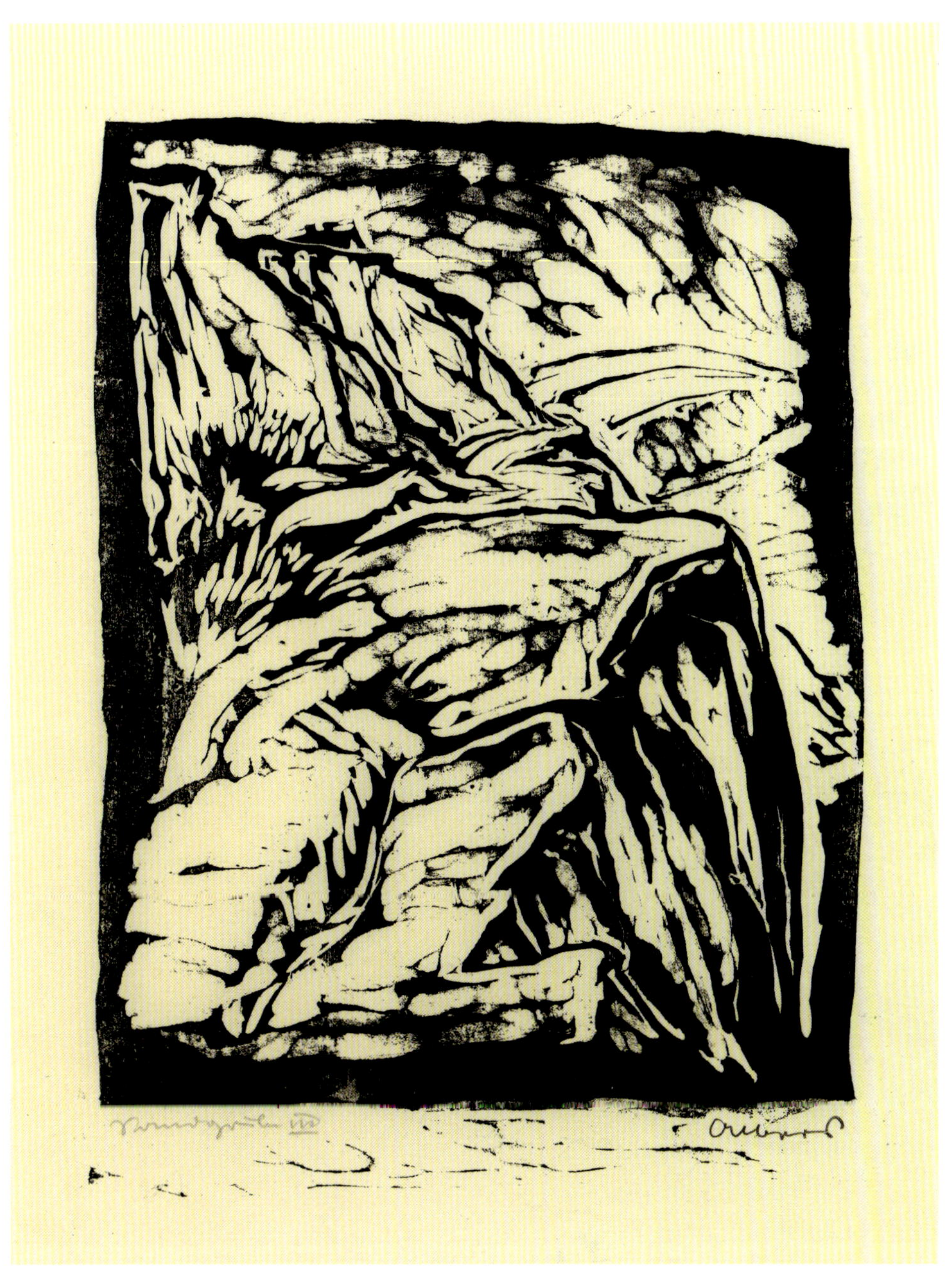

Sandgrube III (Sandmine III), 1916, linoleum cut, paper 45.1 × 33.7 cm, image 26.7 × 21 cm. Josef and Anni Albers Foundation, 1976.4.6

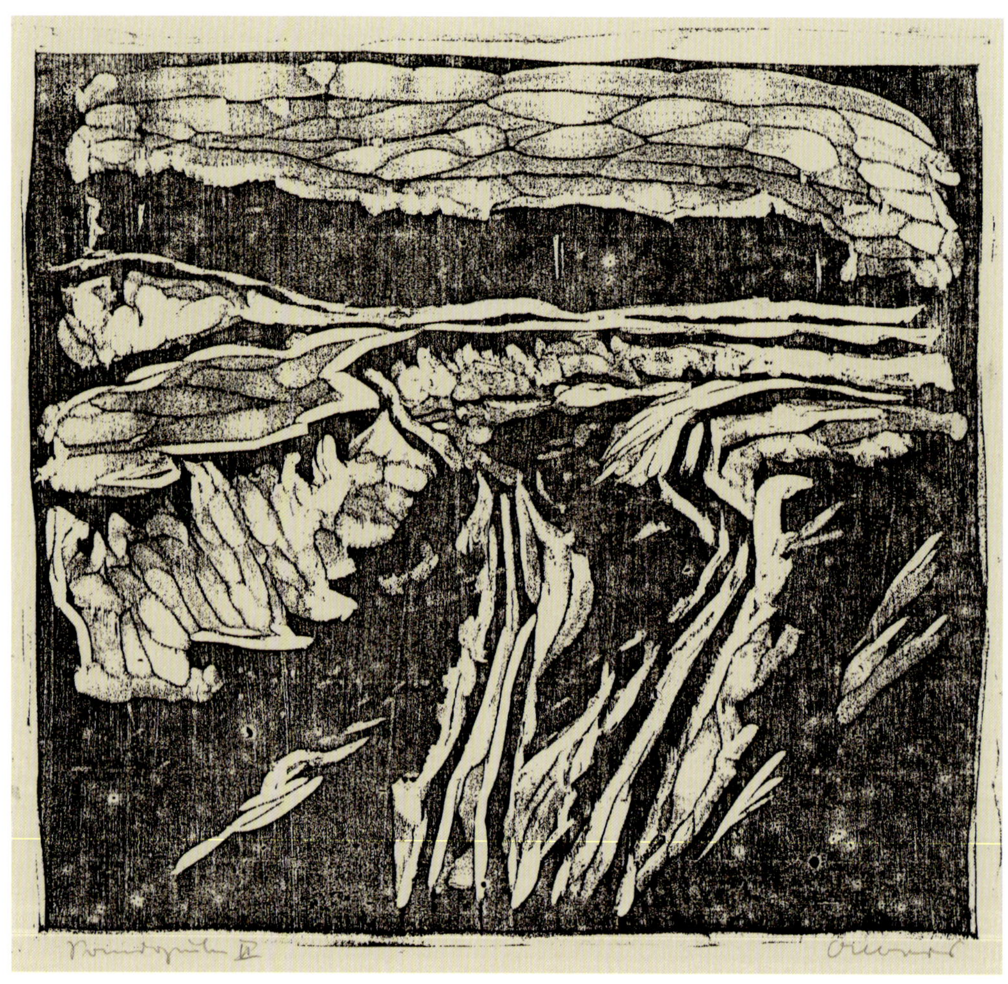

Sandgrube II (Sandmine II), state I, 1916, linoleum cut, paper 26.4 × 28.6 cm, image 23.5 × 26 cm. Josef and Anni Albers Foundation, 1976.4.5a

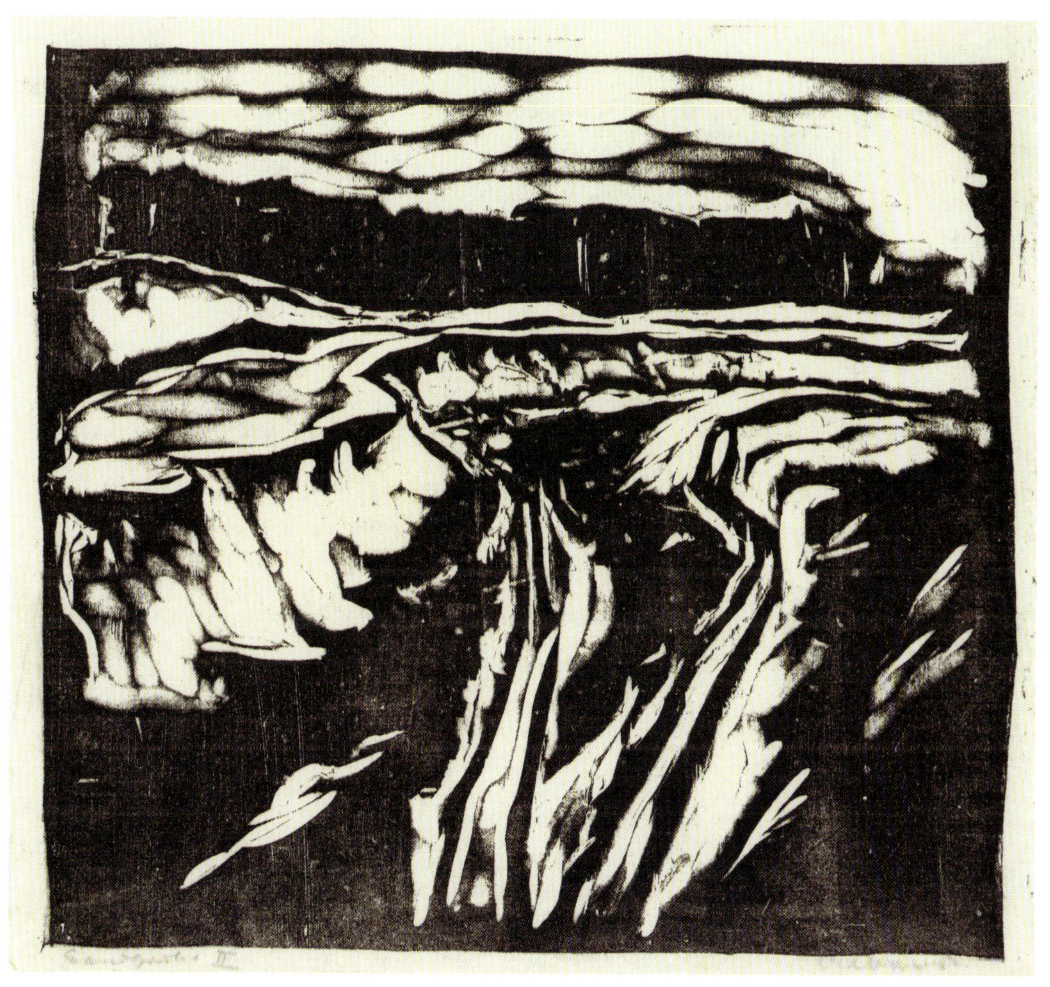

Sandgrube II (Sandmine II), state II, 1916, linoleum cut, paper 26.4 × 28.6 cm, image 23.5 × 26 cm. Josef and Anni Albers Foundation, 1976.4.5b

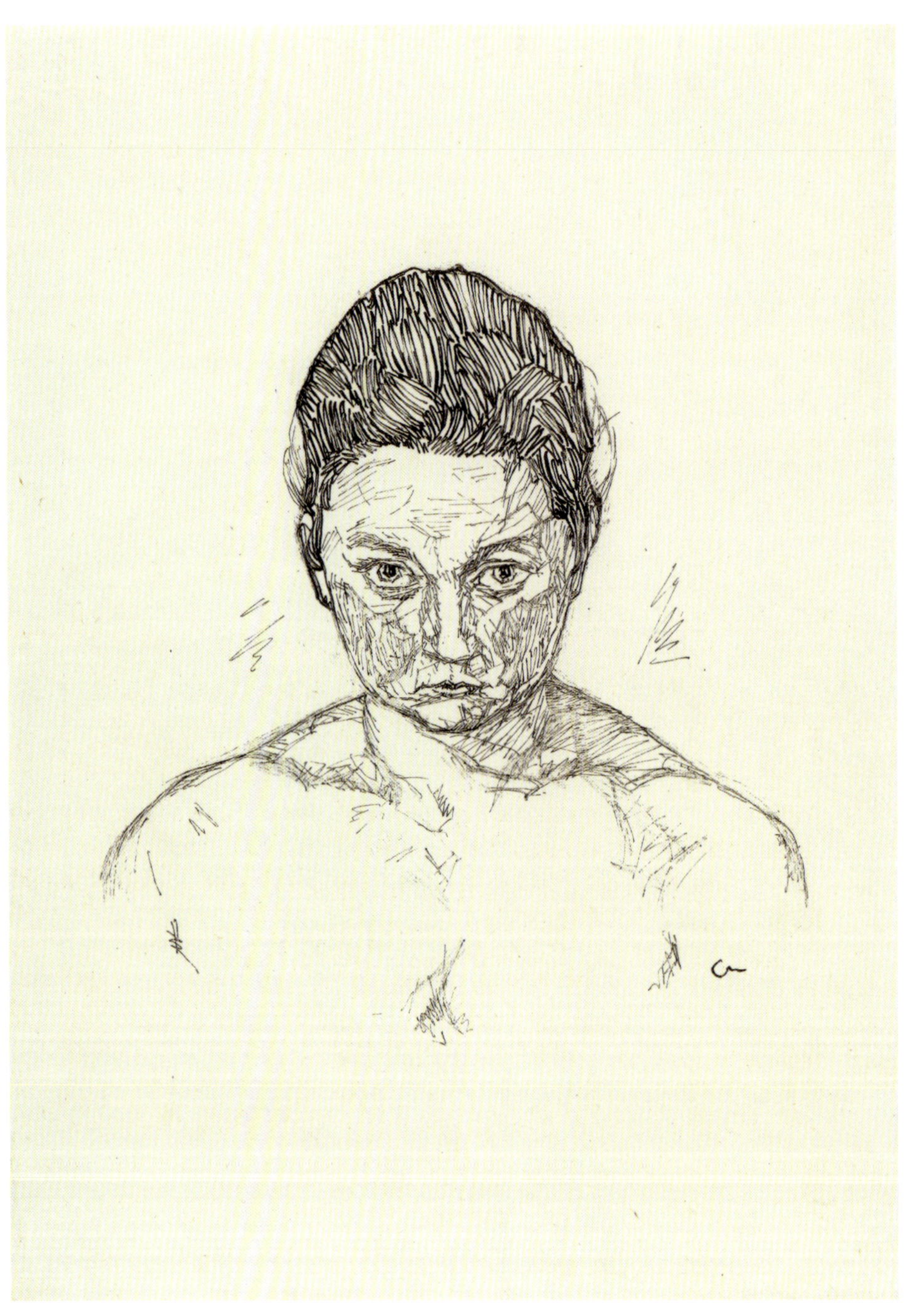

Girl, 1916,
lithograph on stone
with crayon and tusche,
paper 42.5 × 30.5 cm,
image 24.8 × 23.2 cm.
Josef and Anni Albers Foundation, 1976.4.28

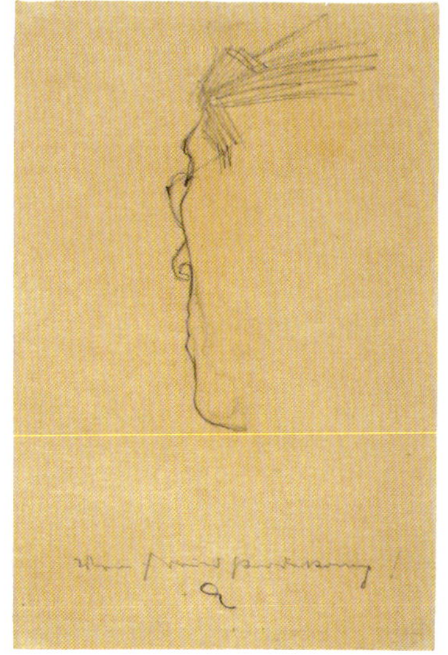

If the early linocuts demonstrate a preoccupation with the subtractive, sculptural relief process, the lithographs are emphatically linked to drawing. Most of the prints are transfer lithographs. There is little evidence that Albers worked directly on the lithographic surface, whether stone or metal plate, without first transferring an image – either complete or in outline – to it. In some cases, the existence of both a drawing in lithographic crayon and an identical lithograph indicates that he traced the image onto the lithographic surface in reverse. This seems to have been the method used for the portraits of Franz Grosse Perdekamp and Aloys Bürger; the 'Rabbit' prints from 1916 (p. 61); and the remarkable *Green Flute* series of the following year (p. 63).

ABOVE *Mein Freund Perdekamp!*, *c.* 1917–18, pencil on paper, 31.8 × 21.6 cm. Josef and Anni Albers Foundation, 1976.3.424

RIGHT Portrait of Aloys Bürger, 1916, transfer lithograph, paper 33.7 × 32.7 cm, image 29.5 × 27.6 cm. Josef and Anni Albers Foundation, 1976.4.29

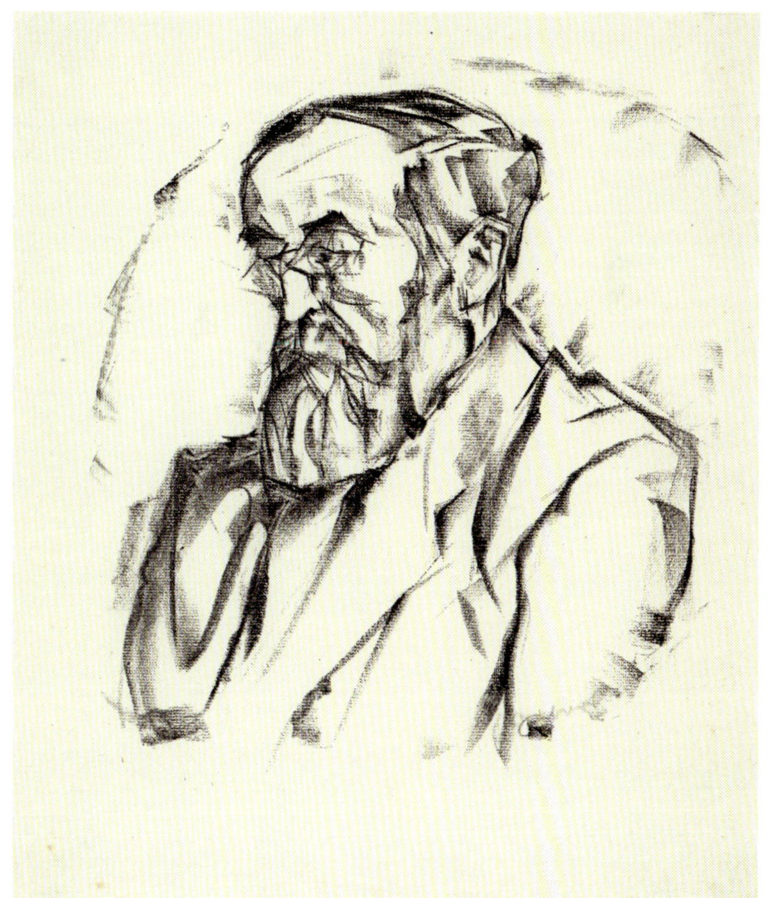

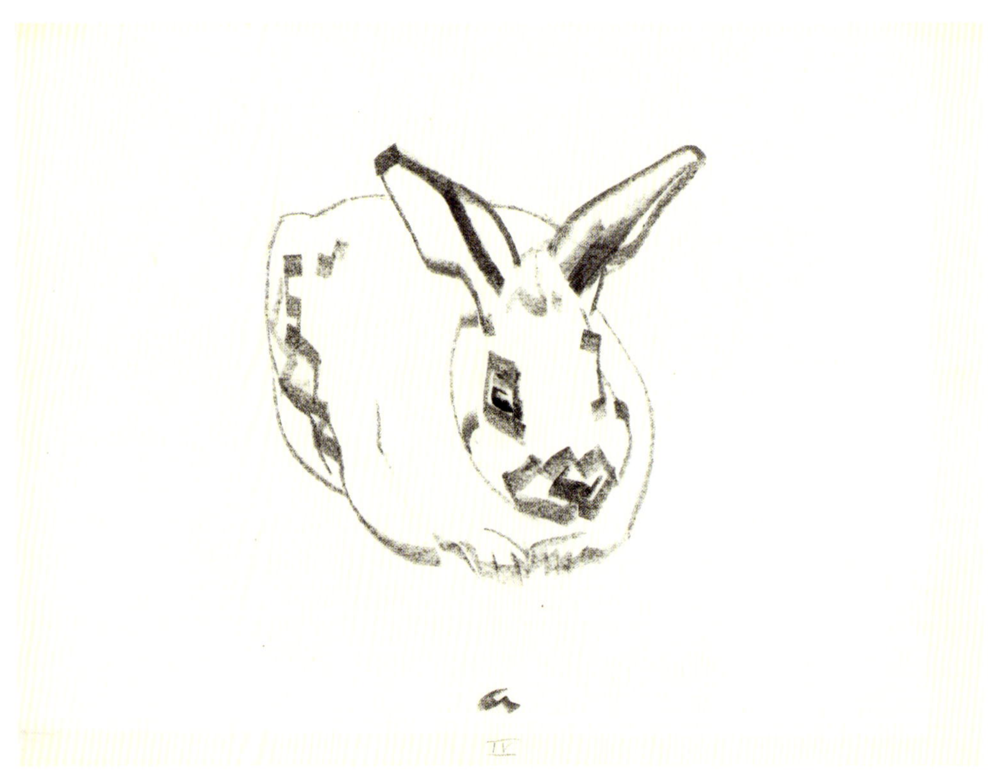

Rabbit, *c*. 1916, lithographic crayon on paper, 26 × 34.6 cm. Josef and Anni Albers Foundation, 1976.3.12

Rabbit, 1916,
transfer lithograph,
paper 27.3 × 33 cm,
image 13.3 × 21 cm.
Josef and Anni Albers
Foundation, 1976.4.24

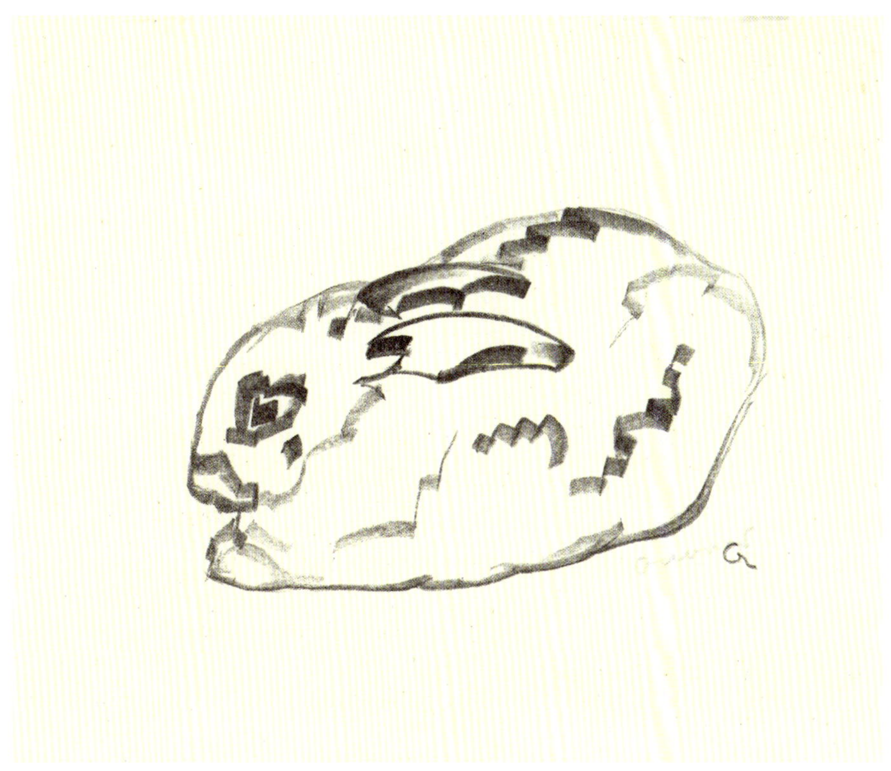

Rabbit, 1916,
transfer lithograph,
paper 26.4 × 31.4 cm,
image 14 × 20.3 cm.
Josef and Anni Albers
Foundation, 1976.4.25

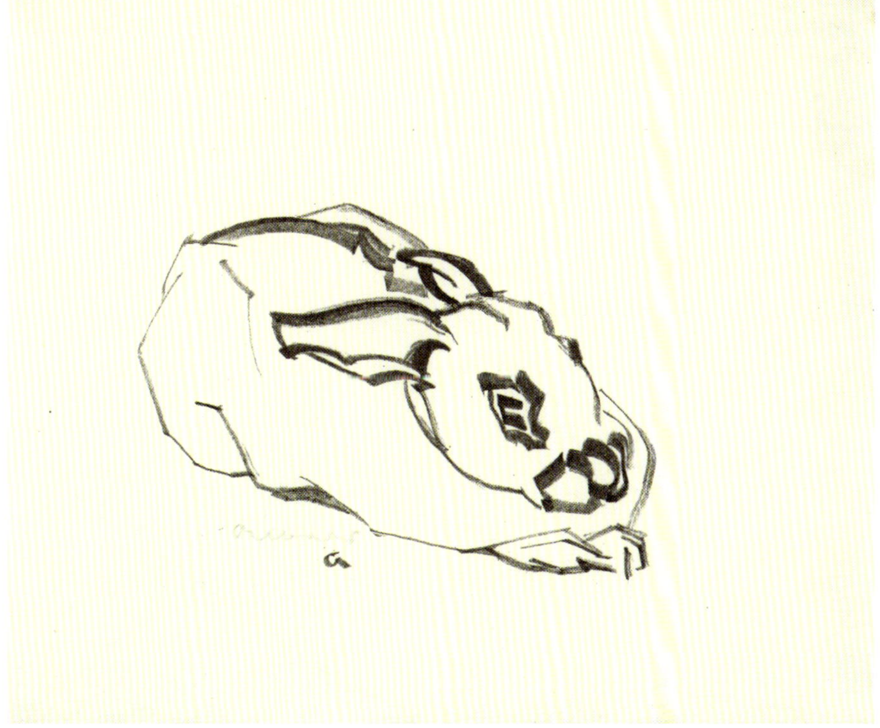

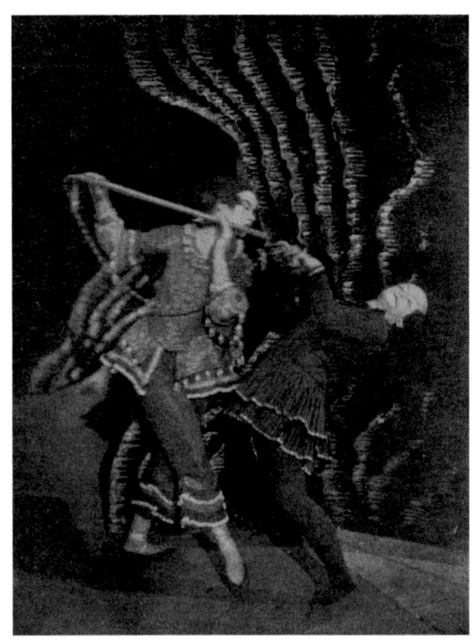

The Green Flute, performed at the Lessing Theater, Berlin, 1925. Theaterwissenschaftliche Sammlung, University of Cologne, Germany

As dramatic in its own way as the sandmines around Bottrop, *The Green Flute*, a pantomime-ballet based on a libretto by Hugo von Hofmannsthal with a score by Mozart, thrilled Albers when he saw it performed in Duisburg in 1916. He reported in great excitement to his friend Perdekamp: 'Dear Franz! If you want to enjoy ... good expressionist theatre art, then you have to be at the Düsseldorf City Theater tomorrow.... They are performing *The Green Flute* (Deutsches Theater Berlin).... I saw it in Duisburg on Friday ... immensely dramatic... You have to go!... I am going to be there for sure.... In wild anticipation ...'.[6] Rarely did Albers communicate his enthusiasms with such passion; even more rarely did he memorialize them overtly in his work.

The production, as described by its set and costume designer Ernst Stern, was pure fantastical illusion and spectacle: a rococo confection set in a version of eighteenth-century China imagined by its German creators. In Stern's lively account, the sets, 'more rococo than Chinese', dripping with golden flourishes, were an organic part of the production.[7] This theatrical experience resulted in a group of delicate and spontaneously evocative, pared-down line drawings, in an idiom entirely different from the sandmine series. Photographs of the production demonstrate how Albers deftly translated the richly ornamental mise en scène into an expressive abstract graphic language. The particular fantasy of the performed spectacle is raised to a universal, graceful, light-handed, and airy series of events. In *The Green Flute* lithographs, the line is soft, spare, and lyrical, and the figures hover and float in an indeterminate pictorial space like the notes of a musical score that have been set free from the rigid horizontal lines of the musical staff. Albers alters the positions of the figures, and prints them singly or in combinations, so that, just like the stage performance that inspired them, they create a sequence of tableaux. Charming and enigmatic, suggestive and abstracted, the cast of *The Green Flute* characters reveals an underestimated playfully sensuous aspect of Albers's work.

6. Josef Albers to Franz Perdekamp, 19 November 1916. Private collection, Germany.

7. Ernst Stern, *Bühnenbildner bei Max Reinhardt* (Berlin: Henschelverlag, 1955), pp. 118–23.

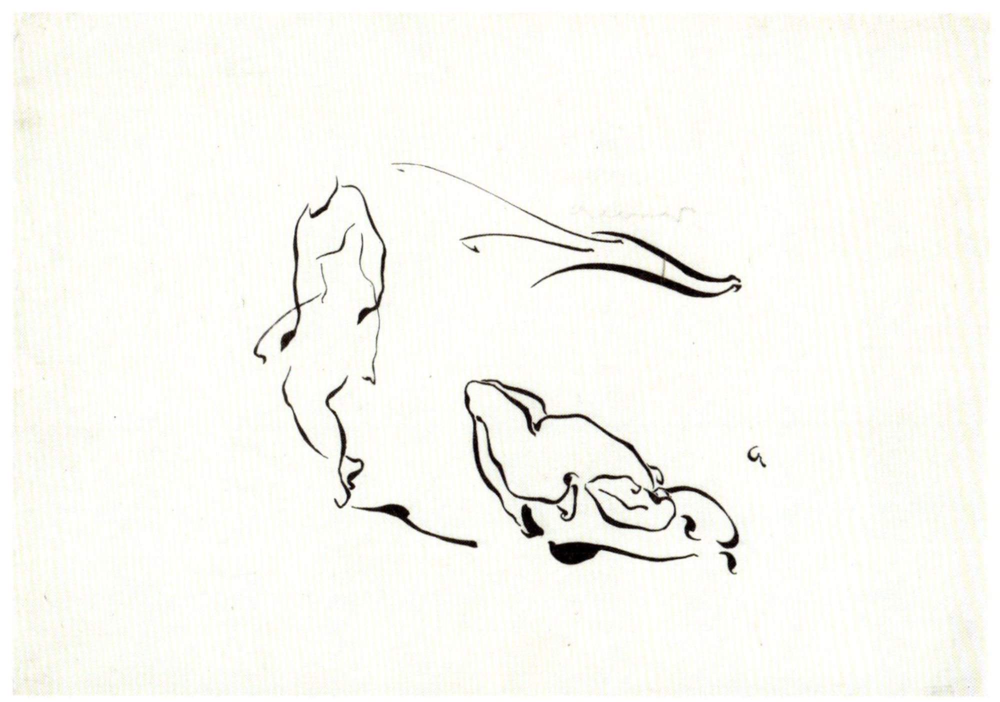

ABOVE *Frightened Pair from a Fairy Tale II*, 1917, lithograph and tusche, paper 34.8 × 49.5 cm, image 19 × 25.4 cm. Josef and Anni Albers Foundation, 1976.4.39

RIGHT Standing figure, 1917, transfer lithograph, paper 31.8 × 21.6 cm, image 15.6 × 7.6 cm. Josef and Anni Albers Foundation, 1976.4.32

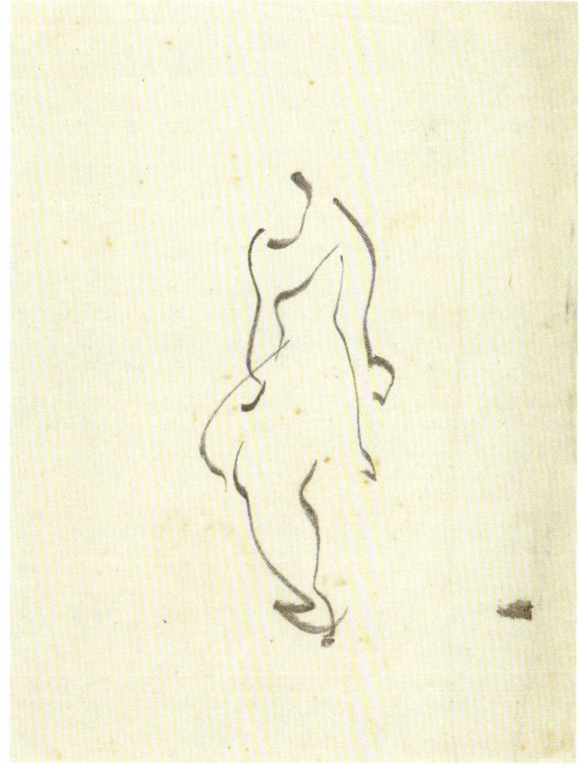

Self-portrait, *c.* 1917–18, lithographic crayon on paper, 48.3 × 39.4 cm. Private collection

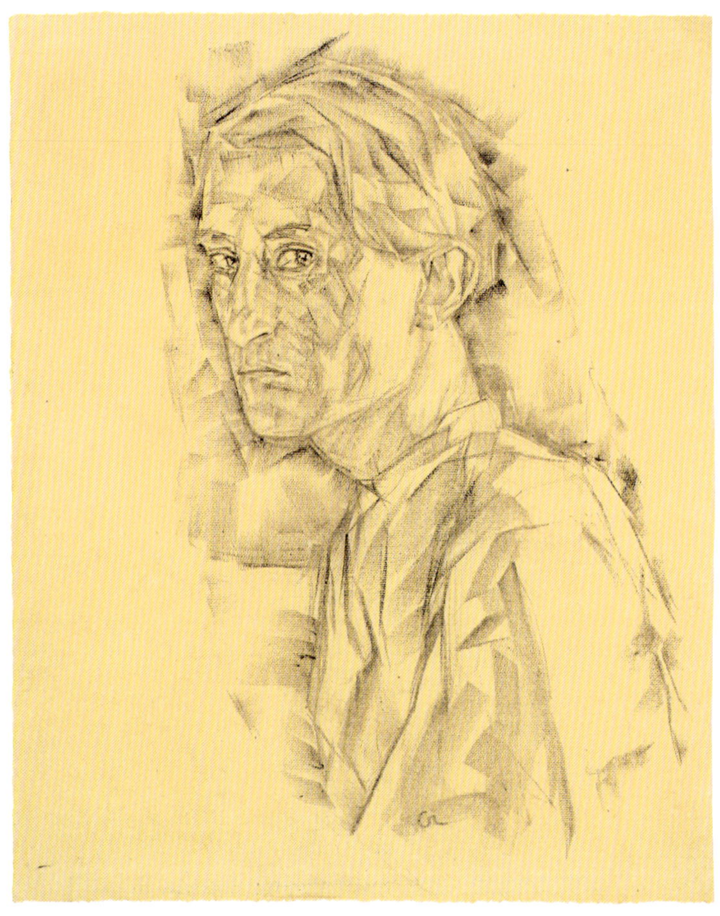

He continued to explore the expressive possibilities of the lithographic process in a large self-portrait of 1917 where a sense of foreboding apparent in the 1916 self-portraits is transformed into the gaze of a serious artist, signalled by fractured strokes reminiscient of Picasso's contemporary Cubist works.[8] Albers provided information about the lithographic process on an almost identical drawing in lithographic crayon. There he wrote below the image 'Stein Verworfen', literally 'stone destroyed'. On the verso of the drawing, apparently at a later date, he wrote the following explanatory note in ink: 'At the bottom of front, it said: "Stein Verworfen" – that is, no [further] prints were made from the stone on which this drawing was transferred.' From this, we have confirmation both that he used a transfer process and that this lithograph, at least, was made from a stone and not a metal plate.

In 1919, Albers took a second leave of absence from his teaching position and travelled to Munich to study painting with Franz von Stuck.[9] In September 1919, two of his prints were exhibited at the Munich gallery Neue Kunst Hans Goltz, which championed Expressionist and other contemporary printmakers.[10] The leave of absence turned out to be permanent. From Munich, Albers went on to Weimar in 1920, eager to enroll at the newly founded design school: the Staatliches Bauhaus. After completing his course of studies there, he remained as a teacher as the school moved first to Dessau in 1925 and then to Berlin in March 1933.

Josef Albers with student, Bauhaus Dessau, *c.* 1927, photographed by Arieh Sharon

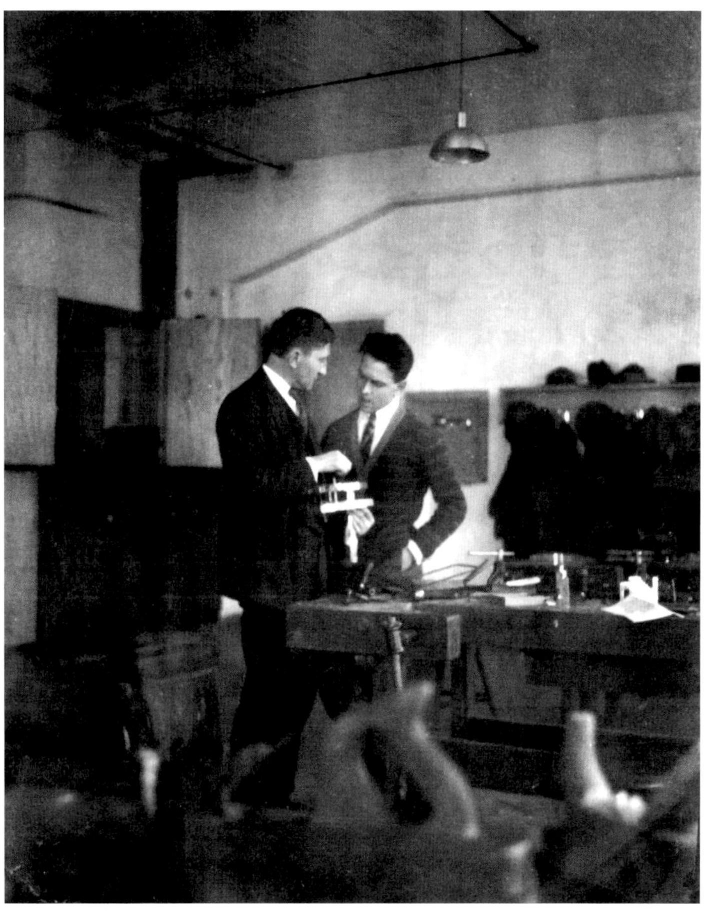

8. Christopher Green has described Picasso's *c.* 1917 works as 'conceptual, geometrical and crystalline', in *Life and Death in Picasso: Still Life/Figure c. 1907–1933* (London: Thames & Hudson, 2009), p. 93.

9. A letter dated 18 February 1919, from the director of the Handwerker und Kunstgewerbeschule in Essen recommending Albers to the Staatliche Kunst-Akademie in Munich indicates that it was about this time that Albers arrived in Munich. Albers remembered that, after passing an entrance test, he entered von Stuck's painting class at the Royal Bavarian Academy of Fine Arts in Munich on 31 May 1919 (J. A. Schmoll gen. Eisenwerth, 'Josef Albers über Franz von Stuck – ein Interview', in *Villa Stuck: Franz von Stuck, 1863–1928* [Munich: Museum Villa Stuck and Karl M. Lipp Verlag, 1984], p. 59).

10. *V. Gesamt-Ausstellung. September – Oktober* (Munich: Neue Kunst Hans Goltz, 1919). This large exhibition included paintings, sculpture, and prints. Two prints by Josef Albers are listed in the catalogue but not identified. One hundred and sixty-three prints by more than sixty artists, including Heinrich Campendonk, Lyonel Feininger, Georg Grosz, Erich Heckel, Paul Klee, Oskar Kokoschka, Franz Marc, Emil Nolde, Max Pechstein, and Egon Schiele were shown. Catalogue information courtesy Dietrich Schneider-Henn Auktion, Munich.

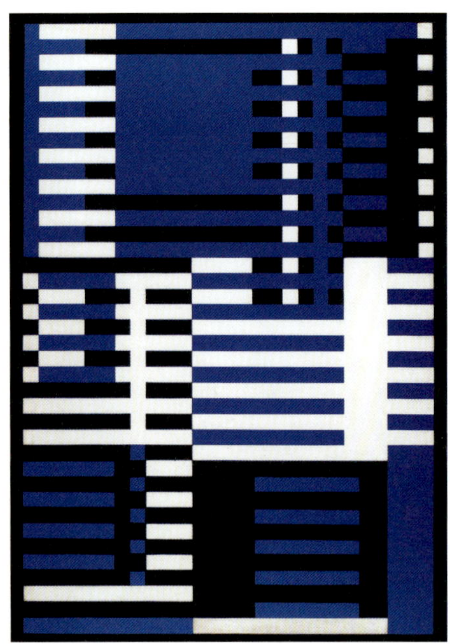

Aufwärts (Upward), *c.* 1926, sandblasted flashed glass with black paint, 44.6 × 31.4 cm. Josef and Anni Albers Foundation, 1976.6.2

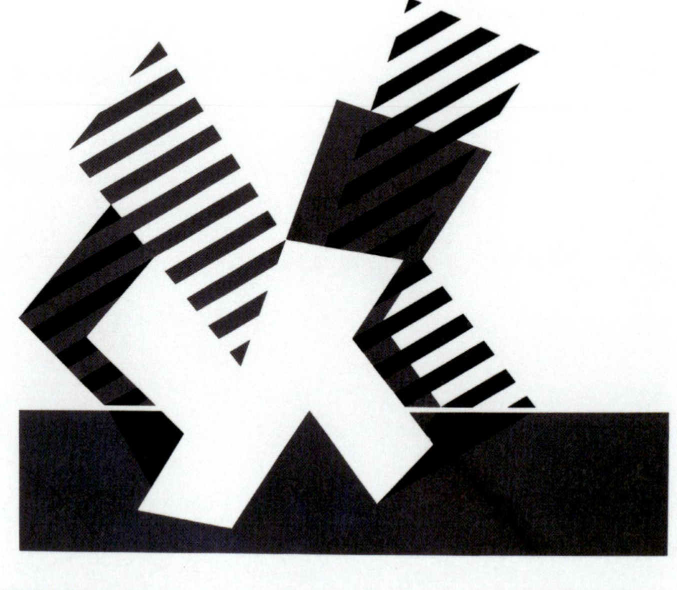

K-Trio, *c.* 1932, sandblasted flashed glass, 47.9 × 54.8 cm. Josef and Anni Albers Foundation, 1976.6.23

Joining the Bauhaus was a life-changing experience. The school valued craftsmanship, experimentation, and invention over style and facility. Group education and practical workshops took precedence over solitary artists cultivating personal styles. Albers worked in stained and sandblasted glass, in typography, photography, wallpaper, and furniture design; and he famously taught the *Vorkurs* – the fundamental preliminary course that established a kind of ethics of form. The Bauhaus was also where Albers met his wife-to-be, Anni. At the time a novice student in the Bauhaus weaving workshop, Anni Albers would become a prominent weaver and textile designer, and eventually a printmaker herself. They married in 1925.

In July 1933, after months of harassment by the Nazi authorities in both Dessau and Berlin, the Bauhaus closed abruptly. Albers now found himself in creative limbo.[11] He no longer had access to

11. The decision to close the Bauhaus was finally taken at a faculty meeting on 19 July 1933. See Hans M. Wingler, *The Bauhaus: Weimar, Dessau, Berlin, Chicago*, ed. Joseph Stein, trans. Wolfgang Jabs and Basil Gilbert (Cambridge, Mass.: MIT Press, 1969), p. 564. The official letter from Mies van der Rohe, then the director of the school, announcing this to the faculty, is dated 27 July and states that the Bauhaus officially closed on 20 July 1933.

Model ti244 armchair, *c.* 1929, laminated beech wood, tubular steel, and canvas upholstery, 72.4 × 58.7 × 72.4 cm. Josef and Anni Albers Foundation, 1992.5.1

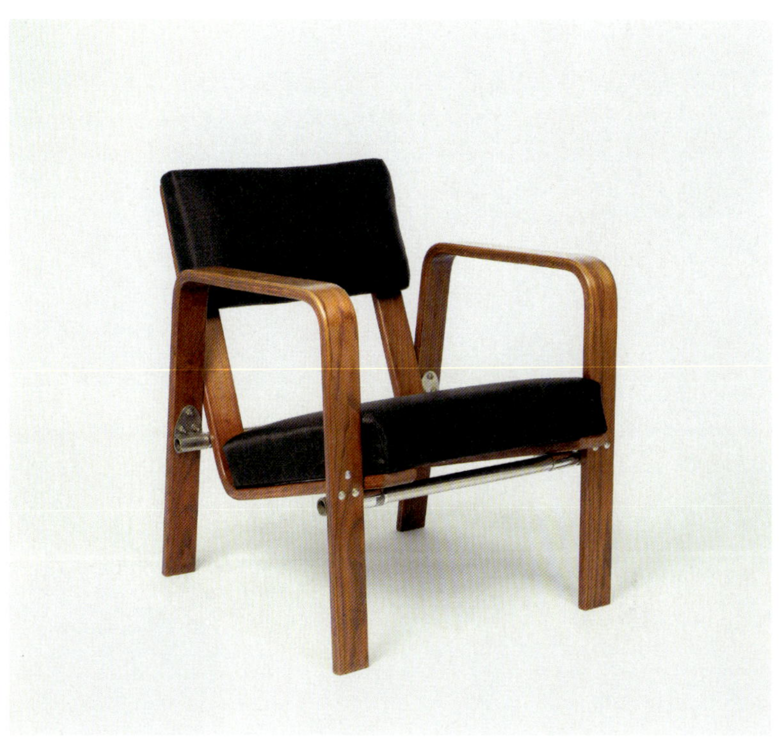

Tea table, *c.* 1928, ash veneer and milkglass, 68.3 × 55.9 × 6 cm. Josef and Anni Albers Foundation. 1976.5.2

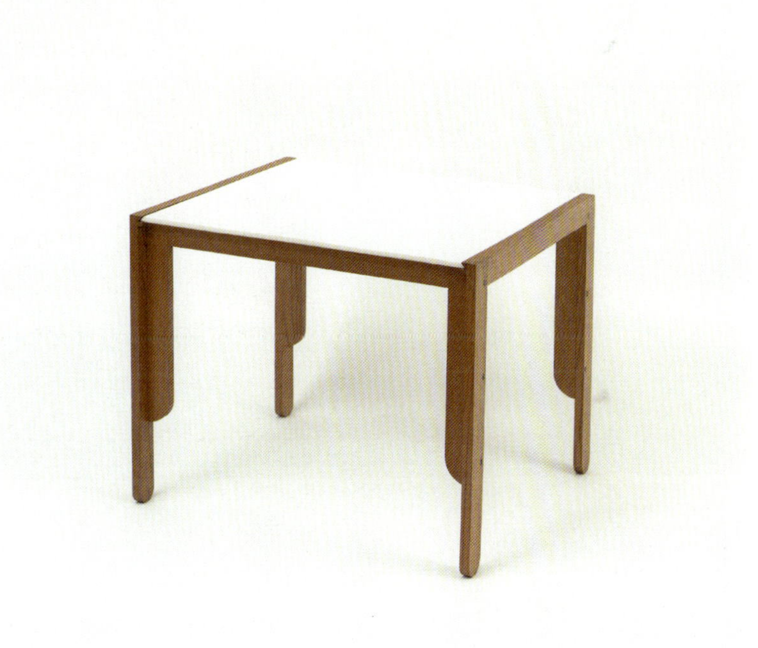

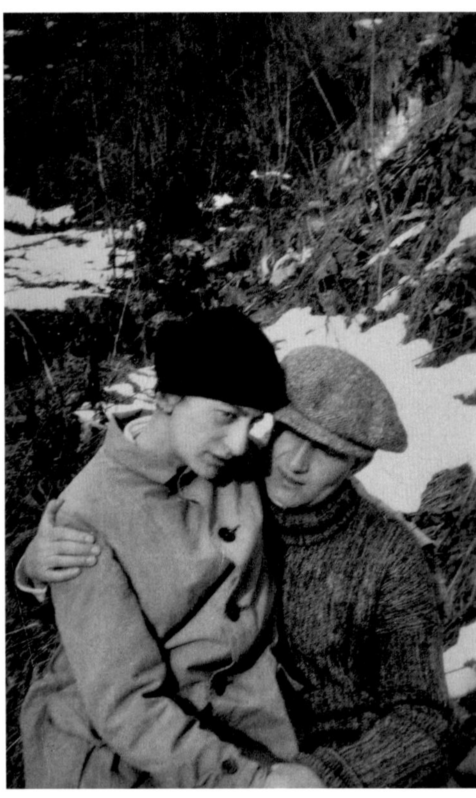

LEFT AND BELOW Josef and Anni Albers, Oberstdorf, Germany, *c.* 1927–8, photographer unknown. Josef and Anni Albers Foundation

BOTTOM Anni and Josef Albers on a studio balcony, Bauhaus Dessau, 1928–9, photographed by Marianne Brandt. Bauhaus-Archiv Berlin

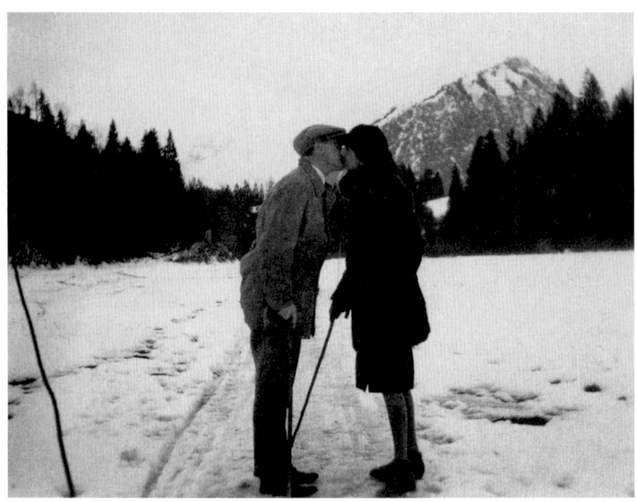

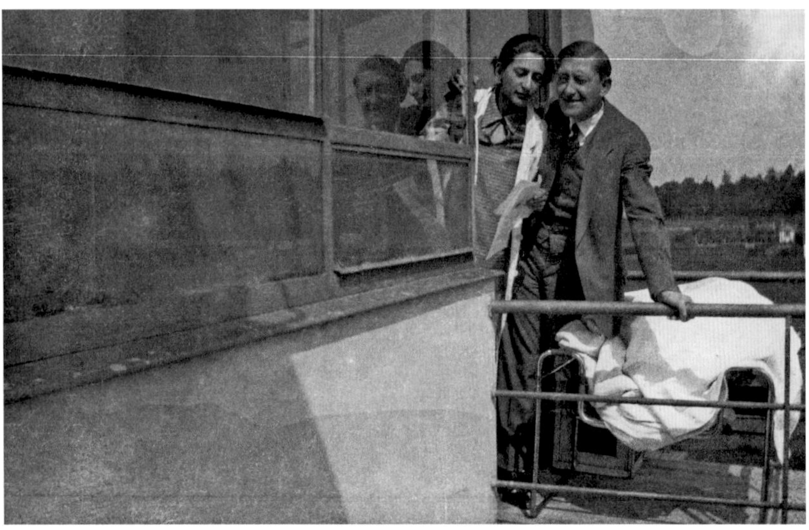

workshop facilities, nor did he have a teaching position or a salary. His association with the Bauhaus made him unemployable in Nazi Germany and his art unsaleable. So he set off in a new direction. Returning to the relief techniques of his earliest work, he began a series of woodcuts. 'I have begun a new chapter: woodcuts and linocuts', Albers wrote, 'this isn't as expensive, since I don't pay for the printing and the paper.'[12] Fortuitously, Anni Albers's family, the Ullsteins, owned Berlin's largest publishing enterprise, and Josef was able to print on the firm's presses.[13] He recorded in his notebooks details of the eight woodcuts, five linocuts, and a single cork relief print that he made in Berlin in 1933.

These relief prints introduced two entirely fresh elements into his graphic oeuvre. First, there is a new technical sophistication and acuity and a changed attitude to materials, the result of his years first as a student and then as a teacher and master at the Bauhaus. Gone, along with any expressive traces, are the anecdotal and pictorially descriptive flourishes of the 1916 relief prints. Second, these works demonstrate a novel conceptual understanding of the image itself and its perception by the viewer, related to gestalt theories of psychology that were becoming increasingly important to Albers.[14] The paired woodcuts *Black Circle* and *White Circle* (pp. 70–1) use an identical format to effect reversals of black and white, figure and ground, real and faux material, that test the viewer's visual alertness. The formats are almost, but not quite, reciprocal. The hatched area of *Black Circle* reproduces the surface grain of the woodblock in the manner of a rubbing or frottage. In *White Circle*, Albers used an artificial method to create an equivalent for the natural surface, as he later explained: 'As far as I know nature does not produce this kind of parallel grain. The woodblock was glued together with appropriate and selected wood strips. Only the central circle and its edged frame have been cut and excavated. The horizontal white lines were not, but were actually soft grain pushed down with a bookbinder's bone folder.'[15]

12. Josef Albers to Ludwig and Maude Gröte, 21 September 1933. Copy in the archives of the Josef and Anni Albers Foundation. Translation by David Blocher.

13. According to Peter Fritzsche, 'Ullstein's mammoth organization reached its zenith during the Weimar years, the "golden age" of the German press.' *Reading Berlin 1900*, (Cambridge and London: Harvard University Press, 1996), p. 212.

14. Theories of gestalt psychology were widespread in Germany in the 1920s and 1930s. Albers reported having attended lectures by the Leipzig gestalt psychologist Count von Dürkheim, at the Bauhaus in 1930 and 1931. The perception of spatial ambiguities in figure-ground relationships, the production of illusions of transparency in overlapping planes, as well as colour perception, were areas of gestalt investigation whose influence is evident in much of the work produced at the Bauhaus.

15. Josef Albers, *Formulation: Articulation*, two portfolios (New York: Harry N. Abrams, 1972), portfolio I, folder 7, page 193 below.

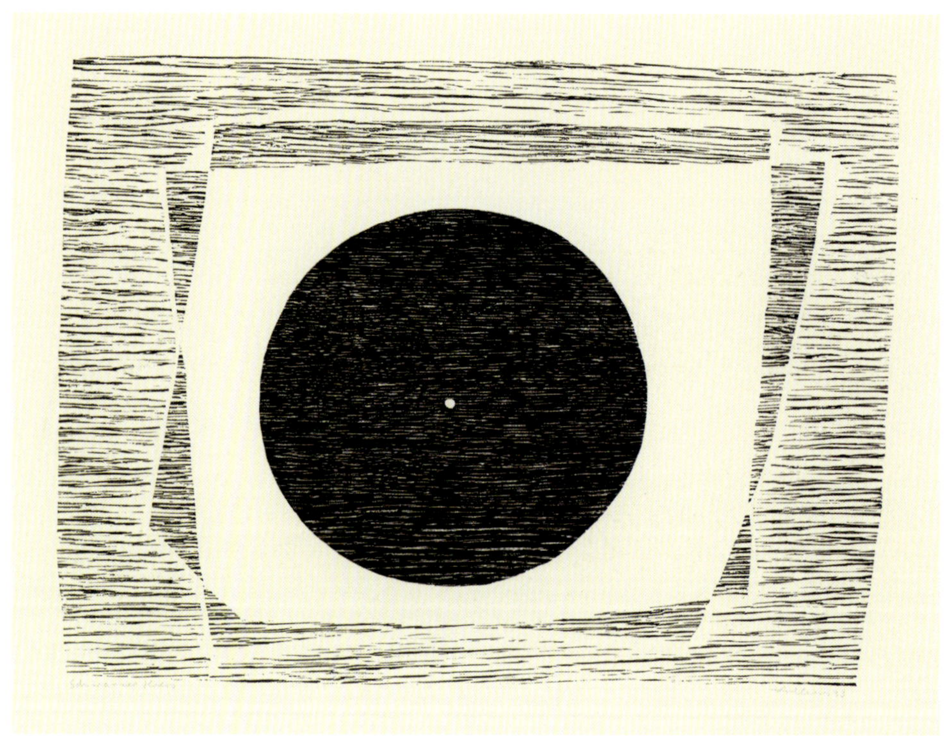

Schwarzer Kreis (Black Circle), 1933, woodcut, paper 35.6 × 50.2 cm, image 25.9 × 35.6 cm. Josef and Anni Albers Foundation, 1976.4.59

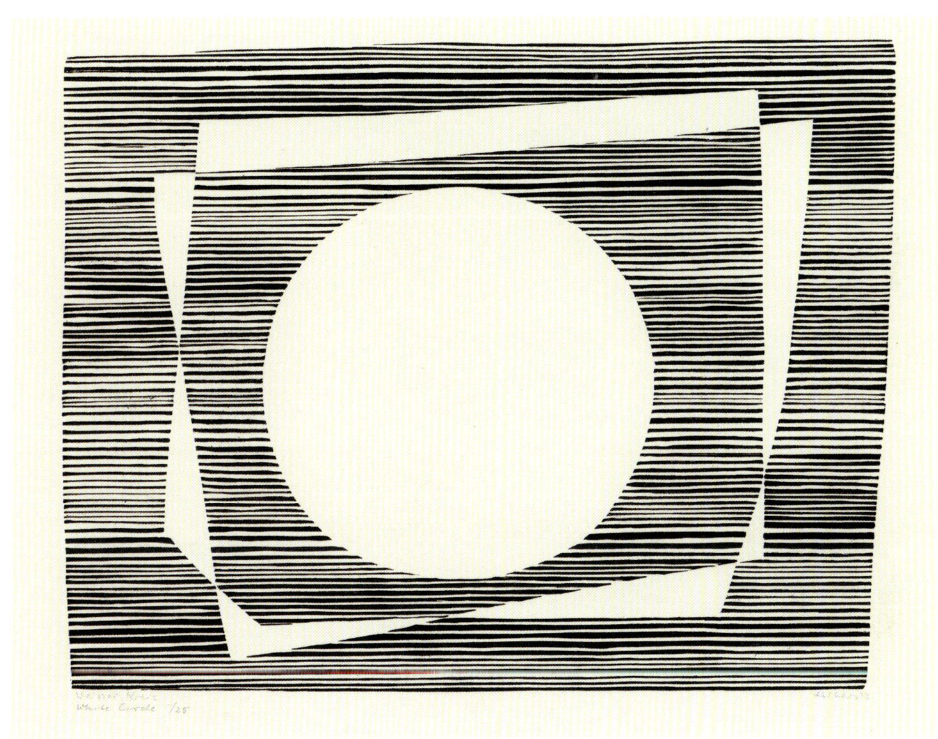

Weisser Kreis (White Circle), 1933,
woodcut, paper 35.6 × 50.2 cm,
image 27.9 × 35.6 cm. Josef and Anni Albers
Foundation, 1976.4.60

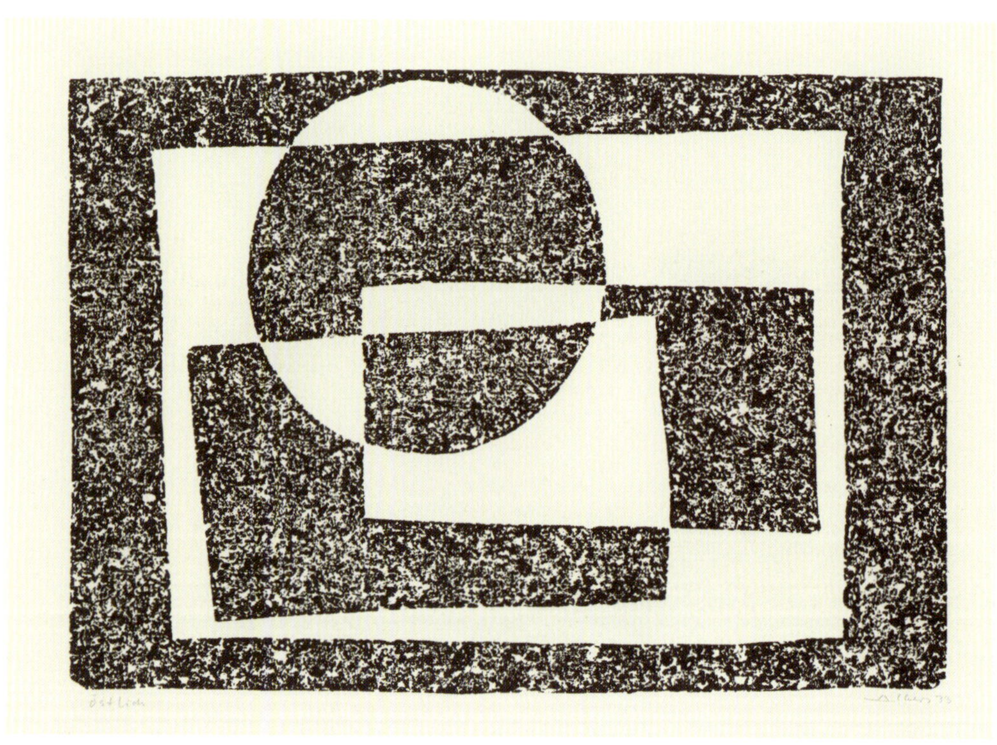

Östlich (Easterly), 1933,
cork relief, paper 35.6 × 50.5 cm,
image 21.6 × 31.1 cm. Josef and Anni Albers
Foundation, 1976.4.66

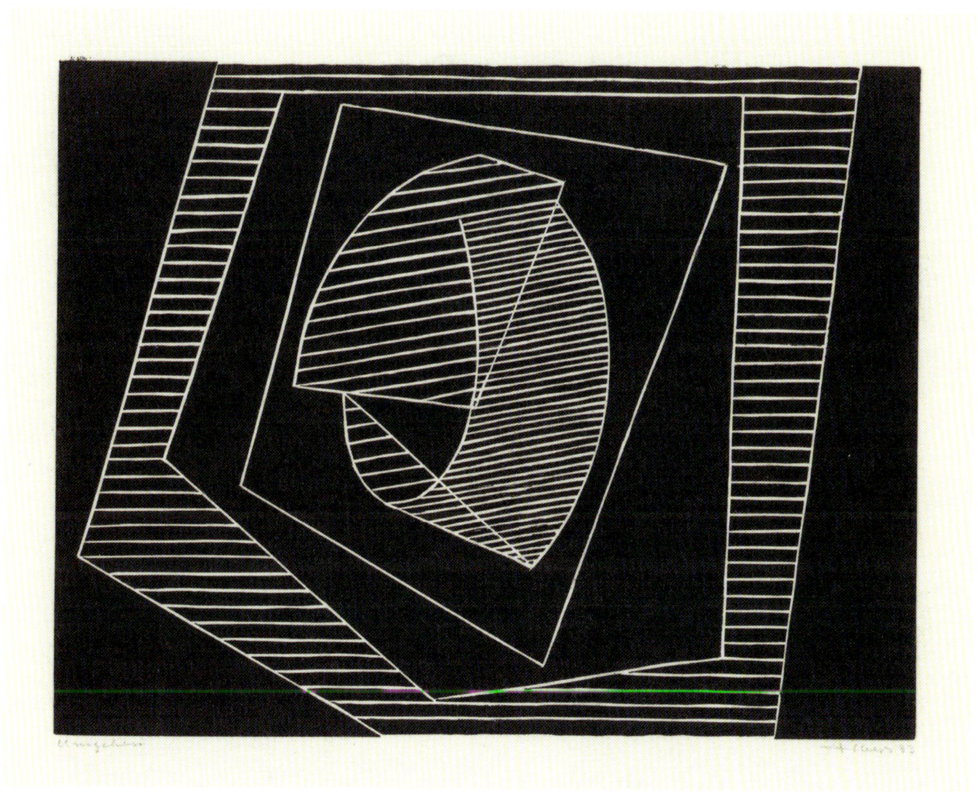

Umgeben (Surrounded), 1933,
linoleum cut, paper 35.6 × 50.6 cm,
image 19 × 25 cm. Josef and Anni Albers
Foundation, 1976.4.67

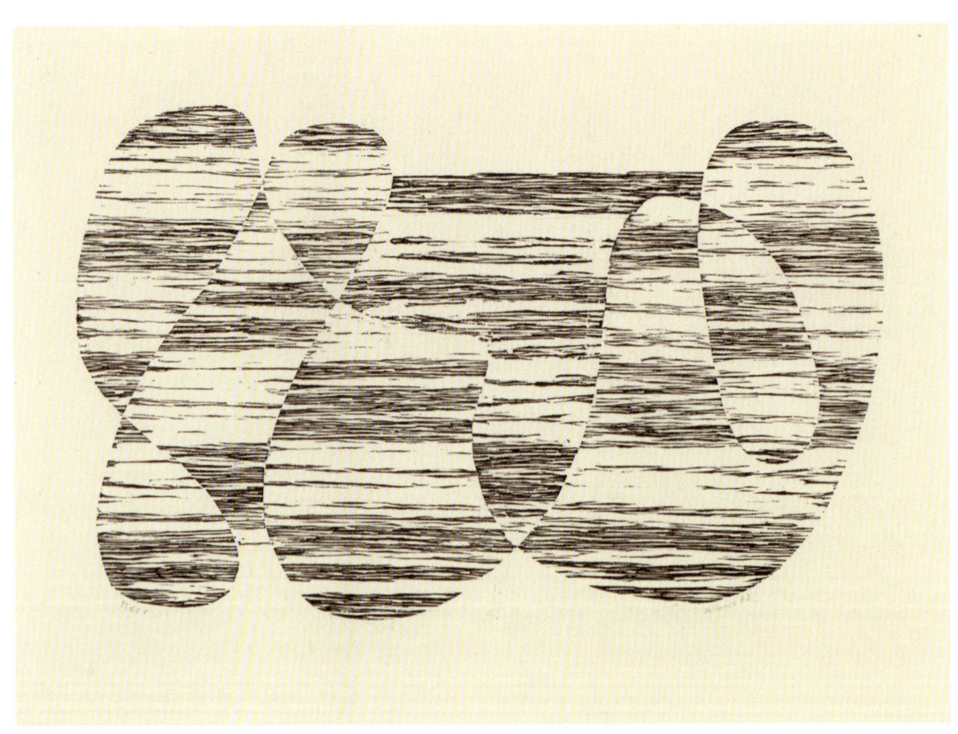

Meer (Sea), 1933,
woodcut, paper 35.6 × 44.8 cm,
image 19.7 × 32.4 cm. Josef and Anni Albers
Foundation, 1976.4.61

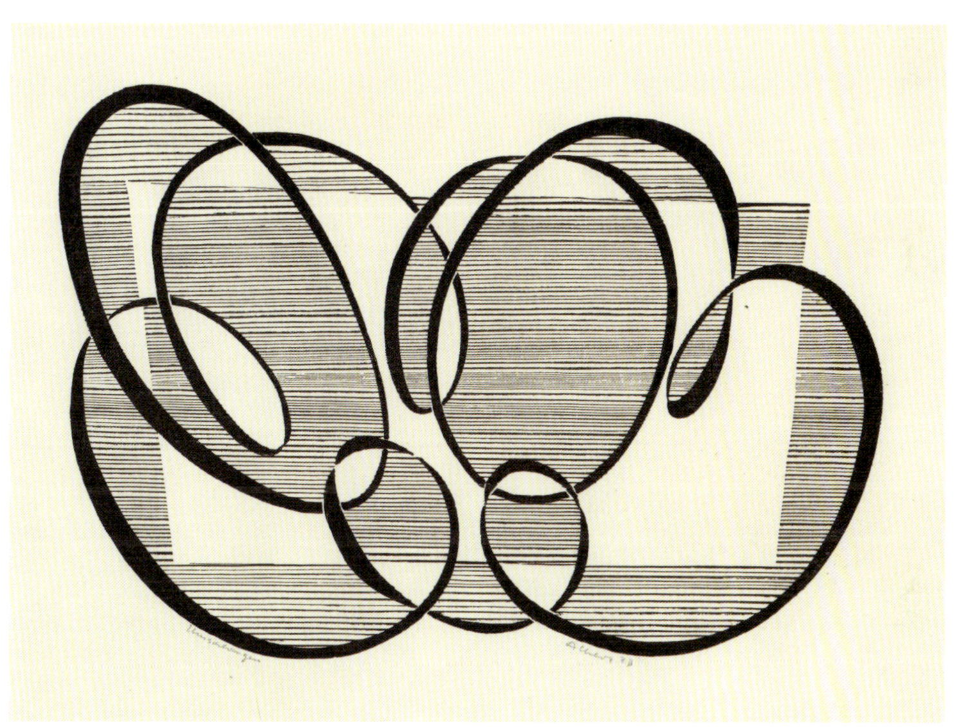

Umschlüngen (Encircled), 1933,
woodcut, paper 34.9 × 50.9 cm,
image 24.1 × 34.3 cm. Josef and Anni Albers
Foundation, 1976.4.62

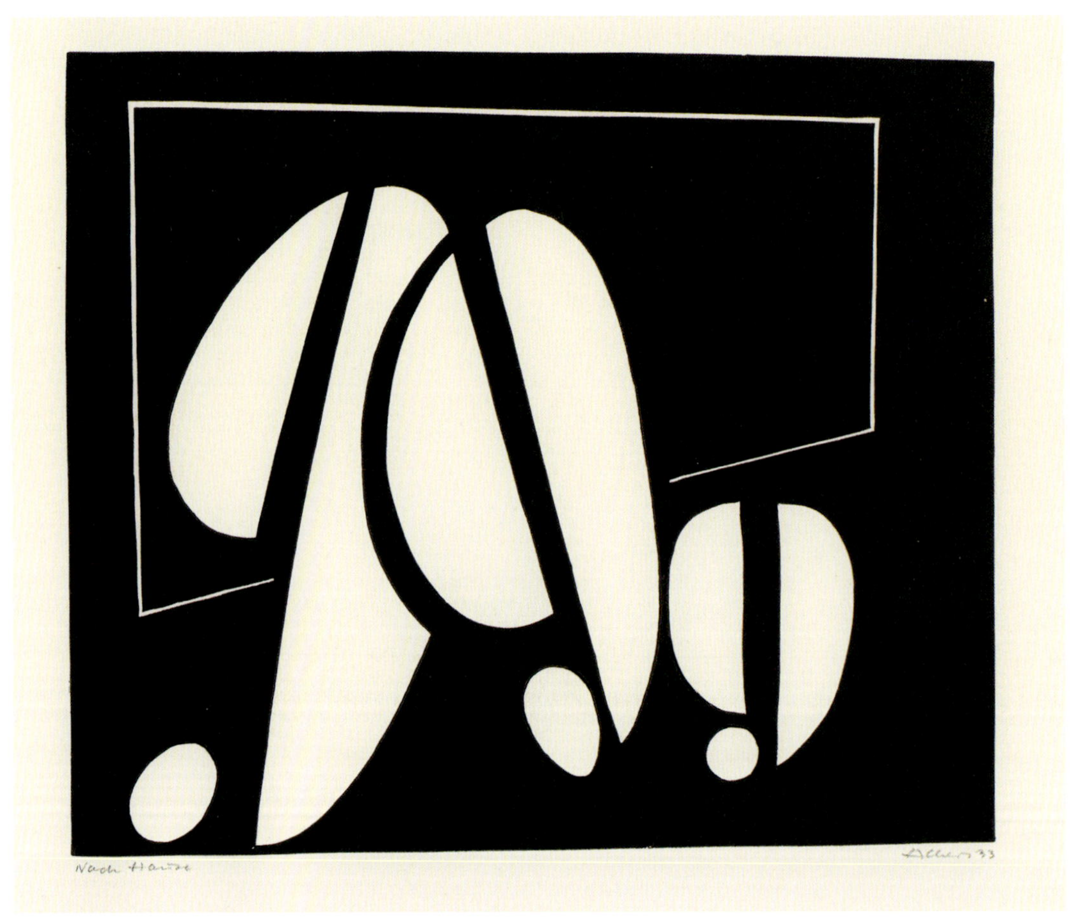

Nach Hause
(Homeward), 1933,
linoleum cut,
paper 32.2 × 50.3 cm,
image 21.6 × 26 cm.
Josef and Anni Albers
Foundation, 1976.4.63

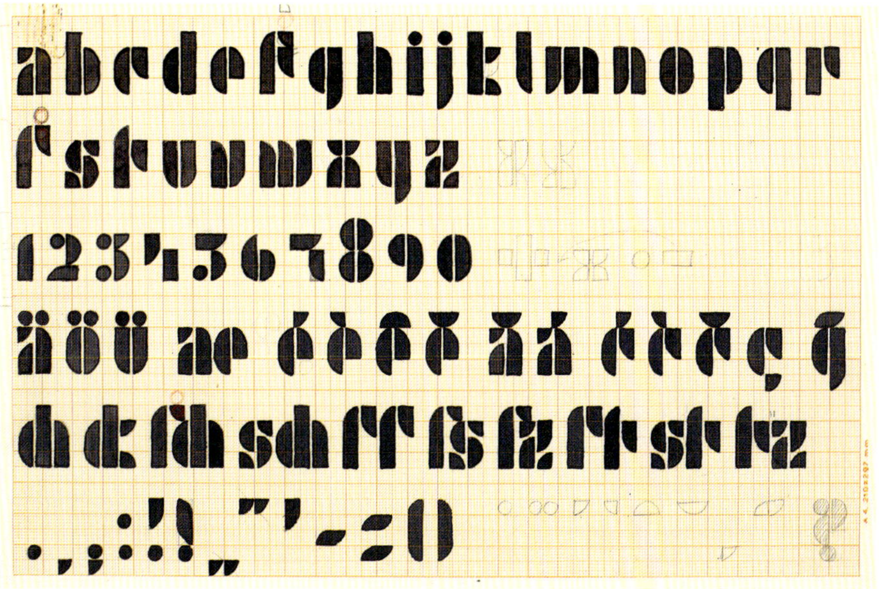

Design for a universal typeface, 1926, pen and ink and pencil on graph paper, 21.8 × 29.8 cm. Josef and Anni Albers Foundation, 1976.3.124

Visual play could also lead to an image that invited a literal reading. The specific arrangement of three figure 9s, modular forms derived from Albers's 1926 design for a universal typeface, when placed in front of a receding quasi-architectural quadrilateral shape, reads as three figures – perhaps father, mother, and child – walking along a street. Albers accordingly titled this print *Homeward*. In works such as *Opera* and *Tents* (pp. 78–9), the artist plays a sophisticated visual game when he juxtaposes contrasting shapes in an abstract composition and then embodies the resulting gestalt in the title. The optical shift between flat surface and the illusion of space in *Tents* foreshadows the spatial plays of line constructions such as *Show Case* (p. 90). Albers's insistence on careful craftsmanship was not mere pedantry. Repeatedly, his work demonstrated that the success of the visual effect depended on perfectly precise execution. In *Tents*, although the mostly triangular shapes have no outlines, their crisply cut borders produce the illusion of converging lines that project the shapes forward from their flat matrixes into the viewer's space.

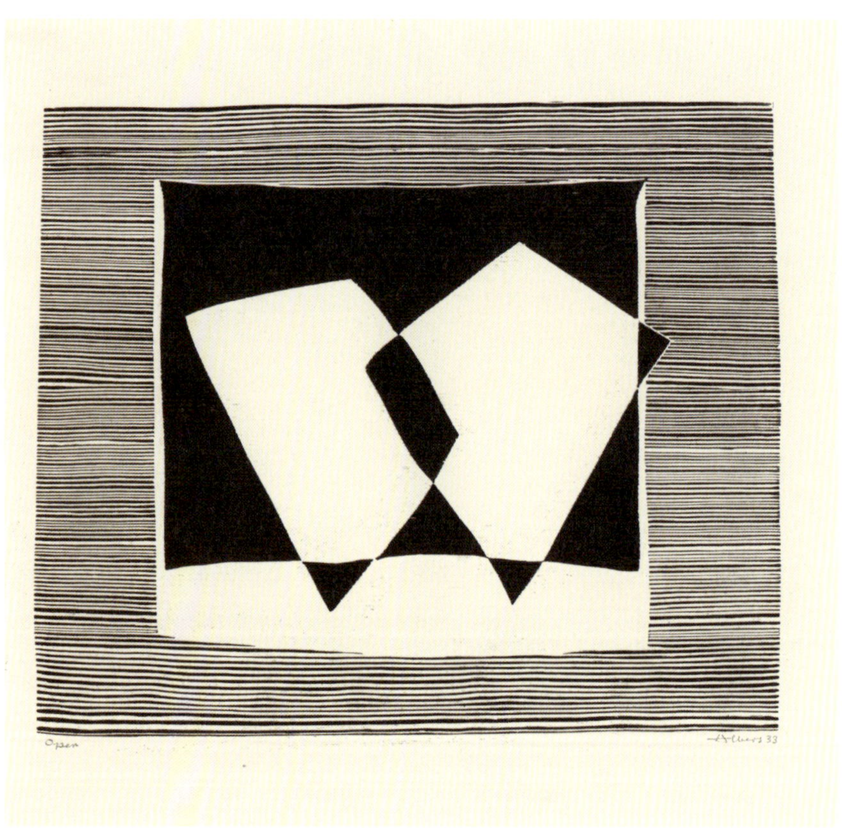

Oper (Opera), 1933, woodcut, paper 32.4 × 44.8 cm, image 24.1 × 29.2 cm. Josef and Anni Albers Foundation, 1976.4.64

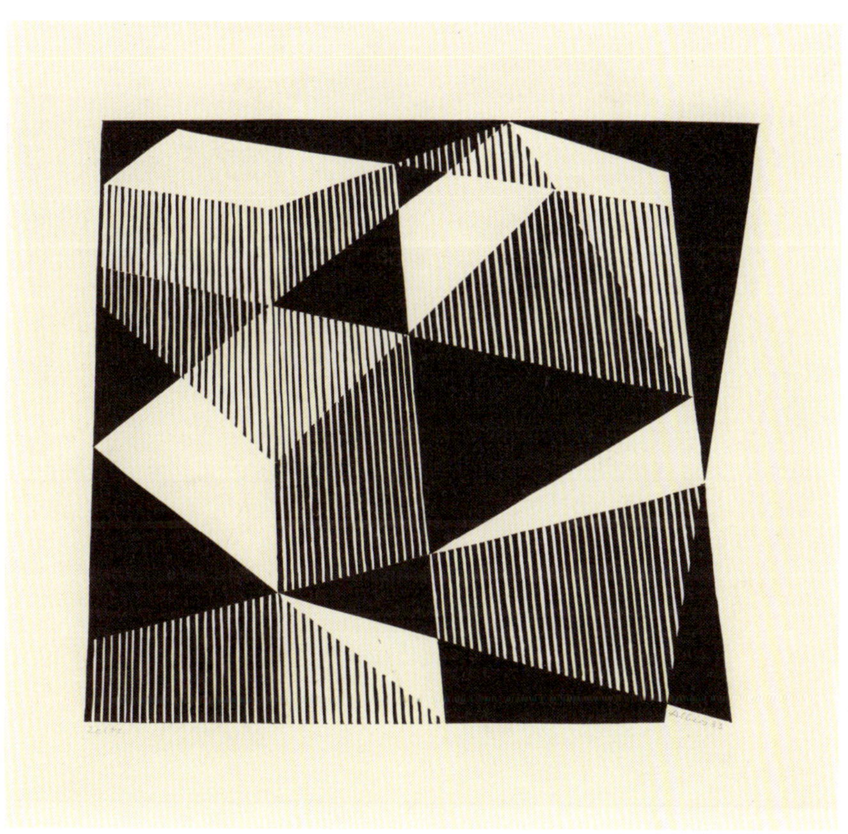

Zelte (Tents), 1933,
woodcut, paper 35.6 × 49.2 cm,
image 23 × 25.5 cm. Josef and
Anni Albers Foundation, 1976.4.65

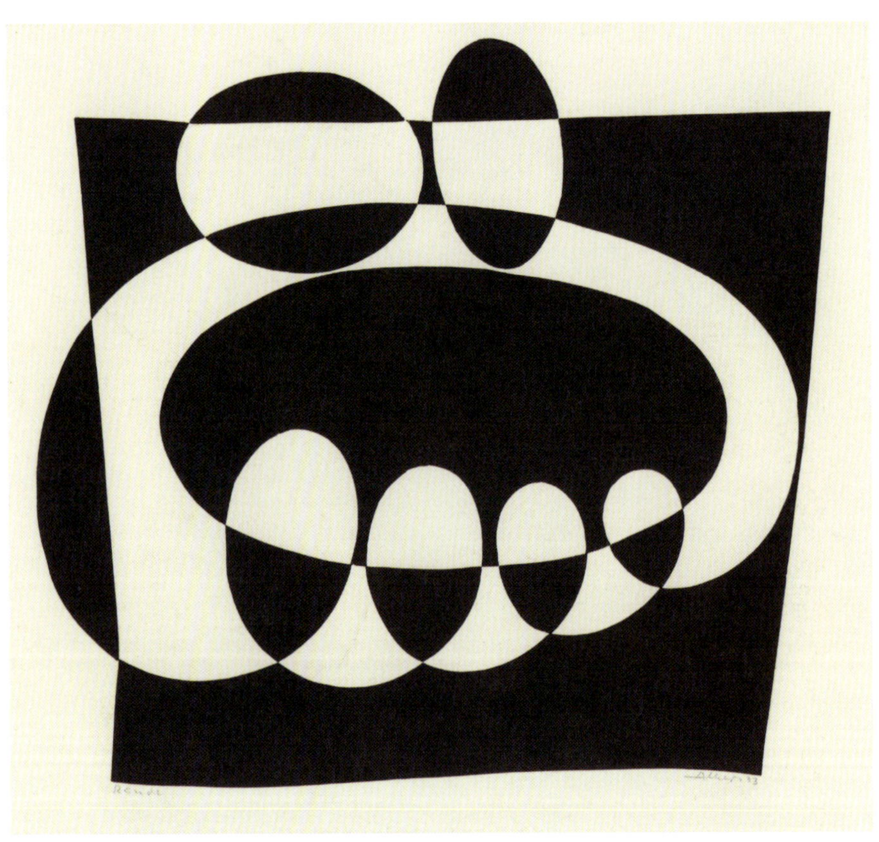

Ründe (Circle), 1933,
woodcut, paper 34.9 × 46.4 cm,
image 26 × 27.9 cm. Josef and
Anni Albers Foundation, 1976.4.68

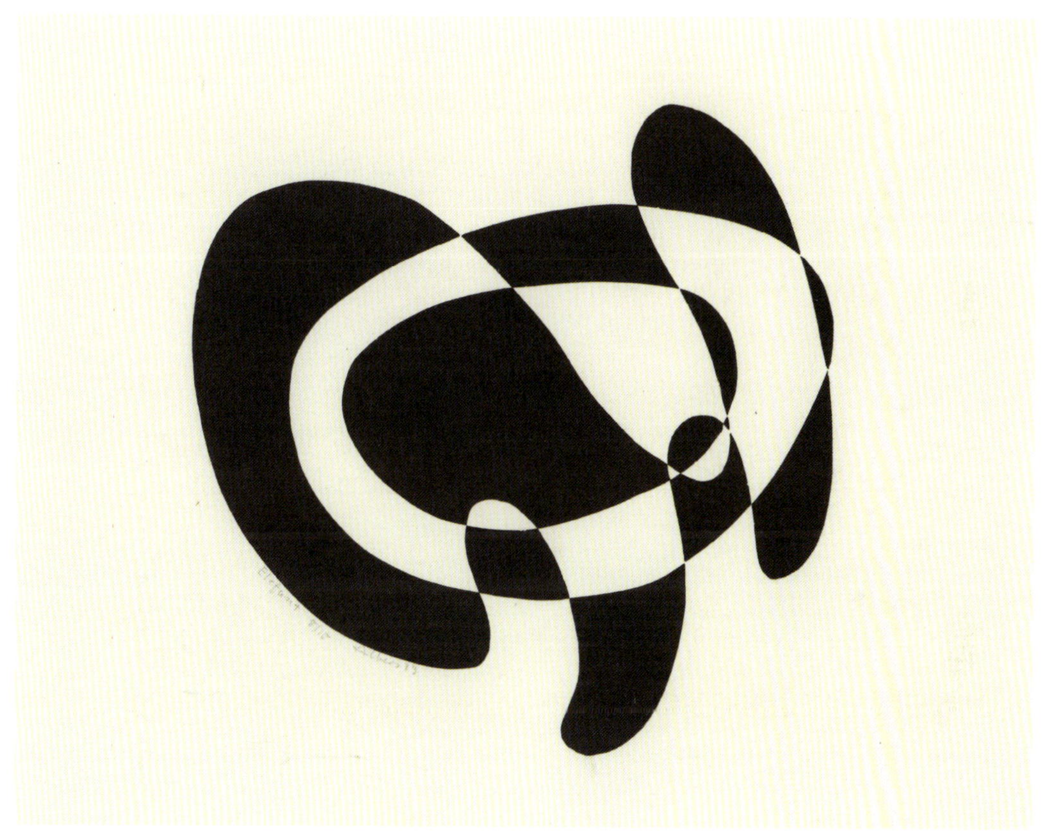

Elefant (Elephant), 1933,
linoleum cut, paper 35.6 × 50.5 cm,
image 20.3 × 20.3 cm. Josef and
Anni Albers Foundation, 1976.4.69

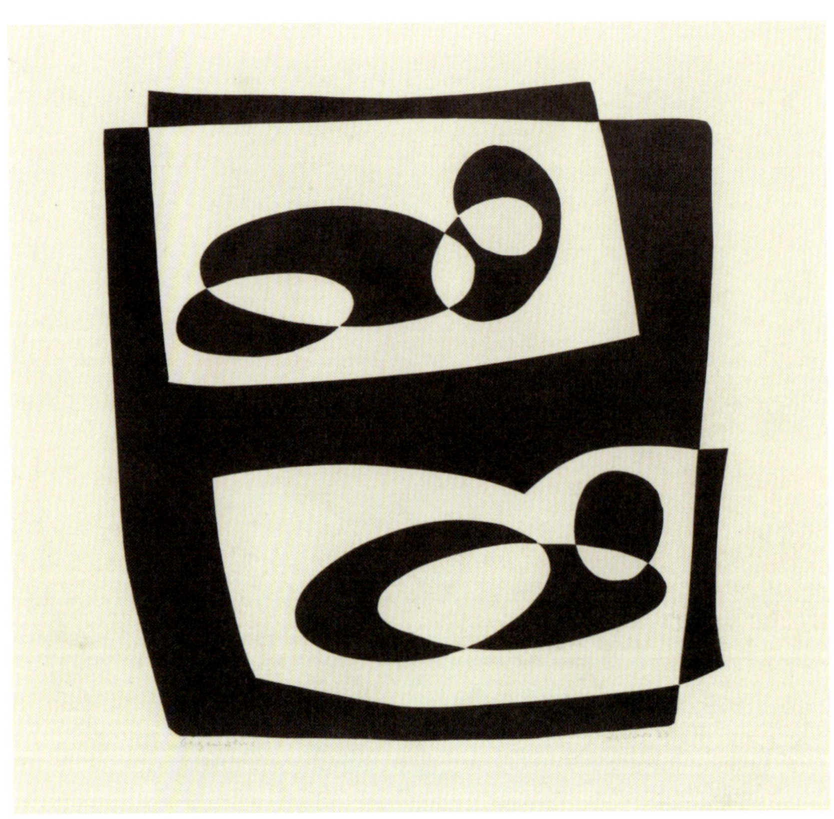

Gegenüber (Opposite), 1933, linoleum cut, paper 34.9 × 44.5 cm, image 25.4 × 25.4 cm. Josef and Anni Albers Foundation, 1976.4.70

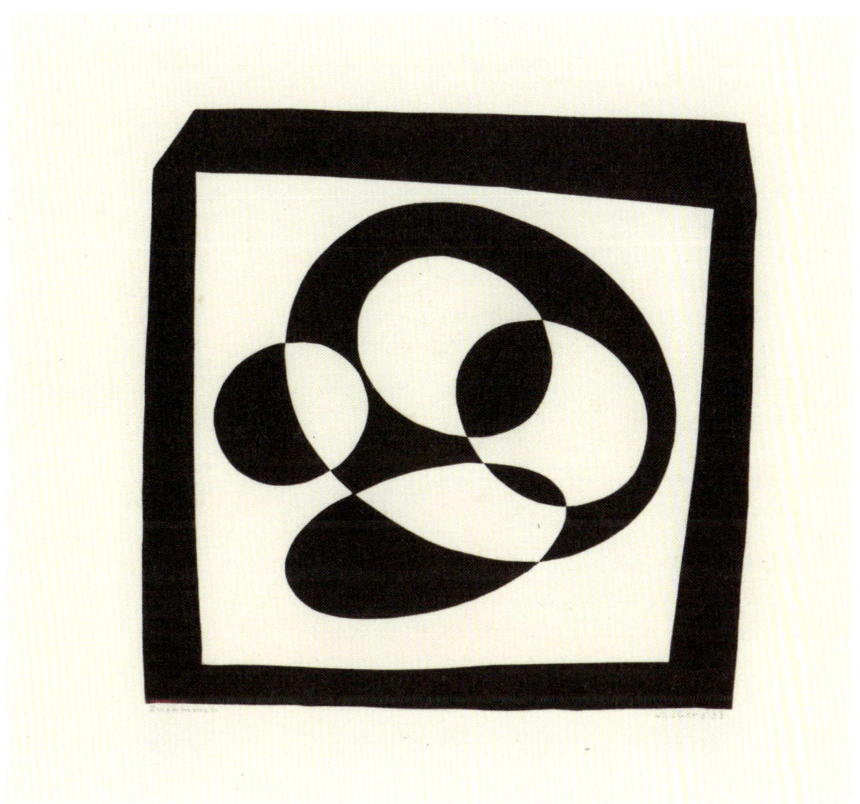

Zusammen (Together), 1933, linoleum cut, paper 33.6 × 43.2 cm, image 21.6 × 22.5 cm. Josef and Anni Albers Foundation, 1976.4.71

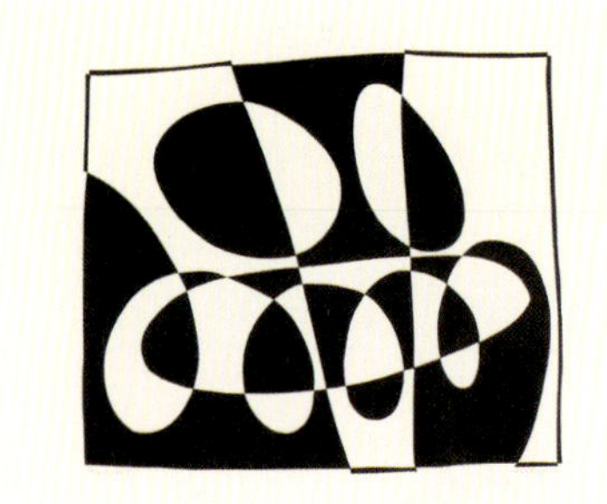

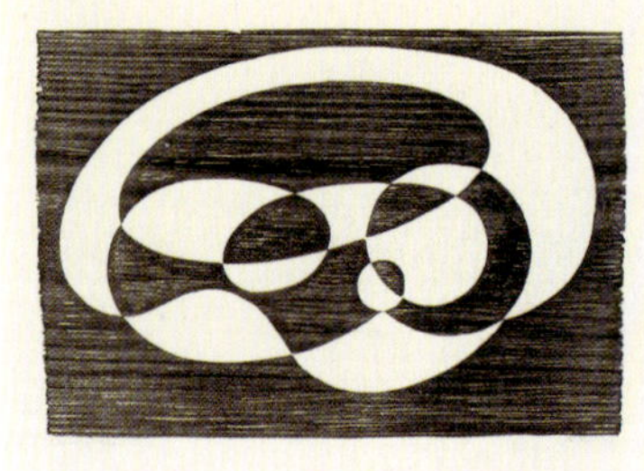

TOP *Aussicht* (Viewing), 1933, linoleum cut, paper 34.9 × 44.5 cm, image 21.6 × 25.7 cm. Josef and Anni Albers Foundation, 1976.4.72

MIDDLE *Aquarium*, 1934, woodcut, paper 25.4 × 35.2 cm, image 18.4 × 26 cm. Josef and Anni Albers Foundation, 1976.4.73

BOTTOM *Cosmic*, 1934, woodcut, paper 33 × 40 cm, image 22.2 × 32.7 cm. Josef and Anni Albers Foundation, 1976.4.80

Soon after the Bauhaus closed, Albers was invited to the United States to establish an art department at Black Mountain College, a newly founded experimental liberal arts college near Asheville, North Carolina. With little hope of employment in Germany, he and Anni seized the opportunity and arrived at Black Mountain College at the end of November 1933. The college would remain their base for the next sixteen years. There, Albers continued the printmaking recently begun in Berlin, but with a significant difference. The Bauhaus had taught him that the motif itself must be an invention, derived from the materials at hand and a rigorous engagement with form. Over the next decade, with ever-increasing confidence, he would produce drawings and printed works that explored the fluidity of organic line and its capacity for engaging the two-dimensional space of the picture plane. These works project an enhanced sensitivity to formal relationships and an intense awareness of the visual field and its context: an awareness that the placement and quality of every line and colour affect every other line and colour.

Though his world had changed abruptly, the change did not at first show up in Albers's work. The 1933 group of relief prints made in Berlin – *Circle*, *Elephant*, *Opposite*, *Together*, and *Viewing* – culminated in *Aquarium* and *Cosmic*, both dated 1934 and thus printed at Black Mountain College. They mark a point of transition from the hard-edged forms and linear geometries associated with his major Bauhaus works in sandblasted glass, which investigated the interplay and exchangeability of figure and ground, to an engagement with evocative line and organic patterns. The 1934 woodcuts and linoleum cuts are not well documented and were most likely printed on a hand press at Black Mountain College.[16] The college did not offer printmaking courses for students, although it acquired a hand press as well as a foot pedal Challenge Gordon platen press, both used mainly for producing administrative documents, concert programmes, and flyers.[17]

16. For an illuminating discussion of the Black Mountain College prints, see Faye Hirsch, 'Albers Prints of the '30s and '40s: Artist's Cheat', *Print Collector's Newsletter*, vol. 26, no. 4 (September–October 1995), pp. 122–5.

17. Mary E. Harris, *The Arts at Black Mountain College* (Cambridge, Mass. and London: MIT Press, 1987), p. 28.

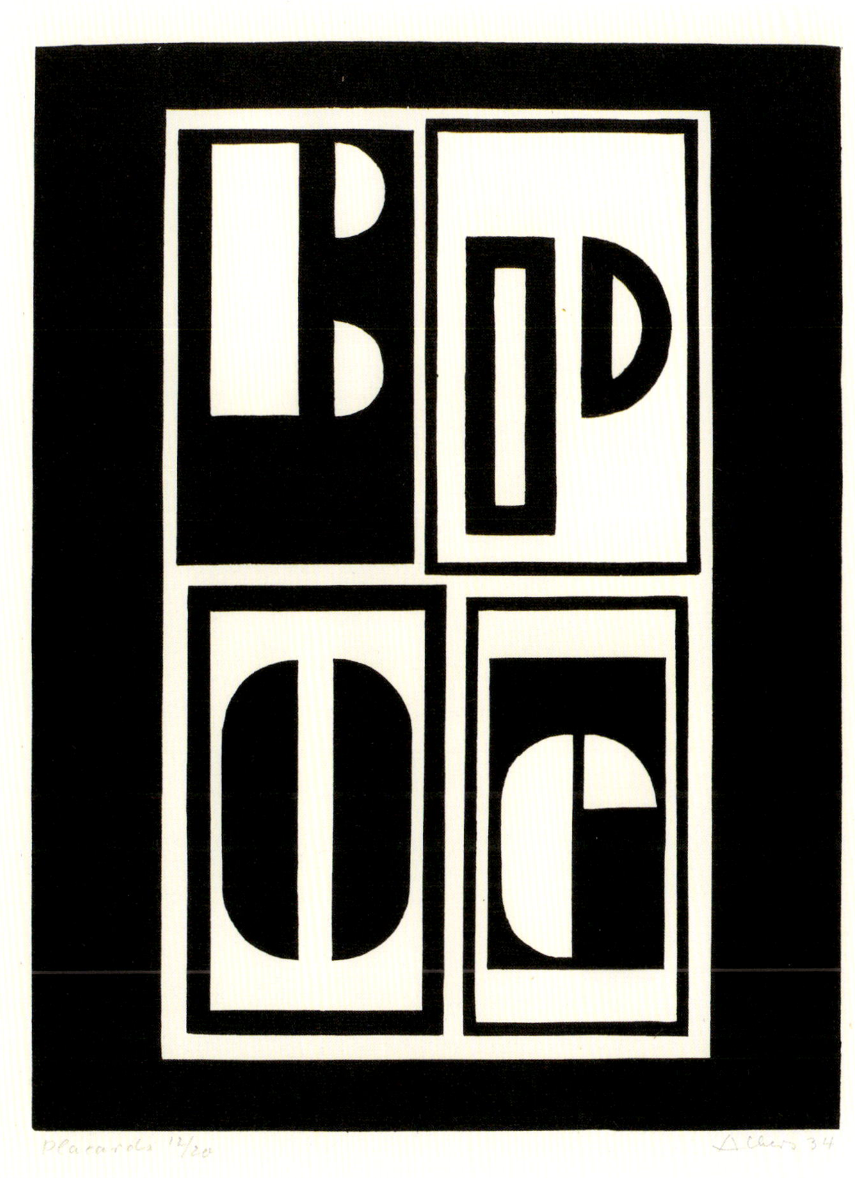

Placards, 1934,
linoleum cut, paper 40.6 × 26.7 cm,
image 29.2 × 22.2 cm. Josef and
Anni Albers Foundation, 1976.4.78

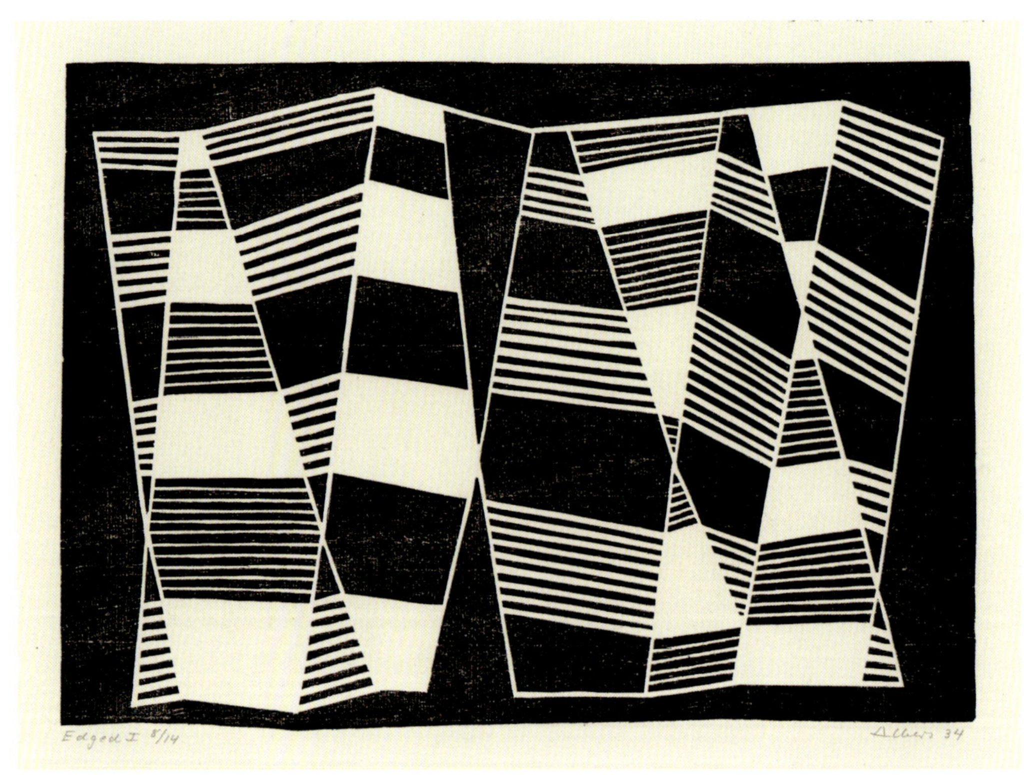

Edged I, 1934,
woodcut, paper 26.7 × 41.3 cm,
image 22.2 × 31.8 cm. Josef and
Anni Albers Foundation, 1976.4.75

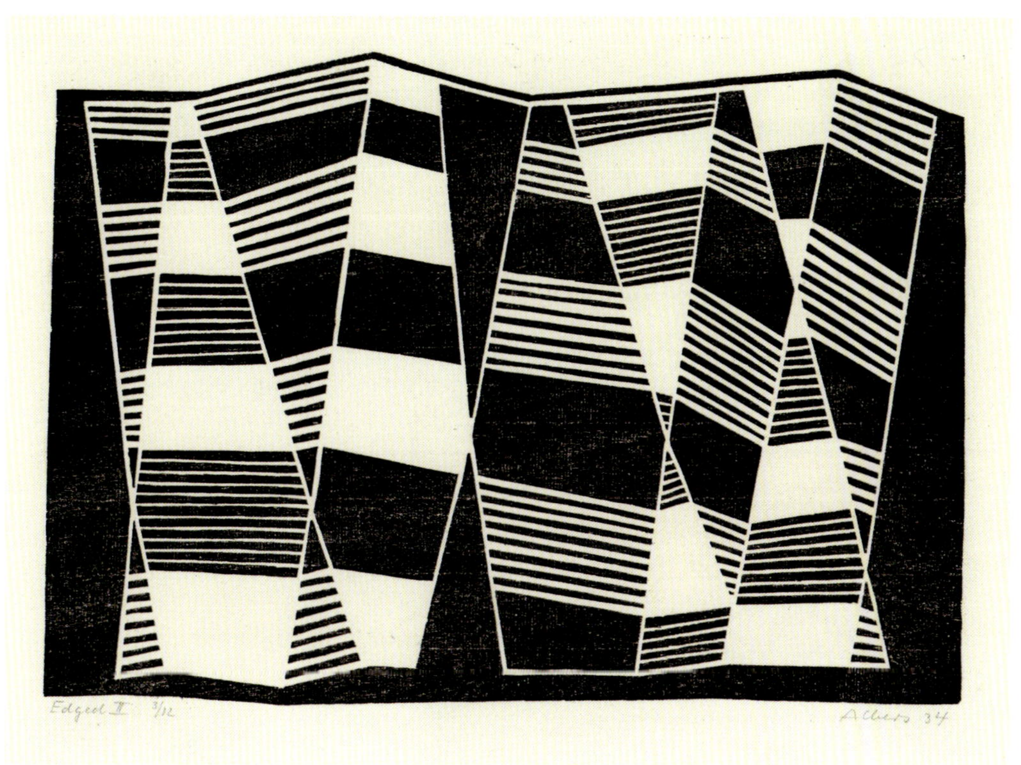

Edged II, 1934,
woodcut, paper 26.7 × 41.3 cm,
image 22.2 × 31.0 cm. Josef and
Anni Albers Foundation, 1976.4.76

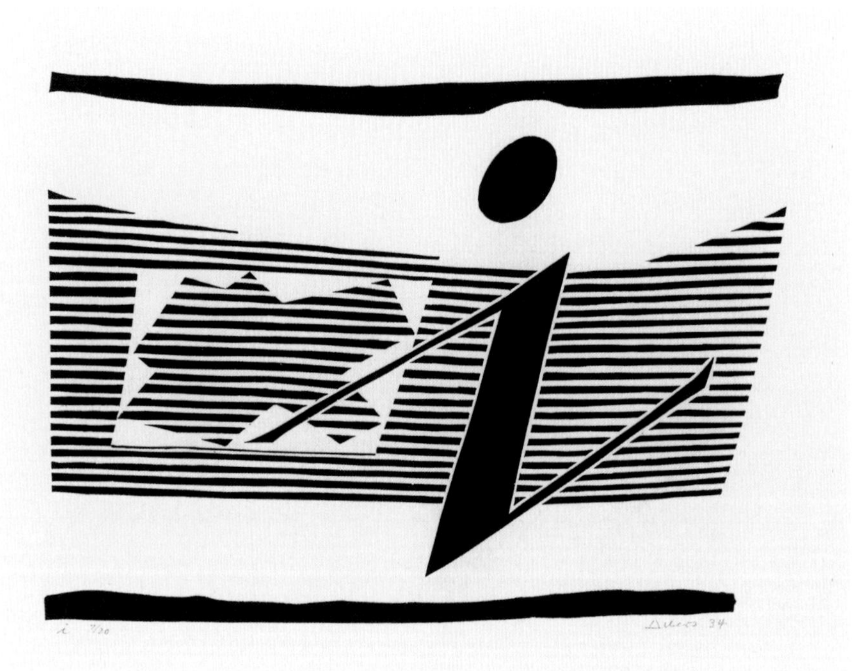

i, 1934,
linoleum cut, paper 35.3 × 38.1 cm,
imago 20.3 × 27.9 cm. Josef and
Anni Albers Foundation, 1976.4.77b

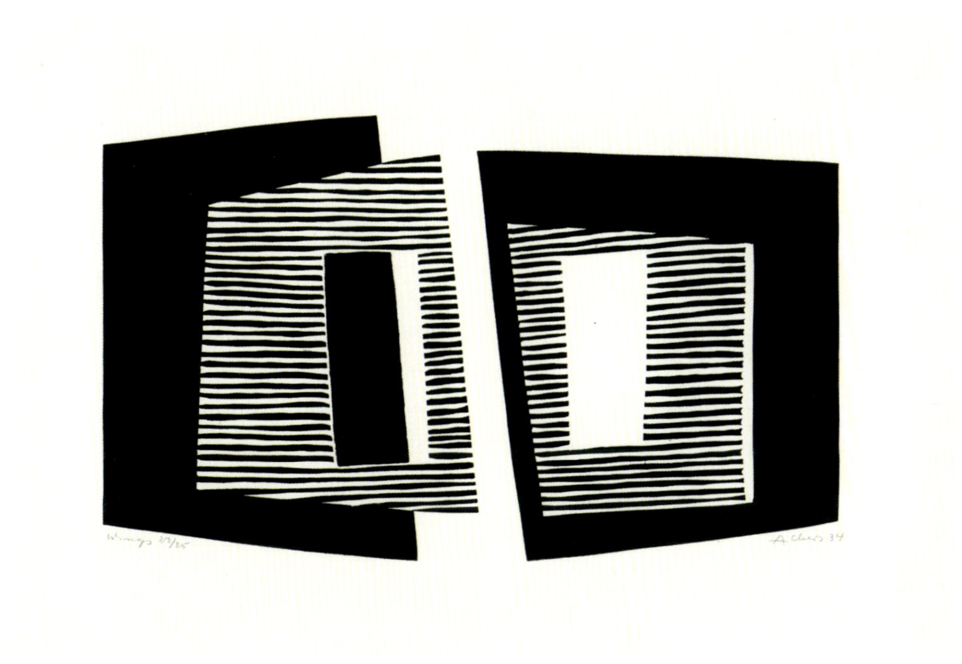

Wings, 1934,
woodcut, paper 26.7 × 41.6 cm,
image 18.4 × 31.1 cm. Josef and
Anni Albers Foundation, 1976.4.81

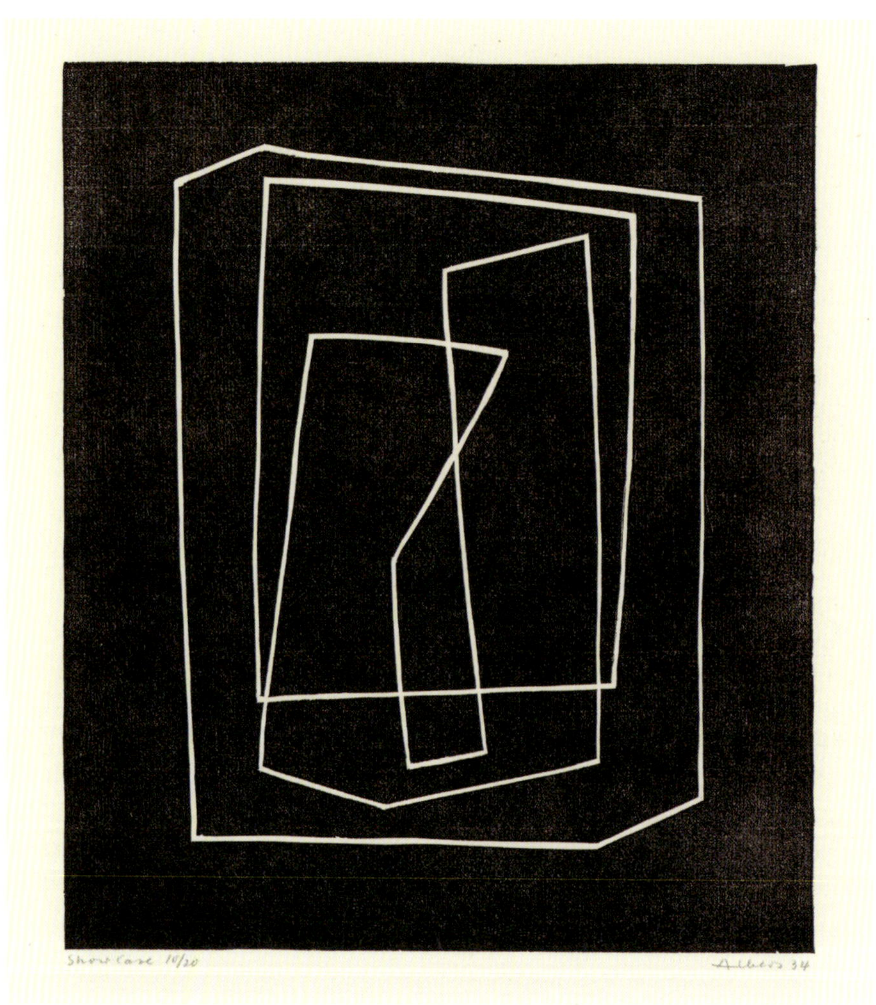

Show Case, 1934,
linoleum cut, paper 38.1 × 35.6 cm,
image 27.3 × 23.8 cm. Josef and
Anni Albers Foundation, 1976.4.82

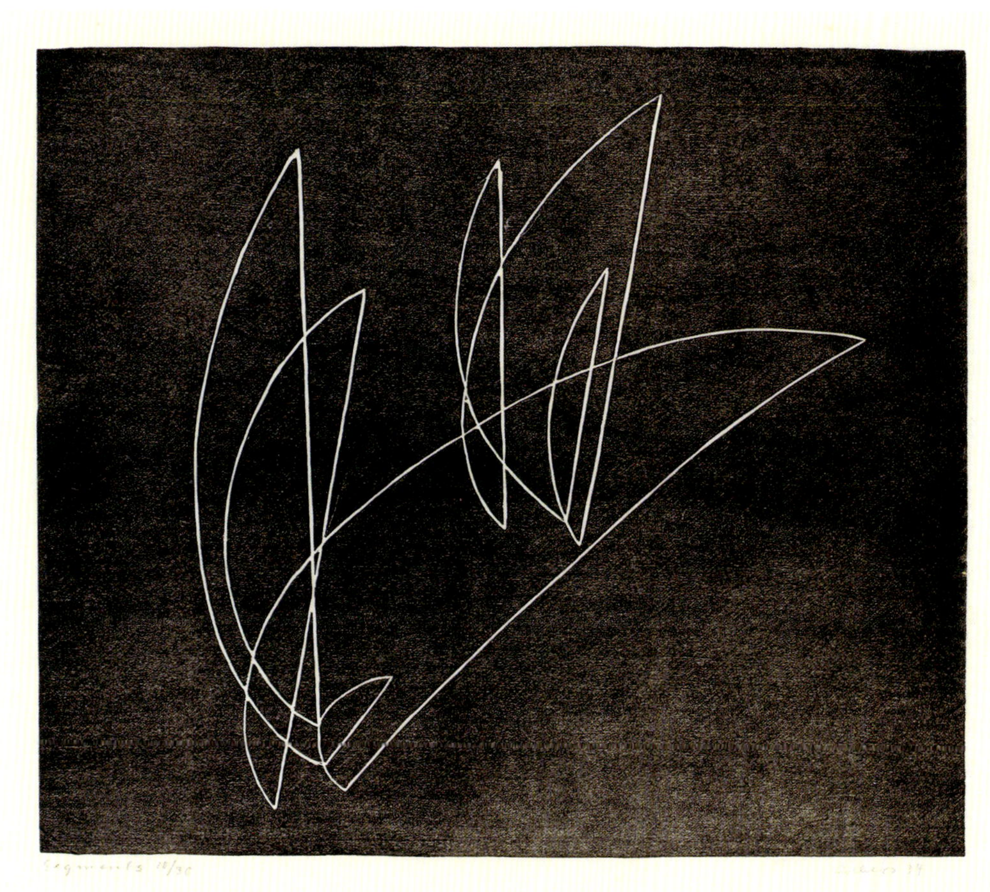

Segments, 1934,
linoleum cut, paper 35.2 × 40.6 cm,
image 24.1 × 28.3 cm. Josef and
Anni Albers Foundation, 1976.4.79

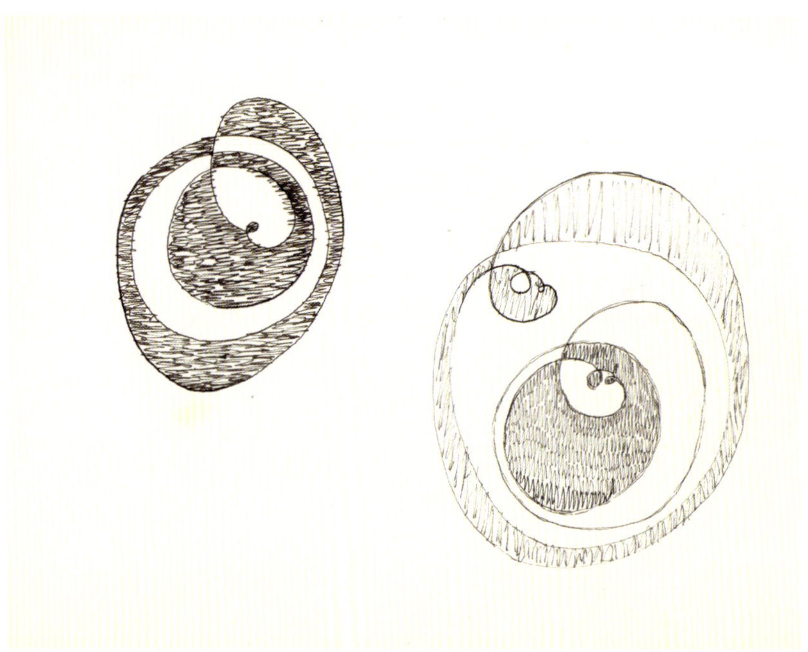

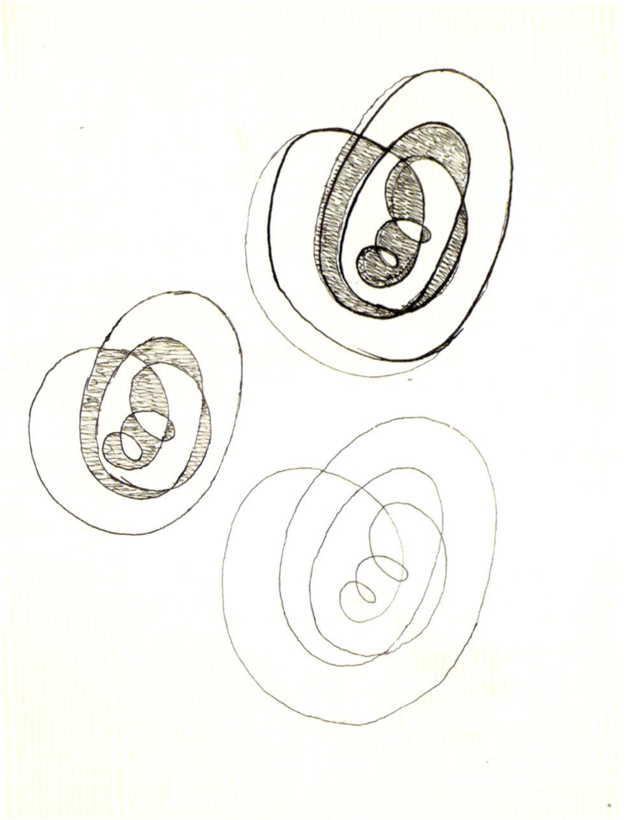

ABOVE Untitled, *c.* 1938, ink on paper, 21.7 × 27.9 cm. Josef and Anni Albers Foundation, 1976.3.688

RIGHT Untitled, *c.* 1938, ink on paper, 27.9 × 21.7 cm. Josef and Anni Albers Foundation, 1976.3.594

Albers's mastery of line was evident in his earliest works. Now, in the 1930s, he would begin to apply that facility in increasingly diverse directions. If we pay close attention to the informal and, at times, tentative drawings of *c.*1938 in which the pencil or pen maps out circular forms with a continuous line, we can follow the movement of the artist's hand in a visceral way.[18] These drawings were made at a time when Albers, recently arrived in the United States, was feeling his way into adapting and developing his Bauhaus teaching for the students at Black Mountain College – a group whose cultural affinities and educational backgrounds were quite different from those of the Bauhaus student population. Albers's encounters with American students thirsty for an educational experience that devalued rote learning, correct answers, and the awarding of points, in favour of experimentation, playful learning, and personal responsibility, inevitably led him towards intensified engagement with changing possibilities in his own work. The organic drawings of the 1930s spawned an undiscovered universe of images – from the Mexico City lithographs of 1939 (pp. 98–101) through the multiple drawings for the 1942 drypoint *Maternity* (pp. 108–9). And then with increasing boldness, to a group of small yet remarkably unrestrained studies, that were concretized in further drypoints *Nippon A* and *Nippon B* of the same year (pp. 106–7).

After his arrival in the United States, Albers actively promoted the exhibition of his prints. In Europe, his former Bauhaus student and colleague Alexander (Xanti) Schawinsky arranged an exhibition of the woodcuts in Milan in 1934. Wassily Kandinsky contributed a text to the catalogue and praised his former colleague for his 'artistic invention' and 'perfect technique'.[19] The first exhibition of Albers's work in the United States was a showing of the woodcut prints at the Addison Gallery of American Art in Andover, Massachusetts, in January 1935.[20] Although printmaking in America had been given a boost in the 1930s through WPA programmes that

18. Think of the way a skilful orchestra conductor can elicit silent head nodding or foot tapping in time with the music.

19. Galleria Il Milione, 23 December 1934 to 10 January 1935.

20. For details about this and other exhibitions of Albers's work in the 1930s, see Brenda Danilowitz, 'Josef Albers and the Reception of Abstract Art in New England 1933–1950', in Boston University Art Gallery, *Josef Albers in Black and White*, exh. cat. (Boston, Mass.: Boston University; Seattle, WA: University of Washington Press, 2000).

Josef Albers, Teotihuacán, Mexico, 1936

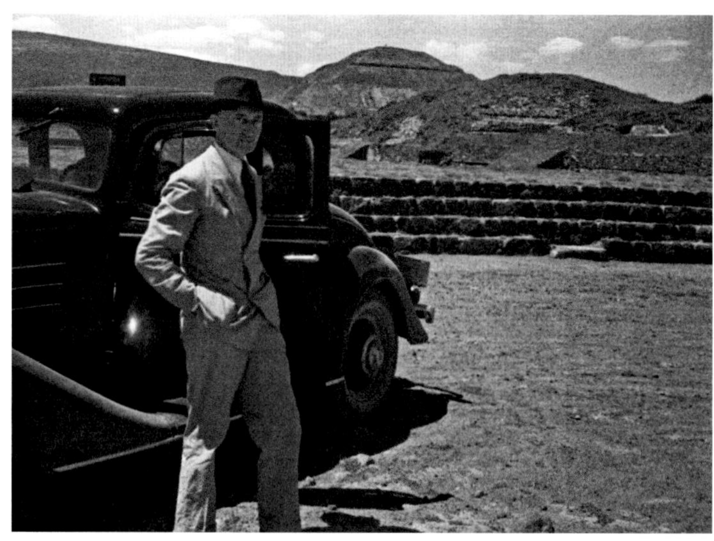

promoted the production and display of socially engaged realist graphic art, an audience for abstract work was less forthcoming. Things were different in Mexico City, where a long tradition of printmaking endured. In August 1936, on the occasion of an exhibition of a group of his woodcuts and gouaches there, Albers was acclaimed in the press as 'one of the founders of abstraction'.[21]

The Alberses first travelled to Mexico in 1935. By 1967 and their last visit, they had made fourteen trips to Mexico and traversed much of the vast country. The effects of these travels, documented in hundreds of photographs, is manifest in Albers's work, in particular in the development of colour in his painting, and in the themes and forms of his print oeuvre.[22] Mexico provided a wealth of visual example in forms that he understood well, as Albers wrote to Kandinsky in 1936: 'Mexico is truly the promised land of abstract art.'[23] Anni Albers had long been interested in the weaving traditions of Latin America, and it was she who planned their 1935 journey. For Josef, always open to revelatory visual experiences, the ancient Zapotec and Aztec sites they visited evoked the sorts of complex architectonic spatial arrangements in the figure–ground pattern motifs of their stonework that had always interested him.

21. *El Nacional*, Mexico City, 16 August 1936. For information about this exhibition, see Brenda Danilowitz and Heinz Liesbrock, *Anni and Josef Albers: Latin American Journeys* (Ostfildern: Hatje Cantz, 2008). Albers's work was well received in Latin America before he established a following in the United States. In 1939, a group of his woodcuts and tempera paintings was shown in São Paulo at the third (and final) Salão de Maio organized by Flávio de Carvalho.

22. For the influence of Latin American art in general and Mexican art in particular on both Josef and Anni Albers, see Danilowitz and Liesbrock, *Anni and Josef Albers: Latin American Journeys*; Neal David Benezra, *The Murals and Sculpture of Josef Albers* (Ph.D. diss., Stanford University, 1983; New York and London: Garland Outstanding Dissertations in the Fine Arts, 1985); James Oles, *South of the Border: Mexico in the American Imagination 1914–1917*, exh. cat. (New Haven: Yale University Art Gallery; Washington and London: Smithsonian Institution Press, 1993); César Paternosto, *The Stone and the Thread: Andean Roots of Abstract Art* (Austin: University of Texas Press, 1996); Virginia G. Troy, *Anni Albers: The Significance of Ancient American Art for her Woven and Pedagogical Work* (Ph.D. diss., Emory University, 1997) and *Anni Albers and Ancient American Textiles: From Bauhaus to Black Mountain* (Burlington, VT and Aldershot: Ashgate, 2002); and Kunstmuseum Bern, *Josef und Anni Albers: Europa und Amerika* (Bern: Kunstmuseum; Cologne: DuMont, 1998).

23. Josef Albers to Wassily Kandinsky, 22 August 1936, letter FK 15, in Centre Georges Pompidou, *Kandinsky–Albers: Une correspondance des années trente* (Paris: Musée National d'Art Moderne, Centre Georges Pompidou, 1998), p. 79 (author's translation).

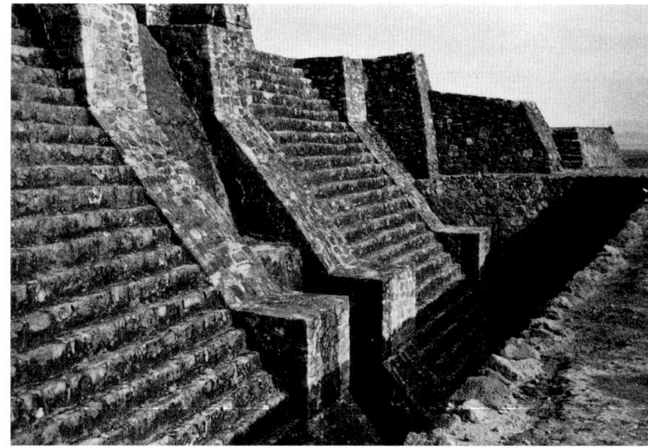

LEFT Pyramid of Teopanzolco, Cuernavaca, Mexico, 1937, photographed by Josef Albers

MIDDLE LEFT AND RIGHT Anni Albers, Monte Albán, Mexico, 1937, photographed by Josef Albers

BOTTOM Josef Albers in front of a relief patterned stone wall at Mitla, Mexico, *c.* 1936–7

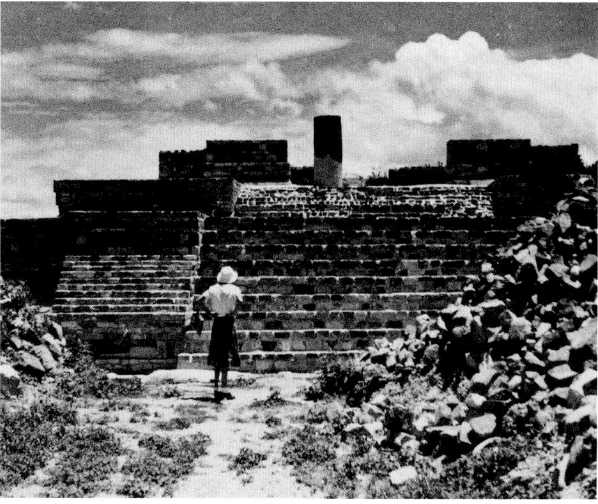

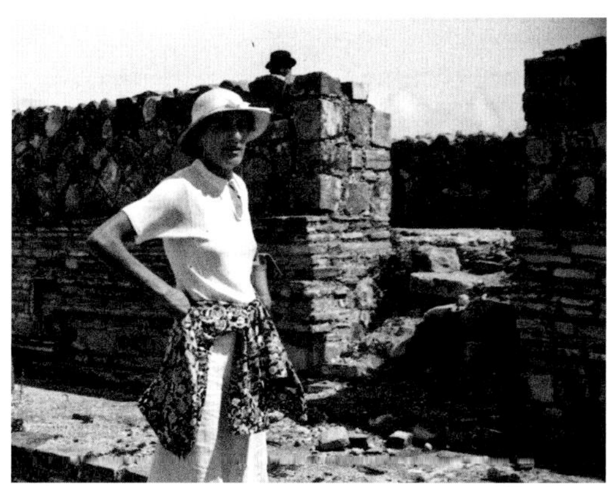

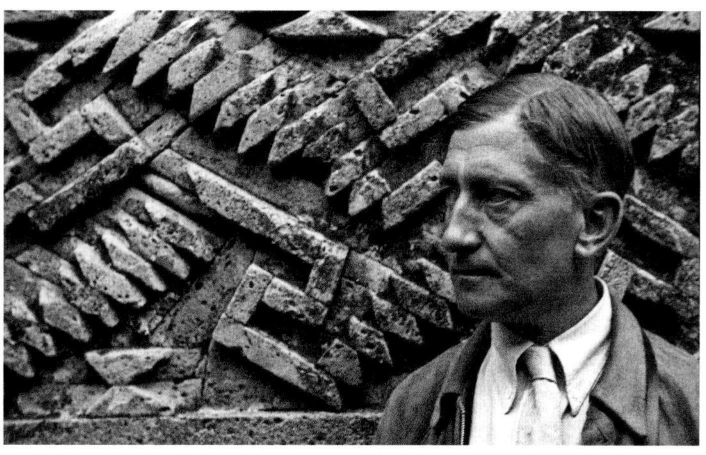

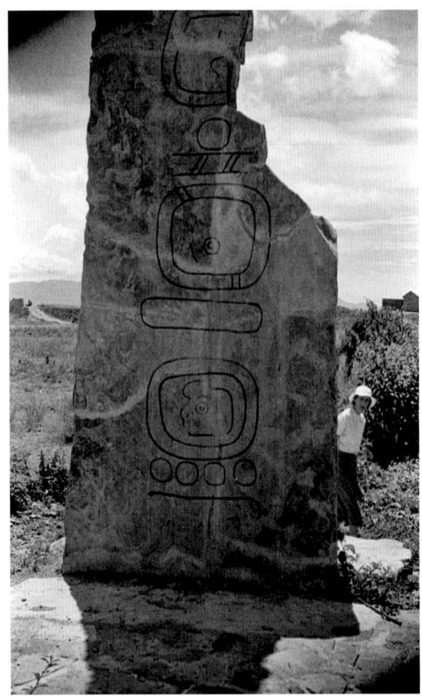

Josef Albers's photograph of a stele at Monte Albán, Mexico, with Anni Albers in the background, 1937

Beyond these structural aspects, which would resonate in his work in the 1940s, the pictorial art of Mexico was replete with relief carvings and inscriptions and ingenious, distinctive, and diverse modelled ceramic figures and objects. In one of Albers's earliest photographs of Monte Albán, the Zapotec site on the outskirts of Oaxaca, Anni looks out from behind a towering stone stele, its surface incised with large enigmatic symbols. The cryptic forms of Mesoamerican glyphs suggested that visual images had the power to codify and contain meaning.[24]

Among Albers's photographs from Mexico are many snapshots of objects in the National Museum of Archaeology, History, and Ethnography (now the National Museum of Anthropology) in Mexico City. Anni described the couple's exploration of the museum's collections where 'the pieces were simply placed side by side in old-fashioned glass cases ... with no attempt at showing them to any advantage.... Since labels were sometimes missing ... it was a challenge to our observation.'[25] One virtue of this informal display was that Josef could capture these intriguing objects from all angles. Thus he not only photographed a large stone frog from frontal and oblique viewpoints, but also documented its striking carved underside in a photograph and a drawing that became a drypoint in 1942.

In 1939, working at the now legendary Taller de Gráfica Popular (People's Graphic Workshop) in Mexico City, Albers made a suite of four lithographs that explored the movement of a continuous line through space (pp. 98–101).[26] These large works isolate the linear elements implicit in works like the earlier *Circle* and *Viewing*. Abandoning the stark contrasts of black and white that dominated those woodcuts, Albers returned to exploiting the possibilities of free drawing that lithographic crayon offered, now making his drawing directly on the lithographic stone. Here his crayon sweeps confidently across the surface in a continuous moving line. In counterpoint to the swirling movement of the line is its deliberately fuzzy quality, emphasized in *Beta* by cross-hatching.

24. Though it was long recognized that the glyphs of the Mayans were a form of writing, it was only in 1950, fifteen years after the Alberses began travelling to Mexico, that these symbols began to be deciphered. See Michael Coe and Justin Kerr, *The Art of the Maya Scribe* (New York: Harry N. Abrams, Inc., 1998).

25. Anni Albers, *Pre-Columbian Mexican Miniatures* (New York: Praeger; London: Lund Humphries, 1970), n.p. She was referring to the old museum housed in a colonial building in the historic centre of Mexico City, which was superseded in 1964 by the present-day National Museum of Anthropology in Chapultepec Park.

26. The Albers spent three months in Mexico in the summer of 1939. It was during this time that Anni Albers's parents finally left Nazi Germany. They arrived in Veracruz towards the end of June after an arduous sea voyage. Josef and Anni met them there.

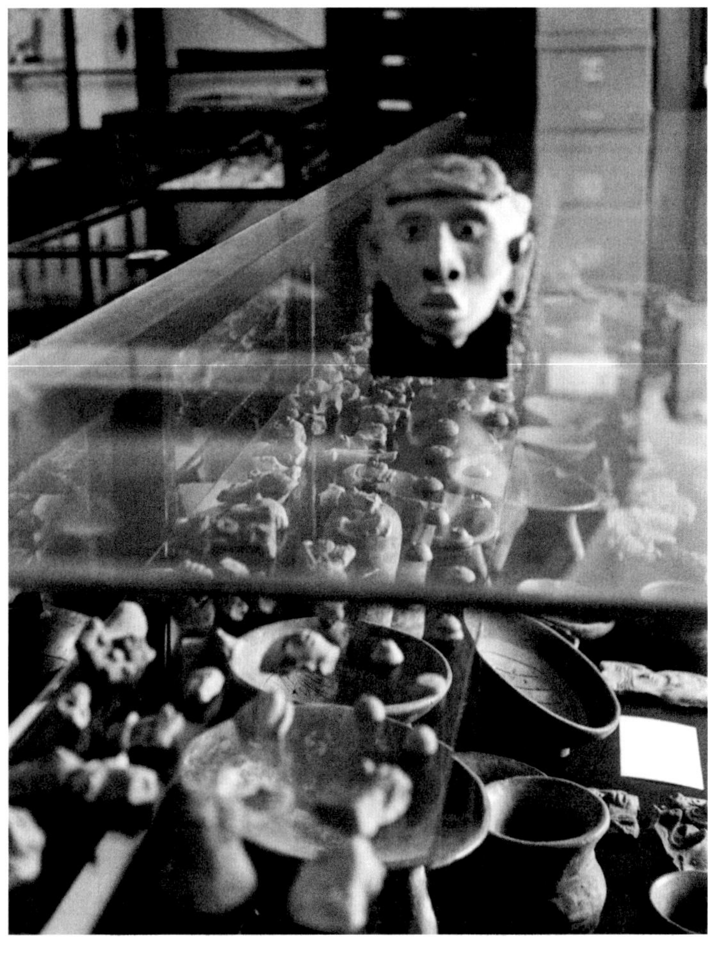

LEFT National Museum of Archaeology, History, and Ethnography, Mexico City, Mexico, 1937, photographed by Josef Albers

BELOW Stone frog in the National Museum of Archaeology, History and Ethnography, Mexico City, Mexico, *c.* 1937, photographed by Josef Albers

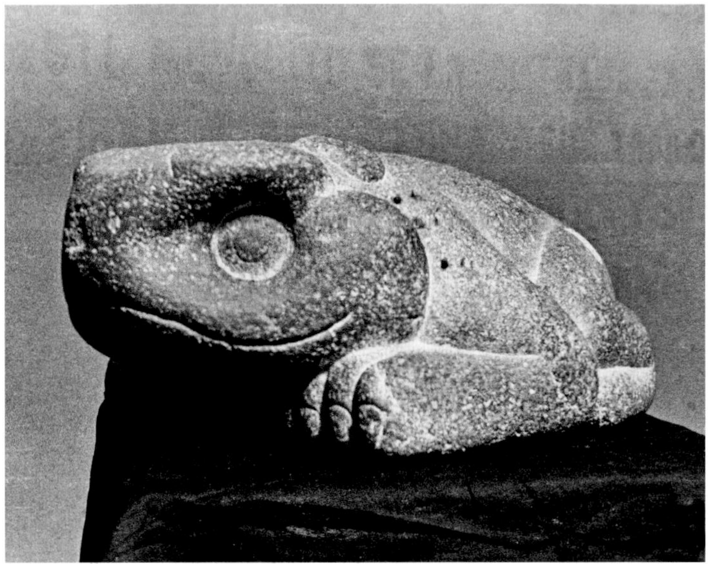

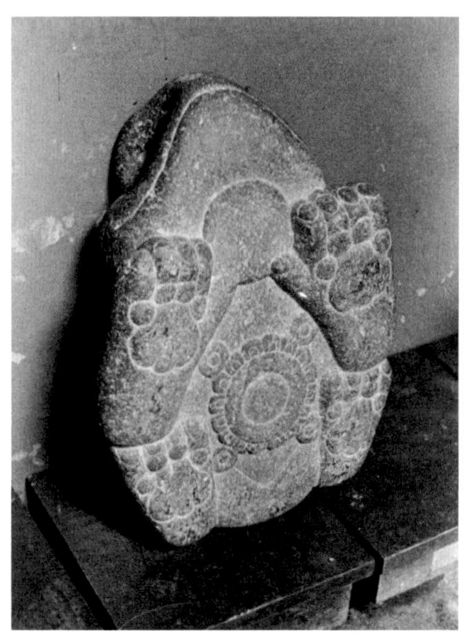

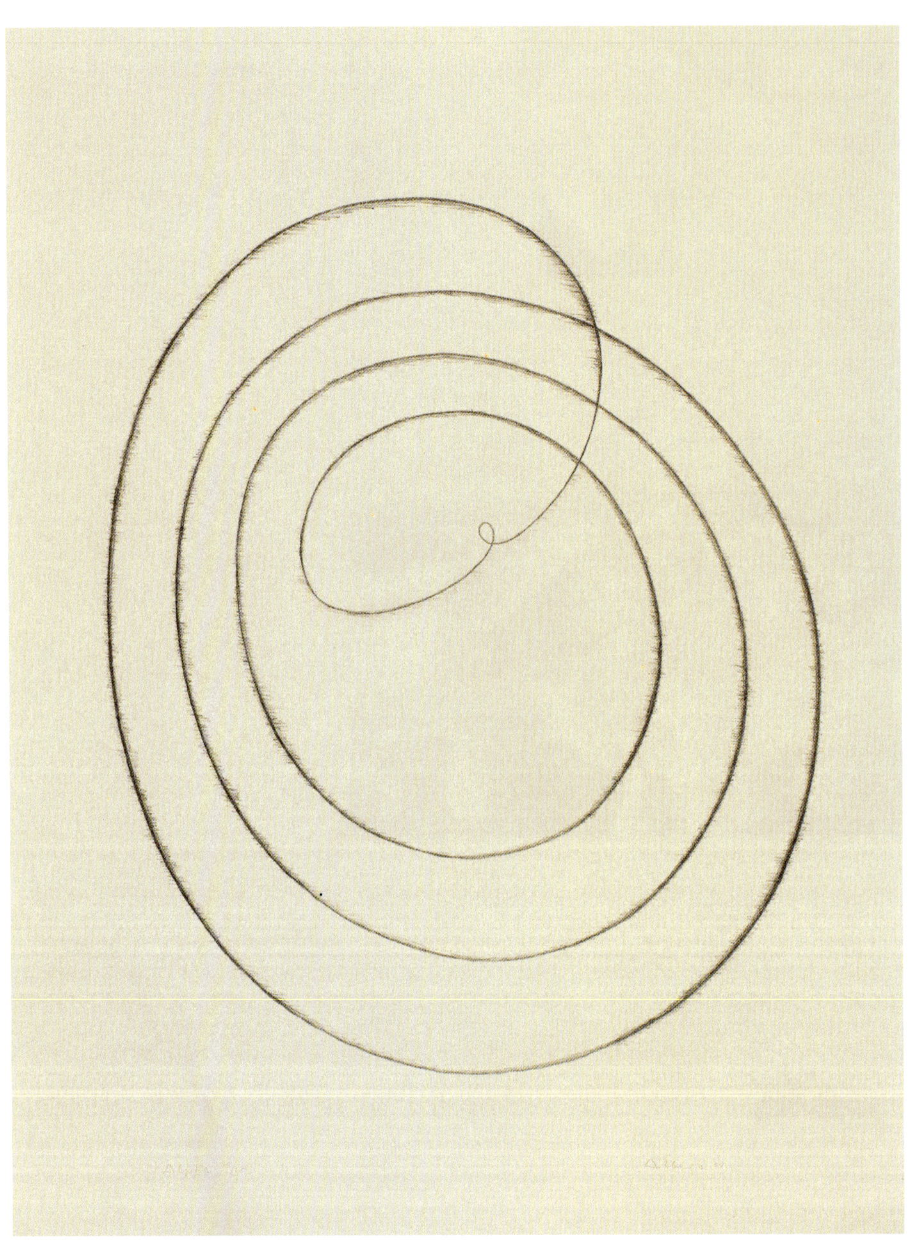

Alpha, from *Mexican Lithographs*, 1939,
lithograph, paper 64.8 × 50.2 cm,
image 36.2 × 30.5 cm. Josef and Anni Albers
Foundation, 1976.4.83

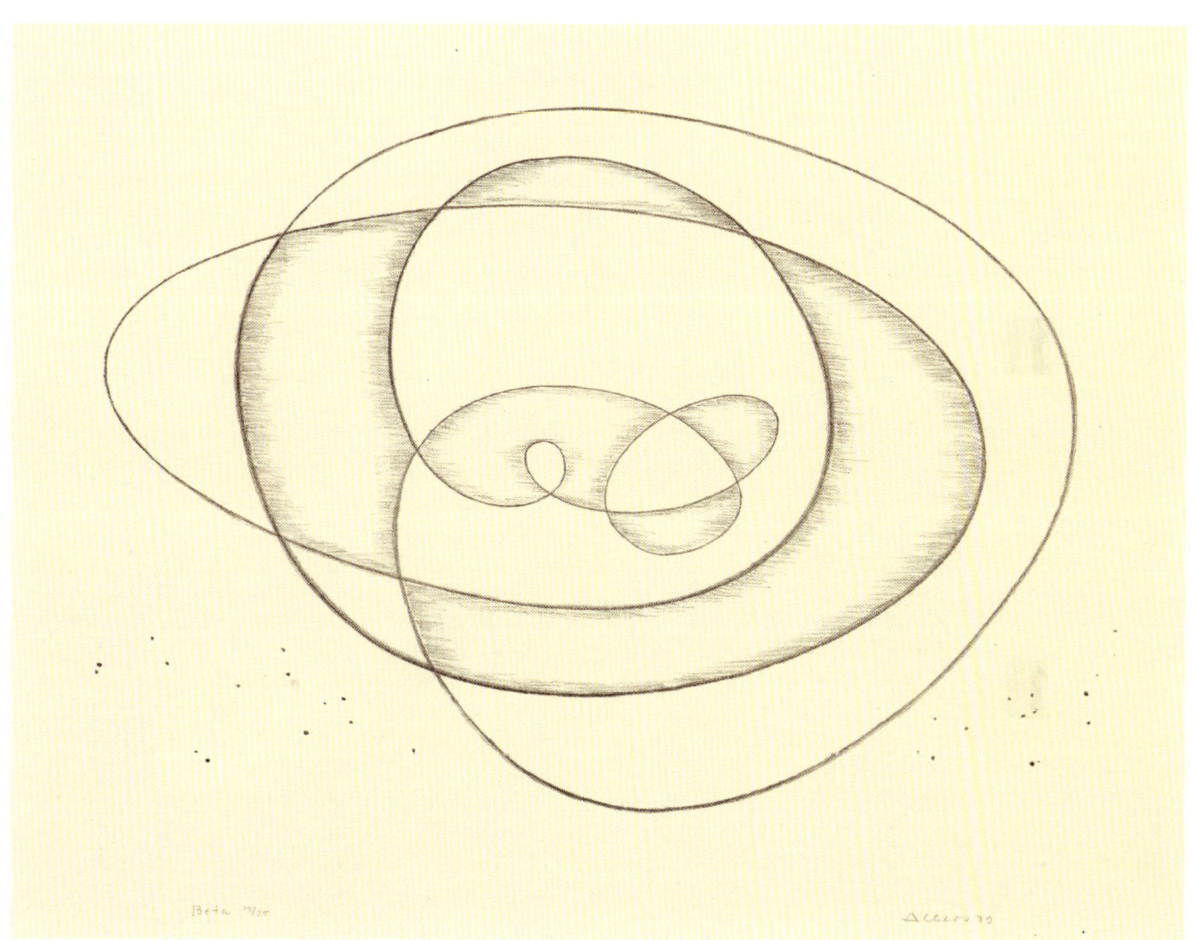

Beta, from *Mexican Lithographs*, 1939, lithograph, paper 50.2 × 64.8 cm, image 27.1 × 38.7 cm. Josef and Anni Albers Foundation, 1976.4.84

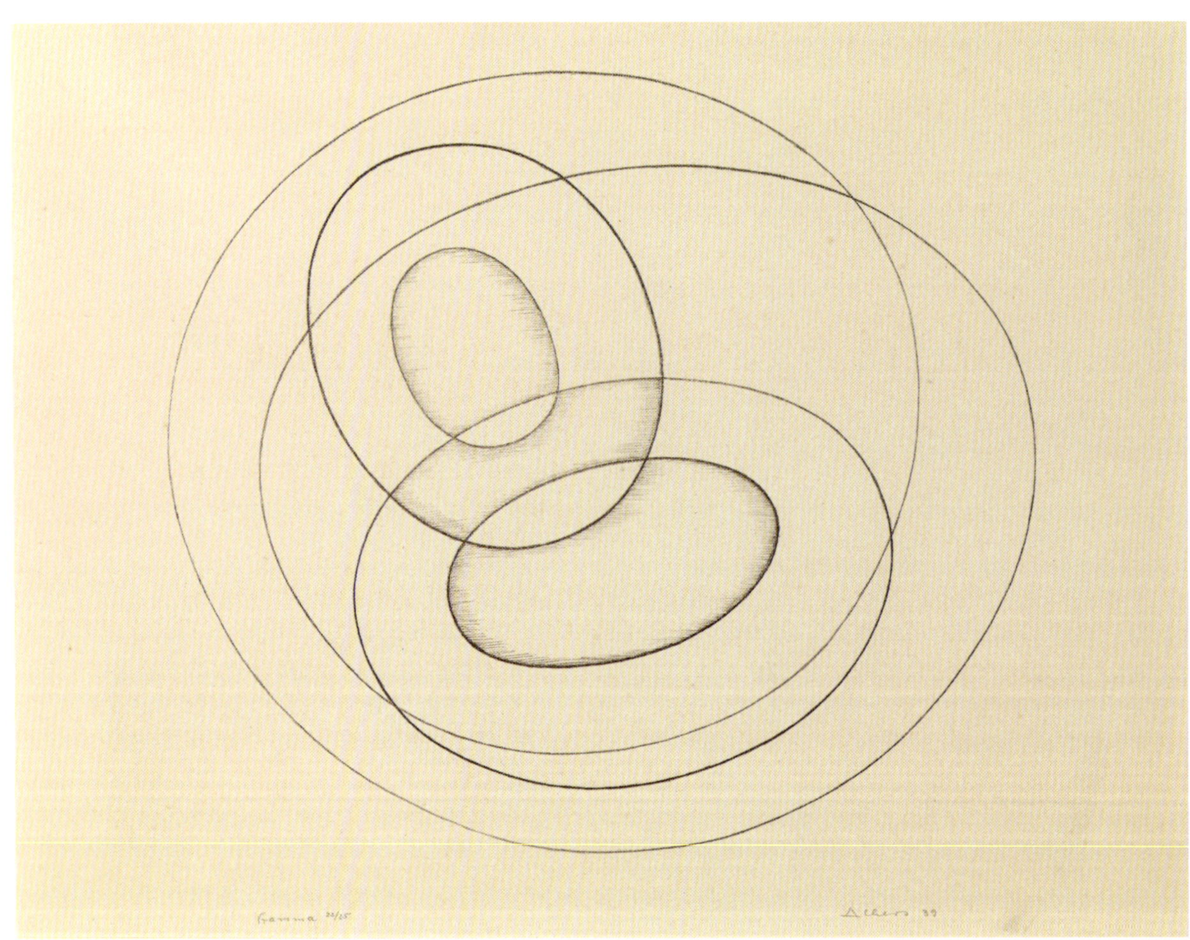

Gamma, from *Mexican Lithographs*, 1939,
lithograph, paper 50.2 × 64.8 cm,
image 31.1 × 35.6 cm. Josef and Anni Albers
Foundation, 1976.4.85

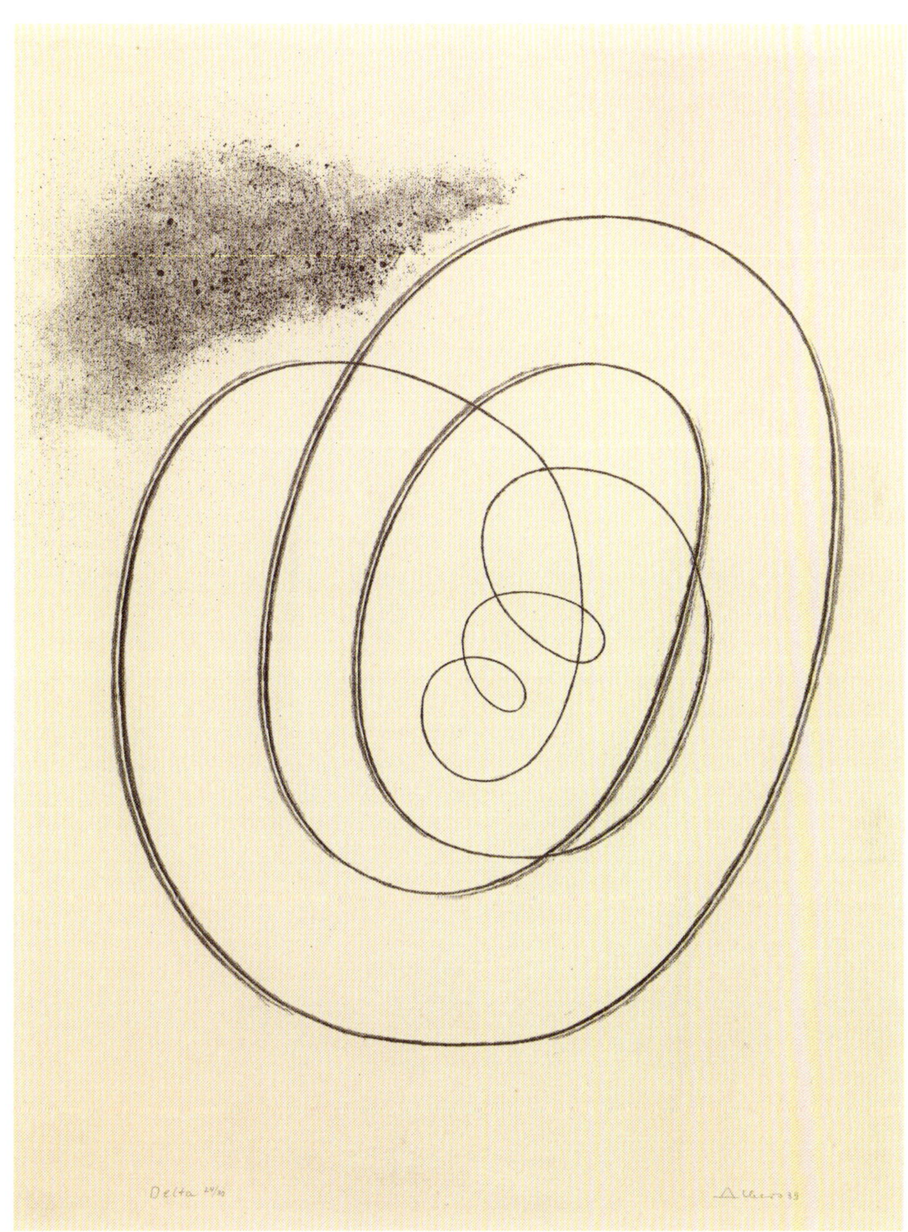

Delta, from *Mexican Lithographs*, 1939, lithograph, paper 64.8 × 50.2 cm, image 35.6 × 34.5 cm. Josef and Anni Albers Foundation, 1976.4.86

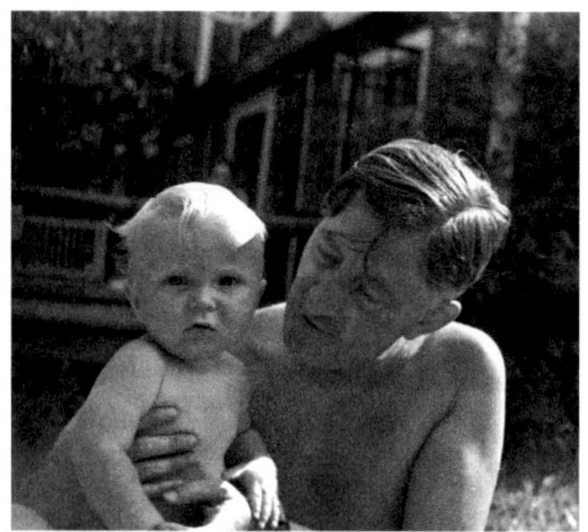

Josef Albers with his godson Eddie Dreier, Black Mountain College, 1938

These Mexican lithographs prepare us for Albers's first experiments with intaglio techniques – the group of small drypoint prints executed at the Art Academy in Mexico City in 1940.[27] In these drypoints and those of 1942, Albers's work reached an enhanced level of freedom and playfulness that suggests that, in addition to the influence of Mesoamerican art, he was intrigued by Surrealism, or at least by some of its processes, at this time.[28] In fact, as inimical as the Surrealist doctrine of chance might have been to Albers's aesthetic of deliberate choice and purposeful execution, there is strong evidence that he regarded the free-associating practices of Surrealism as a legitimate means for opening up not only the minds and the eyes of his students, but his own creative impulses as well. The drypoints fuse the meandering lines of Surrealist automatic drawing with the perceptual reading of abstract form proposed by gestalt theories. There is evidence that Albers actively sought these effects, and on at least one occasion canvassed opinions about the perception of his images.[29]

The drypoint method produced prints with characteristically feathery lines – akin to the textured lines of the 1939 Mexican lithographs. Some prints remained unsigned and others uneditioned, suggesting that, like Albers's search for titles, the prints themselves may have been something of an experiment. In any case, they provide another of those fairly rare glimpses into Albers's very real ability to have fun and inject veiled personal references into his work while inventing with great freedom. *Eh-De* is a pun on 'Eddie', the name of his friends Ted and Bobbie Dreier's baby and Josef's godson, for whom Albers's fondness was well known and recorded in several contemporary photographs.

The drypoints build on the Mexican lithographs in other ways as well. *Maternity* (p. 109) develops the forms of *Alpha*, while *Variants* (p. 111) is a virtuoso variation in six parts on the theme of *Delta*. The foreshortening, intersecting, and overlapping of elliptical forms was one of the key exercises in Albers's drawing classes.

27. On sabbatical leave from Black Mountain College in the 1940–1 academic year, the Alberses returned to Mexico for the fall of 1940 and spent the spring of 1941 in Cambridge, where Josef taught at Harvard's Graduate School of Design.

28. On 17 January 1940, the Galeria de Arte Mexicano in Mexico City opened the *International Exhibition of Surrealism*. Organized by Wolfgang Paalen and César Moro, the landmark exhibition was widely reviewed and had a notable impact on modern art in Mexico. It is likely that the Alberses, who were in Mexico for most of October and November 1940, would at least have heard about the exhibition. See Dafne Cruz Prochini and Adriana Ortega Orozco, 'The 1940 International Exhibition of Surrealism: A Cosmopolitan Art Dialogue in Mexico City, *Dada/Surrealism*, no. 21 (2017), https://doi.org/10.17077/0084-9537.1329, accessed 16 August 2021.

29. On a sheet of notepaper under the heading 'Dry-points – title', Albers noted the responses of three of his Black Mountain College teaching colleagues, all musicians – John Evarts, Edward Lowinsky, and Frederick ('Fritz') Cohen – to images that he listed as 'Lion, Dog, and Dance'. The responses, in the form of musical correspondences, are reminiscent of Kandinsky's ideas about synaesthesia, or correspondences between colours and sounds. Lowinsky has 'scherzo furioso' corresponding to 'Lion' and 'moderato scherzando' corresponding to 'Dog'. Evarts has 'allegro furioso' for 'Lion', 'lento maestoso' for 'Dog' and 'scherzo grazioso' for 'Dancing', which Albers indicated was the drypoint *Rondo*. Cohen's response was not recorded.

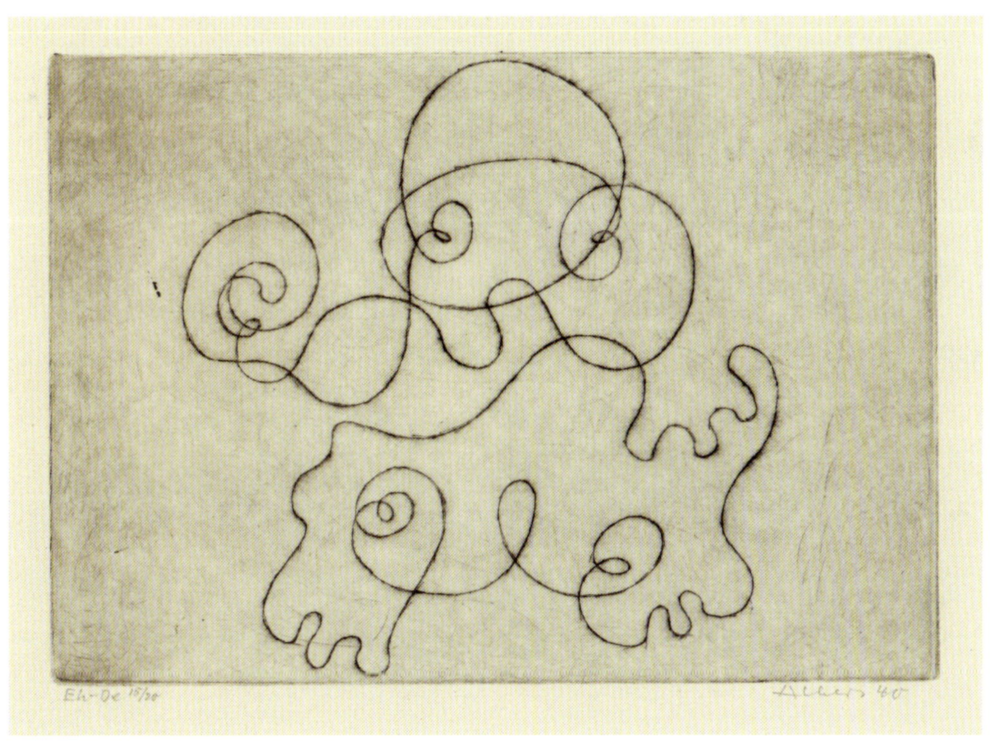

Eh-De, 1940,
drypoint, paper 22.9 × 27.9 cm,
image 14 × 20.3 cm. Josef and Anni Albers
Foundation. 1976.4.88

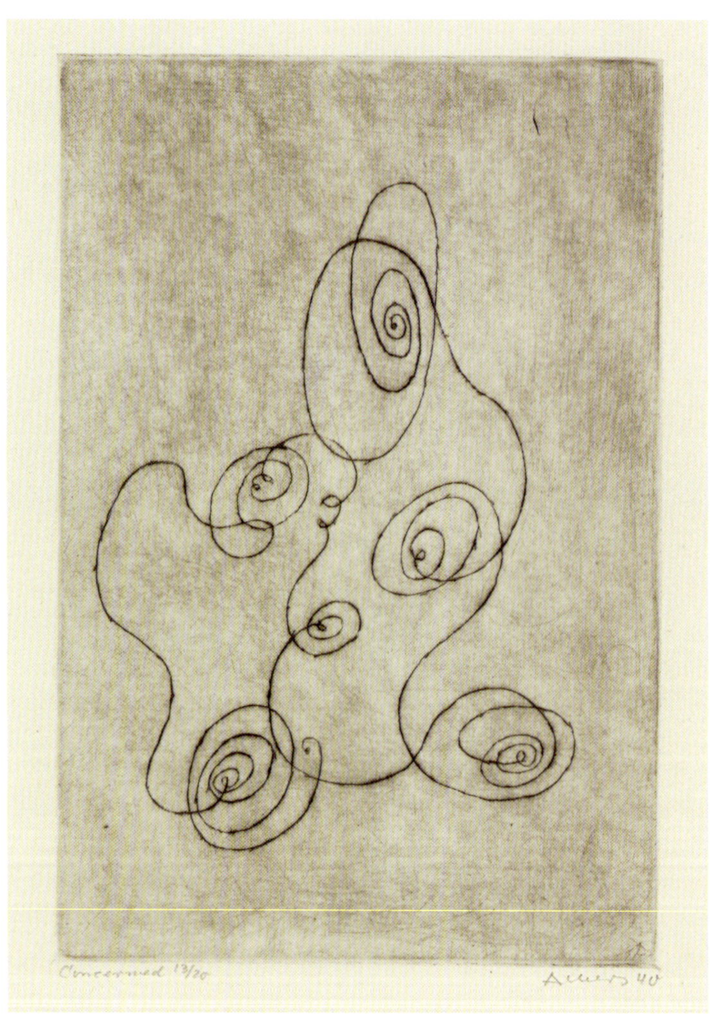

Concerned, 1940,
drypoint, paper 27.9 × 22.5 cm,
image 20.3 × 14 cm. Josef and Anni Albers
Foundation, 1976.4.87

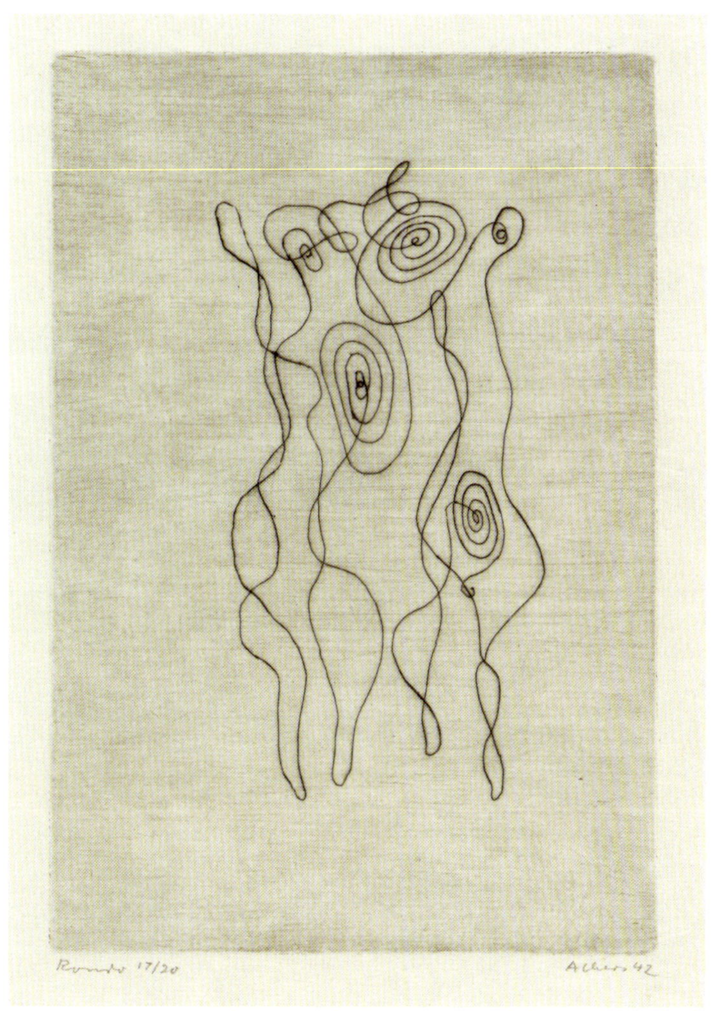

Rondo, 1942,
drypoint, paper 28.6 × 22.2 cm,
image 20.3 × 14 cm. Josef and Anni Albers
Foundation, 1976.4.97

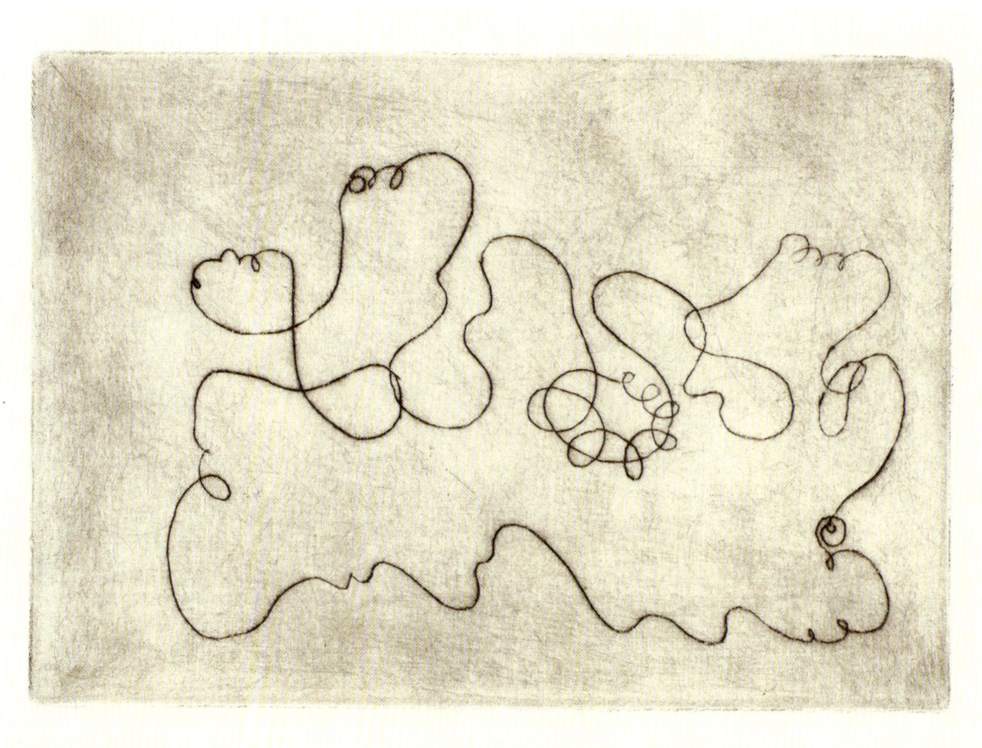

Nippon A, 1942,
drypoint, paper 22 × 29.5 cm,
image 14 × 20.3 cm. Josef and Anni Albers
Foundation, 1976.4.98

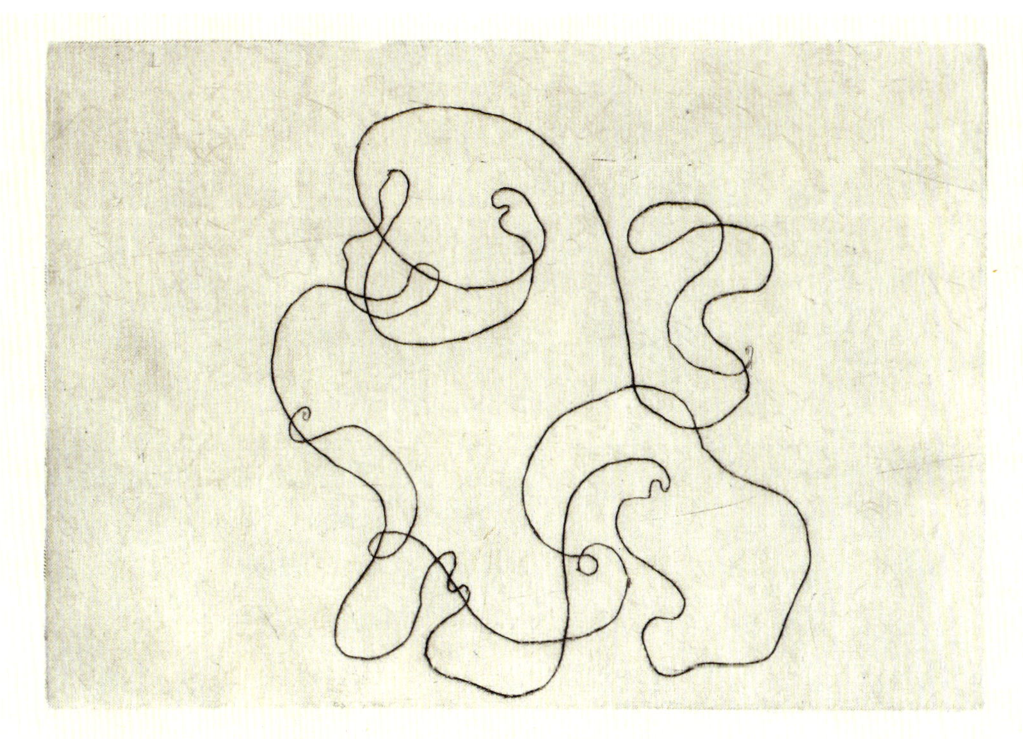

Nippon B, 1942,
drypoint, paper 22 × 29.5 cm,
image 14 × 20.3 cm. Josef and Anni Albers
Foundation, 1976.4.99

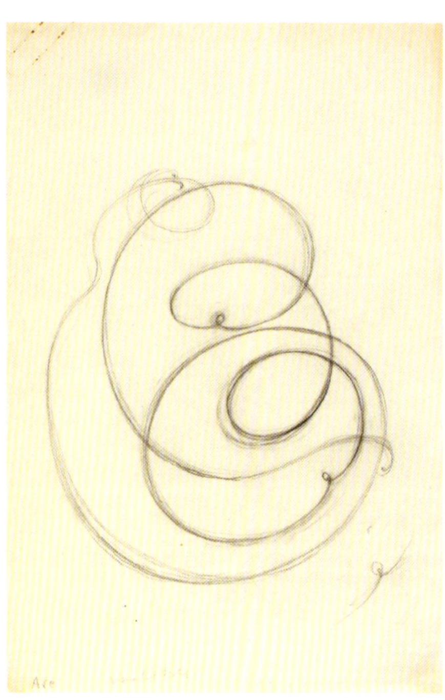

Study for *Maternity*, c. 1942,
pencil on paper, 20.6 × 13.9 cm. Josef and Anni Albers Foundation, 1976.3.252

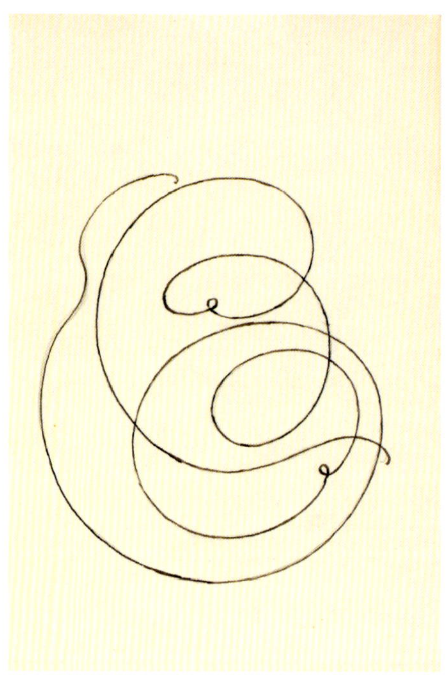

Study for *Maternity*, c. 1942,
ink and pencil on paper, 20.6 × 13.9 cm. Josef and Anni Albers Foundation, 1976.3.253

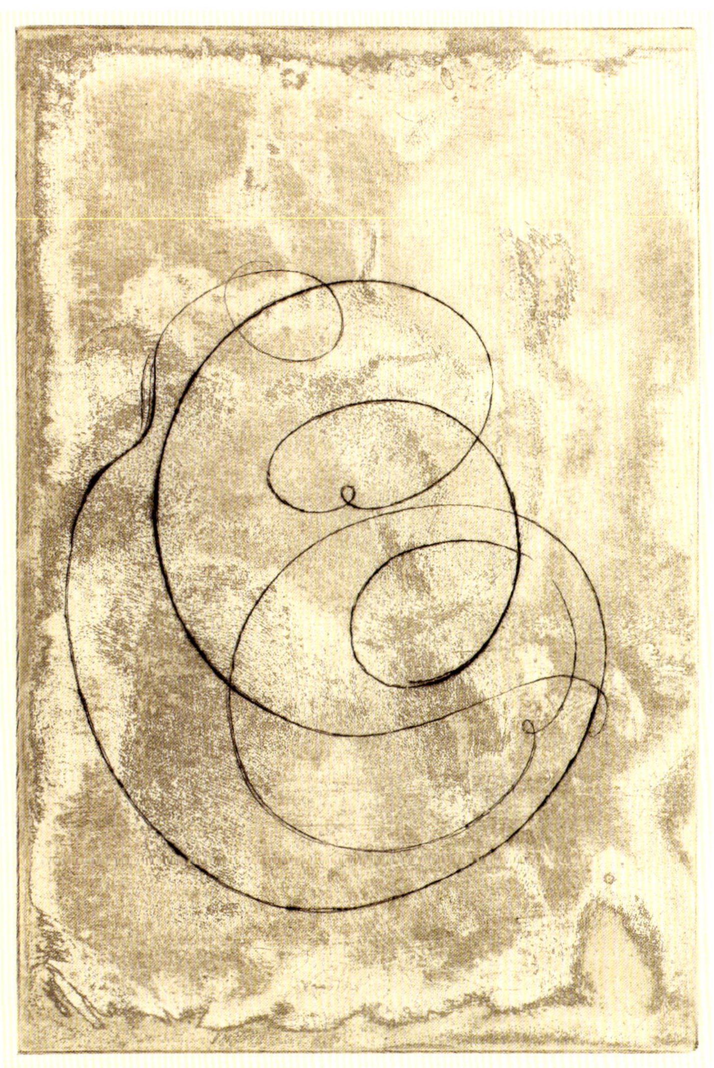

Maternity, 1942,
drypoint, paper 32.9 × 25.2 cm,
image 20.3 × 13.7 cm. Josef and
Anni Albers Foundation, 1976.4.96

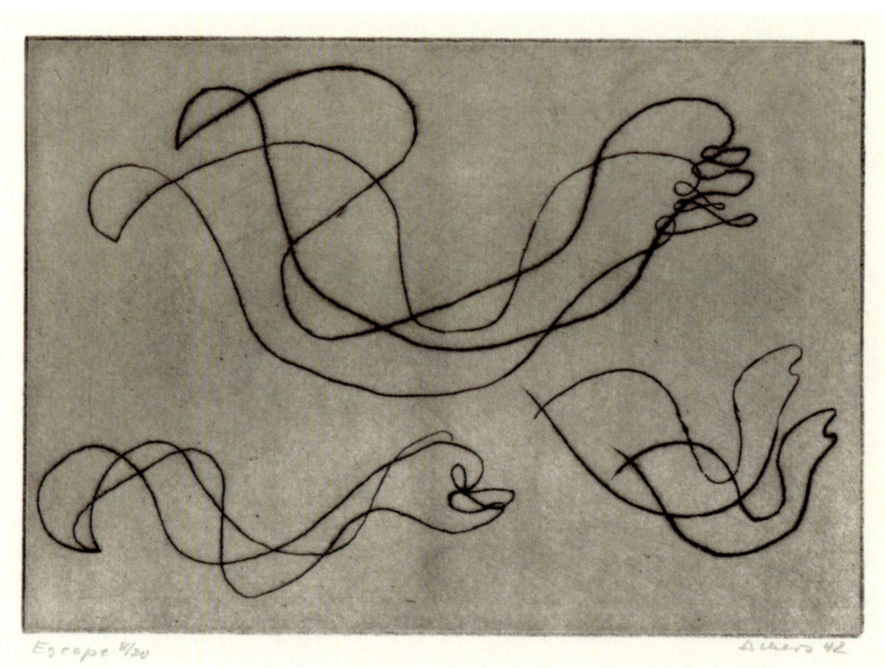

Escape, 1942,
drypoint, paper 20 × 26 cm,
image 14 × 20.3 cm. Josef and Anni Albers
Foundation, 1976.4.92

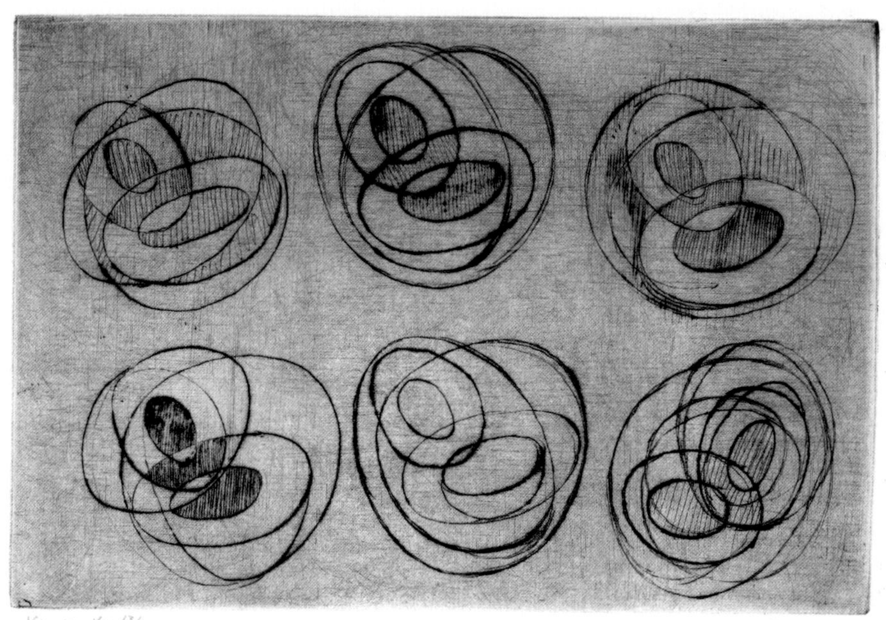

Variants, 1942,
drypoint, paper 21 × 27.3 cm,
image 15.3 × 22.5 cm. Josef and Anni Albers Foundation, 1976.4.93

Variants elevates a classroom exercise to the animated activity of a vital set of forms that move in and out and around each other, perpetually shifting in space and challenging the viewer's eye to keep pace. The effect is intensified by the variety of sketchy marks made by the drypoint stylus.

Albers had not given up on geometry, however. He had been using pure line to manipulate the rectangular picture formats since the mid-1930s, and lines re-entered his prints with the *Graphic Tectonic* series of 1942. Albers spent the spring semester of 1941 in Cambridge, Massachusetts, where, at Walter Gropius's invitation, he taught architecture students at Harvard's Graduate School of Design. There he began a new series of pen-and-ink drawings on graph paper, in which he explored the illusionistic effects that could be obtained with unmodulated lines. He distilled these drawings into a suite of nine *Graphic Tectonics* printed from zinc lithographic plates the following year by Reinhard Schumann, a skilled German emigré printer who lived in Hickory, North Carolina.[30] The *Graphic Tectonics* move sharply away from the free and organic abstract forms of the drypoints to anticipate the *Multiplex*, *Transformation*, and various *Structural Constellation* series that, alongside a growing interest in colour, would dominate from the late 1940s on.

The series title *Graphic Tectonic* suggests an apparent contradiction that Albers may have set out to resolve. 'Graphic' relates to drawing, while 'tectonic' refers to structure. His notes on the subject make clear that with the *Graphic Tectonics* he intended to challenge received ideas about the aims, nature, and process of drawing. Whereas the graphic process conventionally relies on a modulated line to produce an illusion of space and volume on a two-dimensional surface, Albers used groups of precisely drawn unmodulated thick and thin lines in the *Graphic Tectonics*. The tools and materials used to create these lithographs – ruler, pen and ink, and smooth zinc lithographic plates – ensured a precision and uniformity more readily associated with machine-made than with handmade objects.

30. See Hirsch, 'Albers Prints of the '30s and '40s.' Hirsch interviewed Schumann's widow, Eva Schumann, in 1995. In a postcard dated 23 November 1941, Reinhard Schumann wrote asking Albers to send the completed plates to him in High Point, North Carolina.

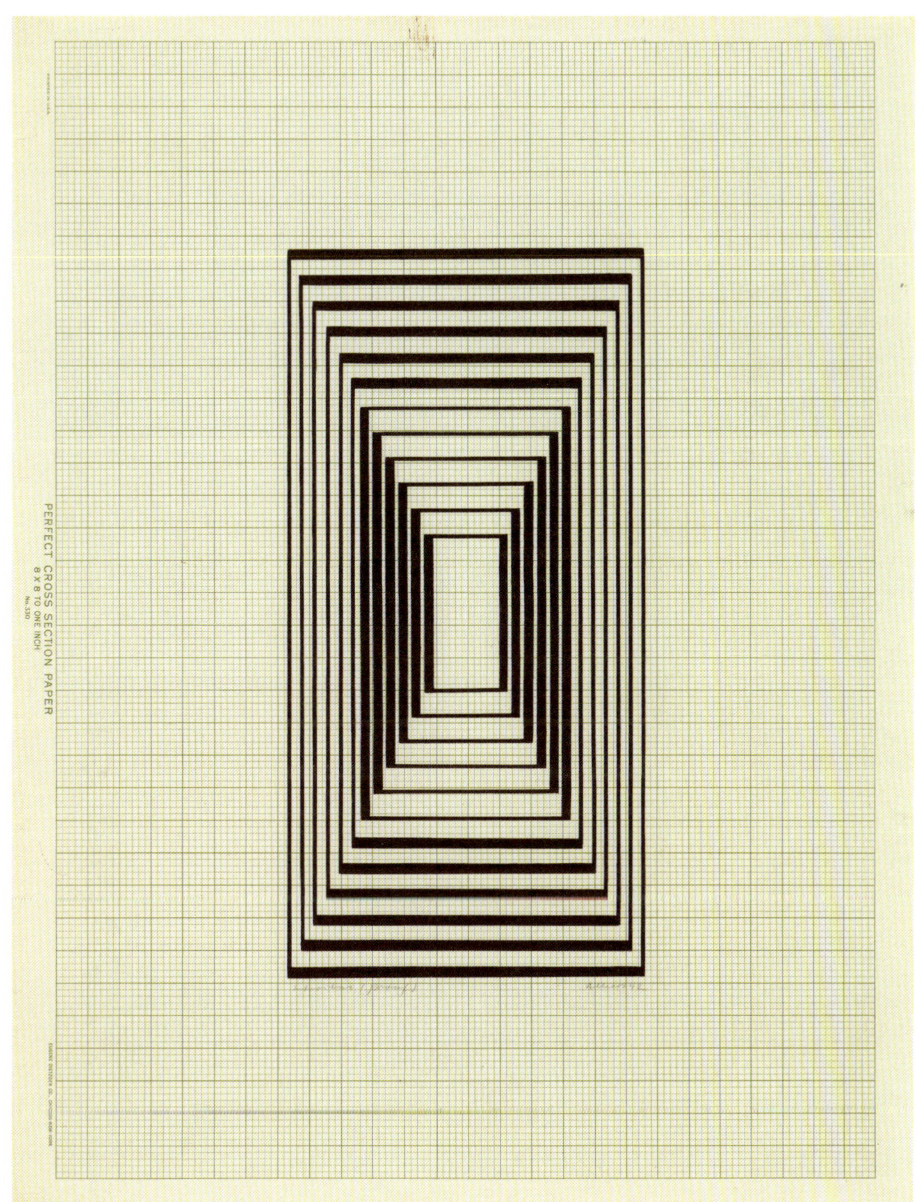

Introitus (unnumbered proof), 1942, lithograph, paper 61 × 48.3 cm, image 35.6 × 17.8 cm. Josef and Anni Albers Foundation, 1976.4.102

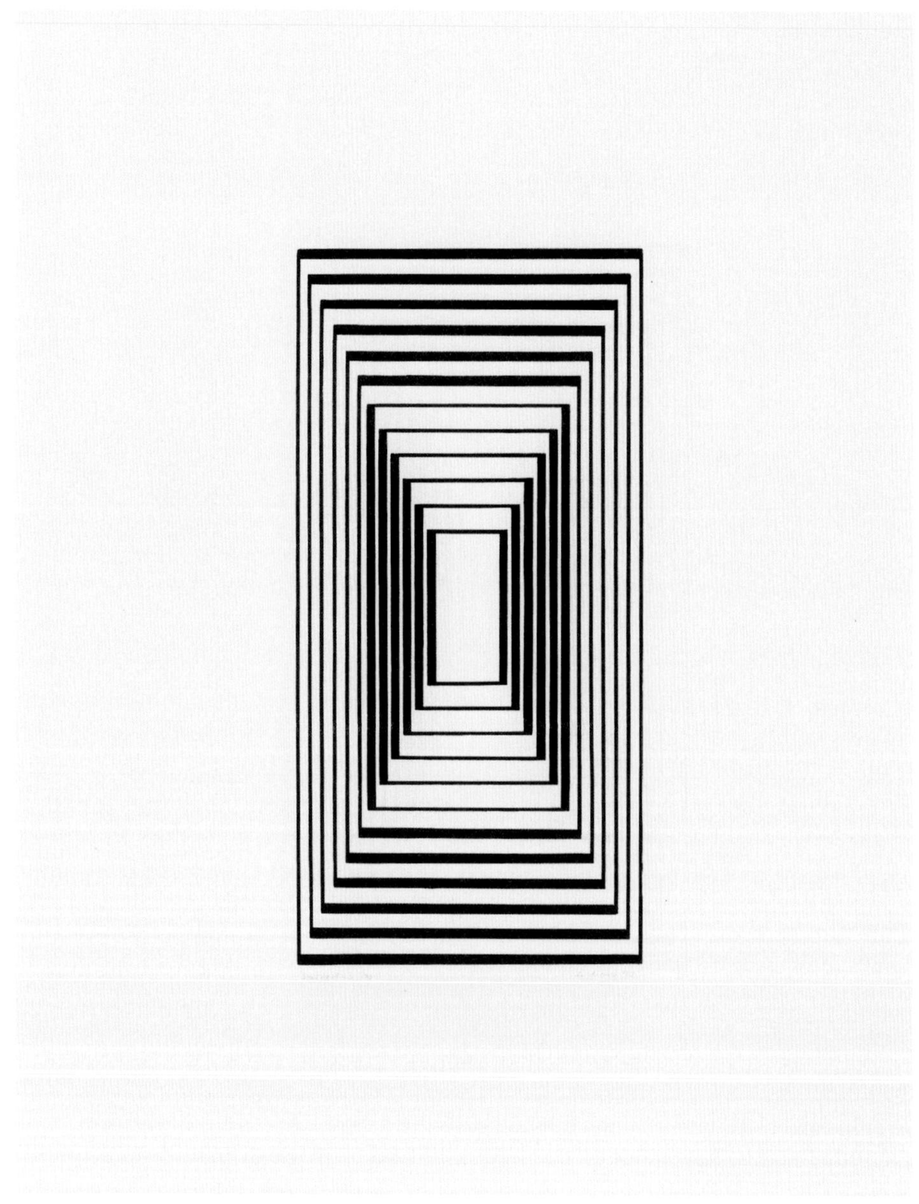

Introitus, 1942,
lithograph, paper 61 × 48.3 cm,
image 35.6 × 17.8 cm. Josef and Anni Albers
Foundation, 1976.4.102

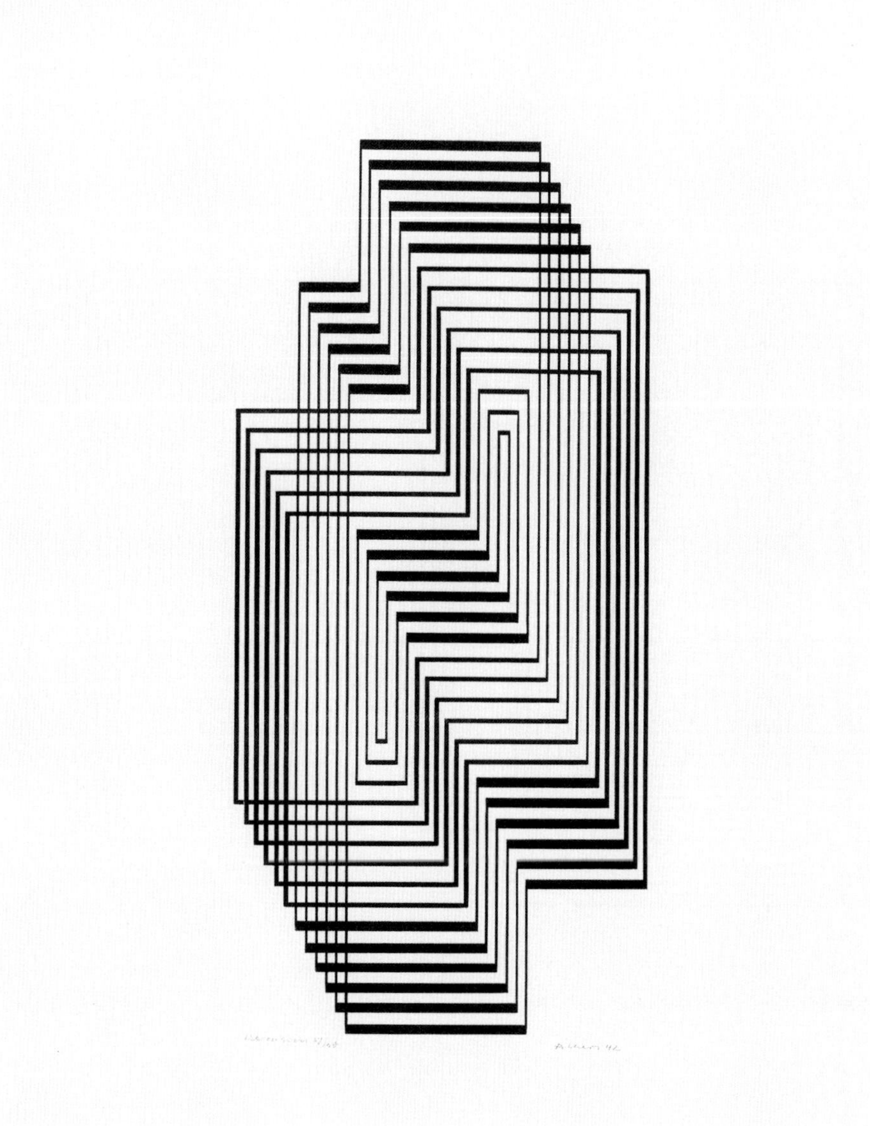

Ascension, 1942,
lithograph, paper 61 × 48.3 cm,
image 43.8 × 20.6 cm. Josef and
Anni Albers Foundation, 1976.4.100

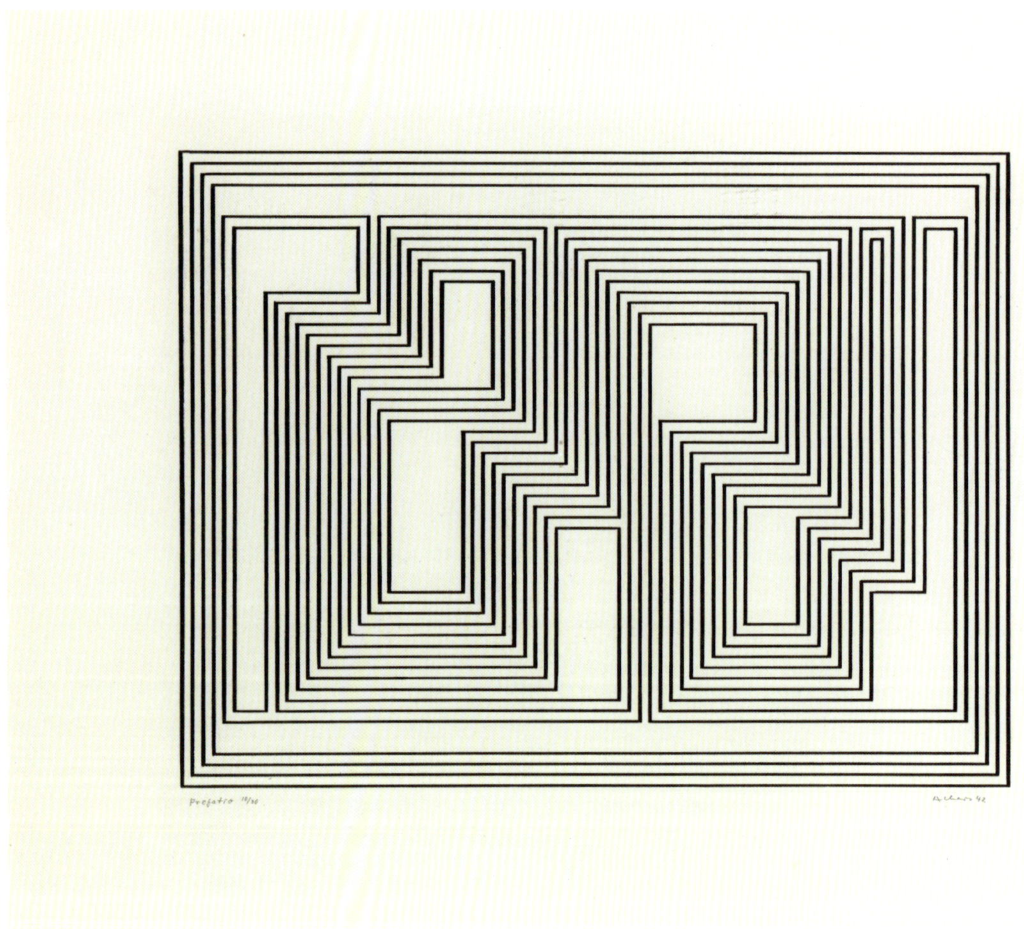

Prefatio, 1942,
lithograph, paper 48.3 × 61 cm,
image 29.8 × 40 cm. Josef and Anni Albers
Foundation, 1976.4.103

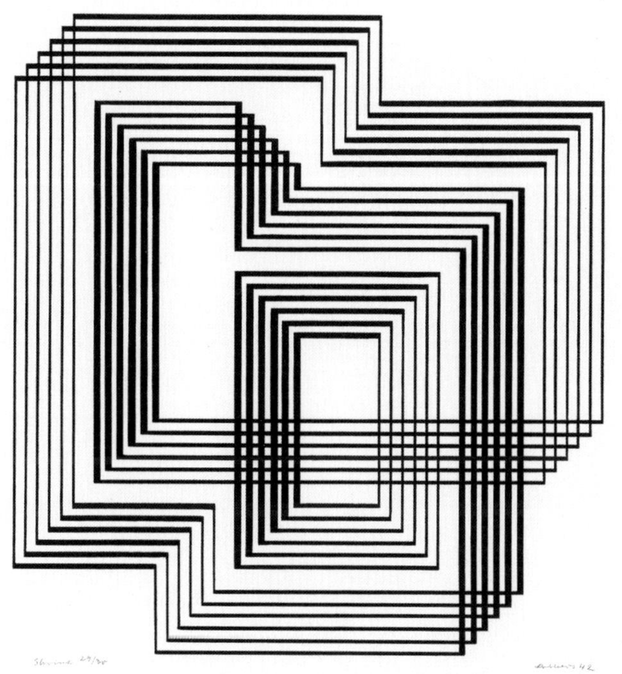

Shrine, 1942,
lithograph, paper 61 × 48.3 cm,
image 33 × 31.4 cm. Josef and Anni Albers
Foundation, 1976.4.106

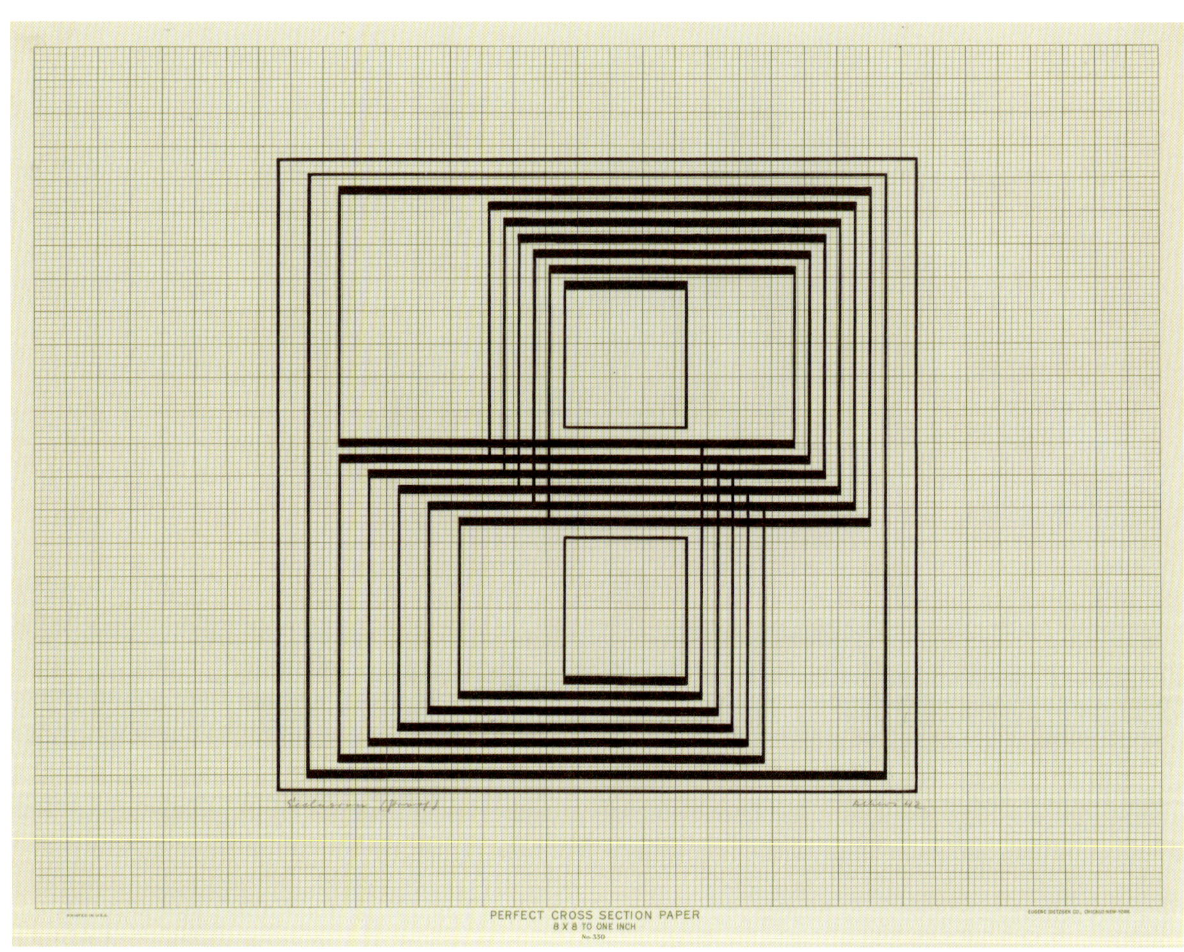

Seclusion (unnumbered proof), 1942, lithograph, paper 48.3 × 61 cm, image 30.5 × 31.7 cm. Josef and Anni Albers Foundation, 1976.4.105

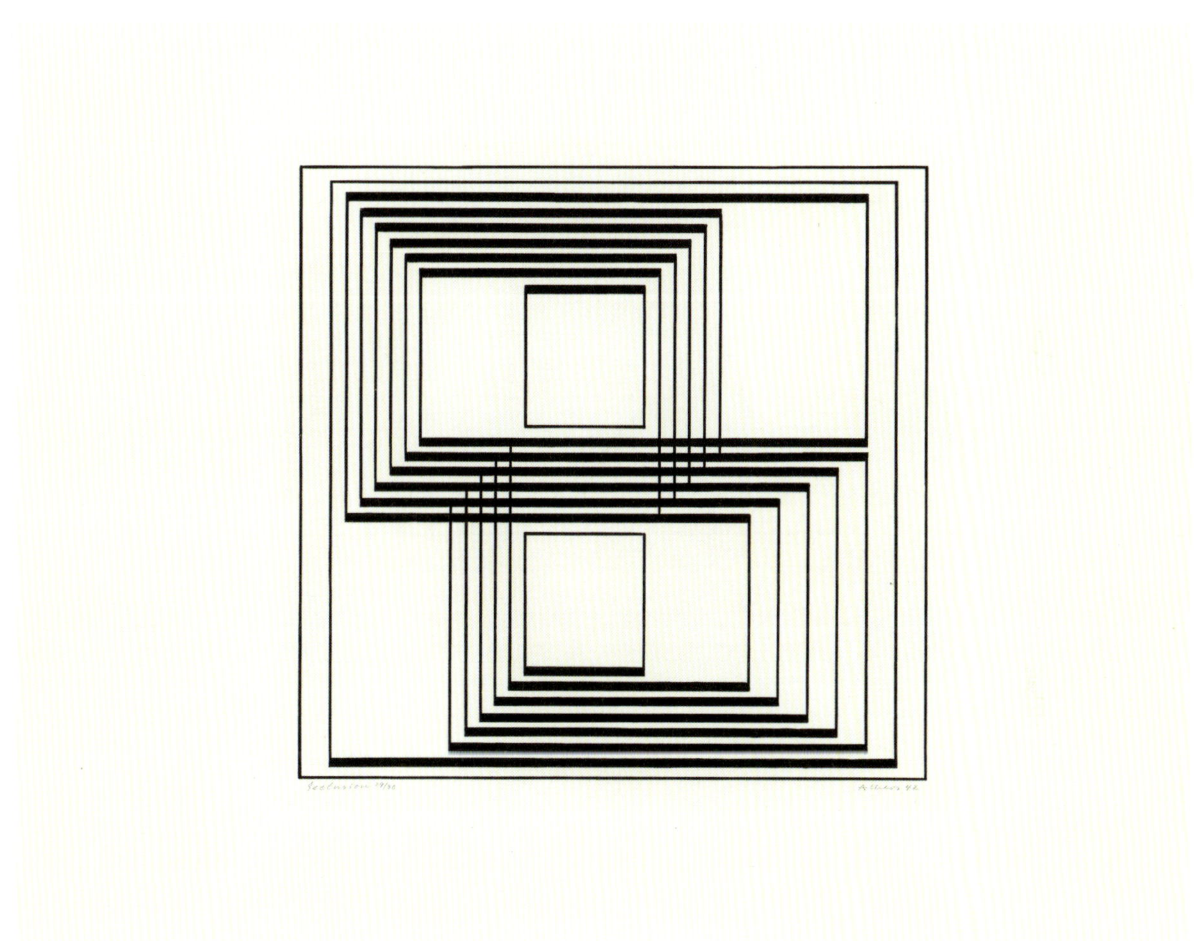

Seclusion, 1942,
lithograph, paper 48.3 × 61 cm,
image 30.5 × 31.7 cm. Josef and
Anni Albers Foundation, 1976.4.105

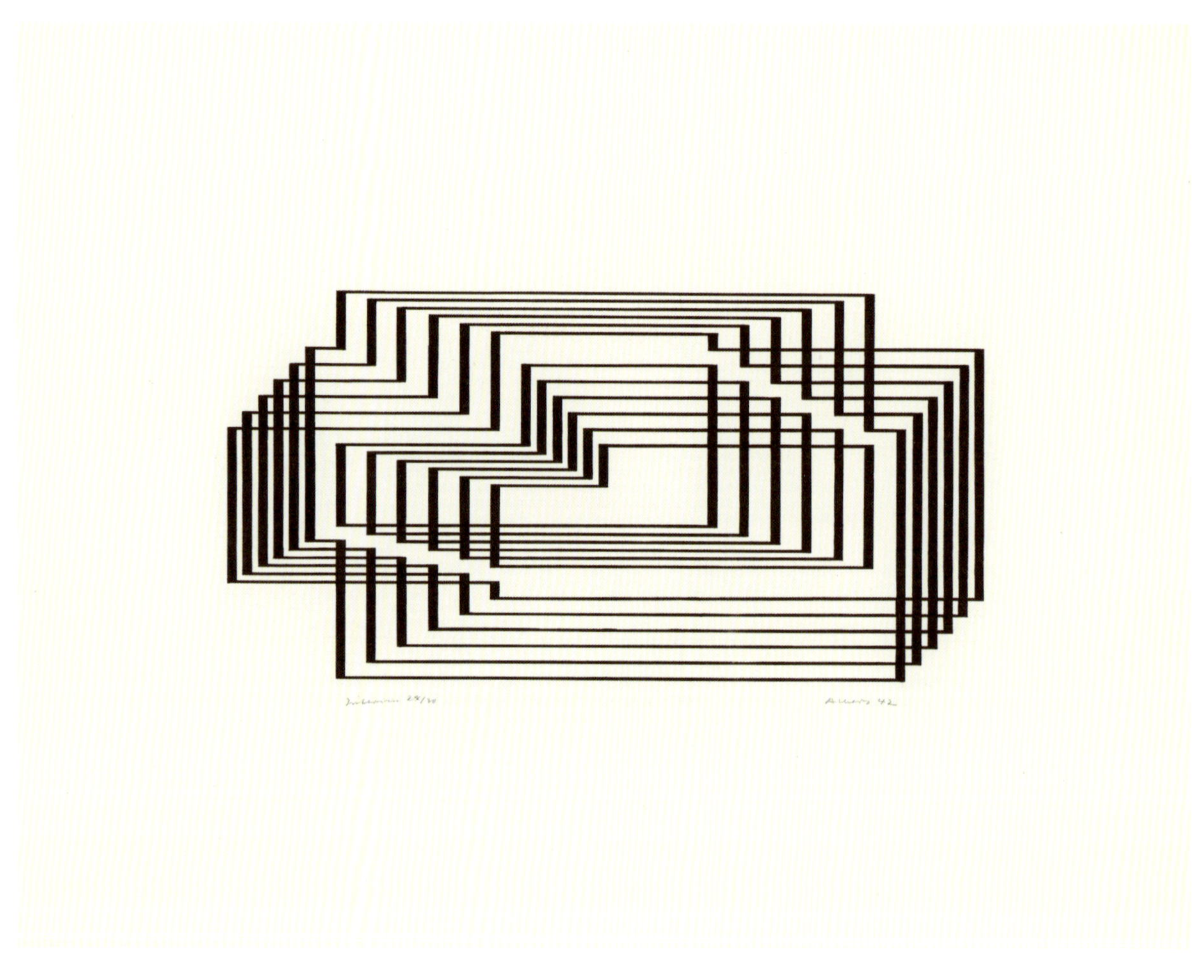

Interim, 1942,
lithograph, paper 48.3 × 61 cm,
image 19.4 × 38.7 cm. Josef and
Anni Albers Foundation, 1976.4.101

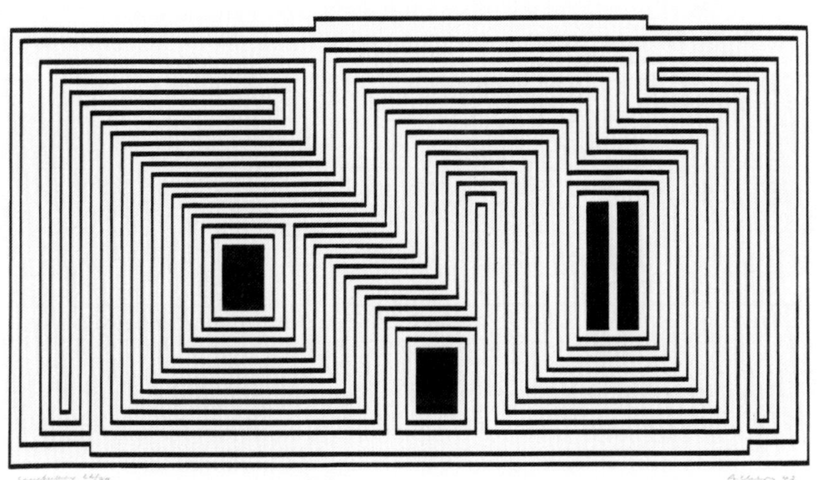

Sanctuary, 1942,
lithograph, paper 48.3 × 61 cm,
image 22 × 40 cm. Josef and
Anni Albers Foundation, 1976.4.104

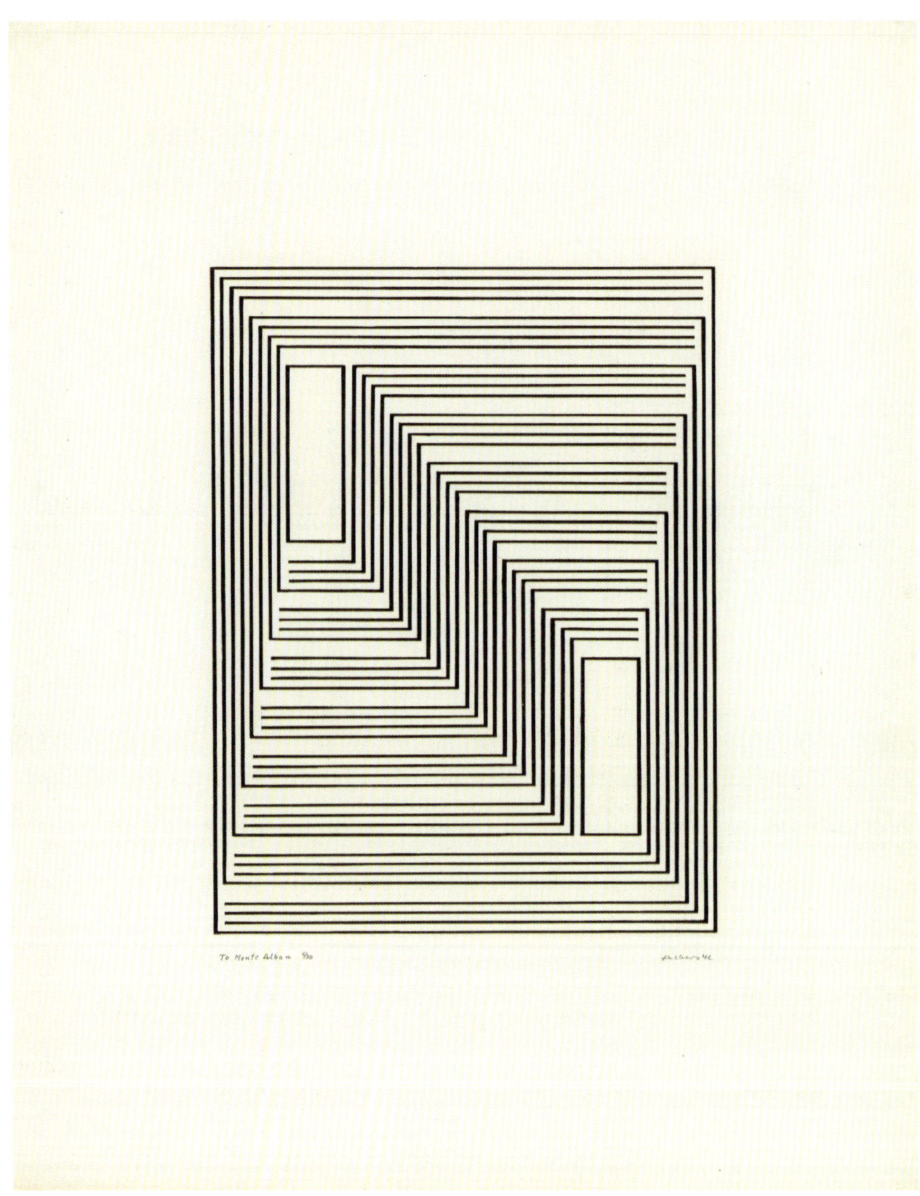

To Monte Alban, 1942, lithograph, paper 61 × 48.3 cm, image 33.7 × 26.7 cm. Josef and Anni Albers Foundation, 1976.4.107

Monte Albán, Mexico, *c.* 1937, photographed by Josef Albers

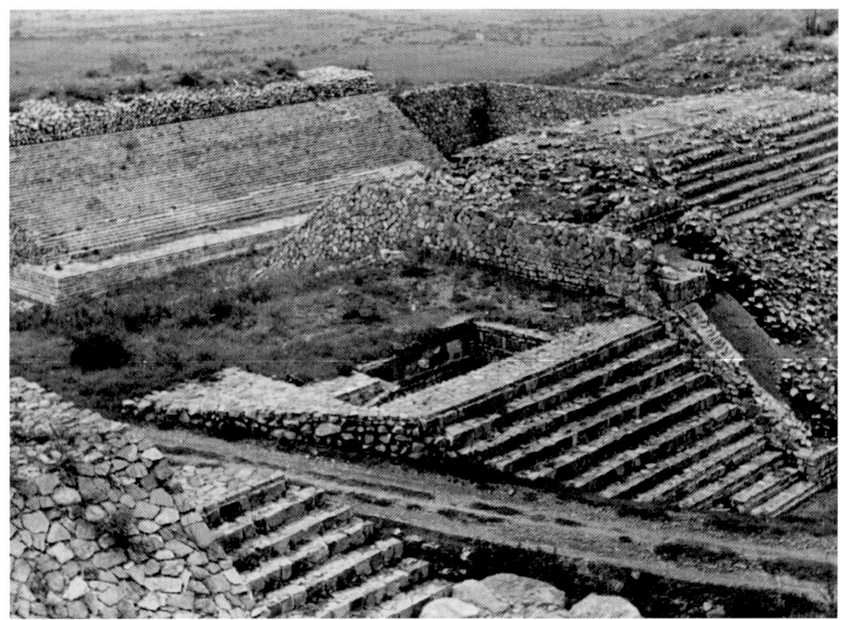

Within these constraints Albers's deft manipulation of thick and thin lines, and of the intervals between them, created brilliantly illusionistic compositions that animated the page and created movement from depth to surface and from light to dark tones. This, he wrote, proved it 'unjustified to evaluate and reject lines without modulations as an un-artistic means for graphic art', and put in question 'a belief that "hand-made" is better than machine or tool made'.[31] The nine *Graphic Tectonic* lithographs hover between the iconic *Introitus* and the suggestive *To Monte Alban*. Albers acknowledged the affinities between the forms of pre-Columbian architecture and his own tectonic forms, and a comparison of one of his many photographs of the eponymous site makes it explicit in *To Monte Alban*.

My wife and I are great admirers of old Mexican art, architecture, and pottery, and we went many times to study them, and Monte Albán is one of the most beautiful sites. I would say it competes with the Acropolis. And there is the same thing; pyramid next to pyramid.... So I thought, that's a nice homage to Monte Albán.[32]

31. Albers, statement on the *Graphic Tectonics* (1943), in Margit Staber (ed.), *Josef Albers: Graphic Tectonic*, exh. cat. (Cologne: Galerie der Spiegel, 1968), n.p.

32. Albers's response to a question from an interviewer who asked: 'I noticed that one of your *Graphic Tectonics* is entitled *To Monte Alban*, could you explain why?' Audio-taped interview with Marion Gore, July 1964, cited in Benezra, *Murals and Sculpture of Josef Albers*, p. 22. Anni Albers's wall hanging *Monte Alban*, 1936, is a similar 'homage'.

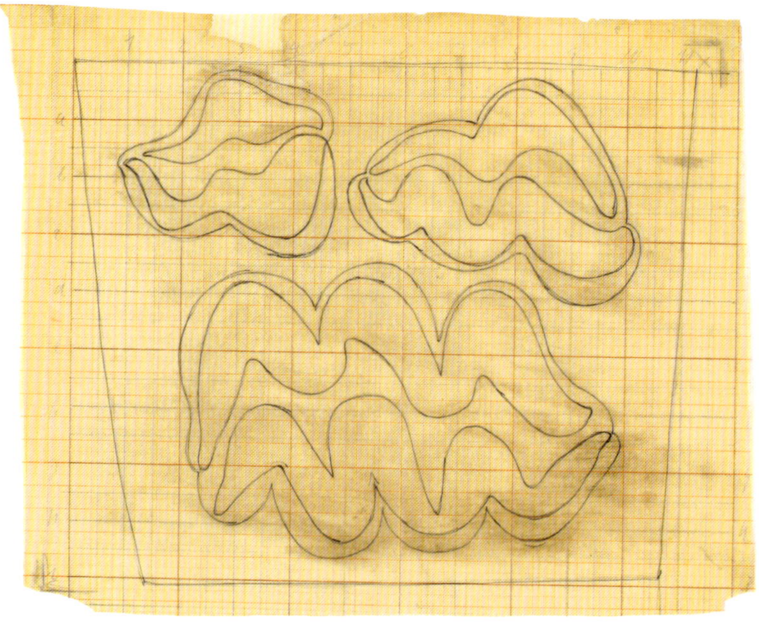

Study for *Adjusted*, 1944, pencil on paper, 26 × 31.5 cm. Josef and Anni Albers Foundation, 1976.3.241

This response is revealing also of Albers's use of titles. Never intended as descriptive, their relation to the work was metaphoric – adding another level of meta-perception to the viewer's experience. Albers, who wrote poems and was fascinated by etymology, invited his audience to contemplate the words that accompanied his works. Among the *Graphic Tectonic* titles are *Introitus* and *Prefatio* taken from Catholic ritual, and *Sanctuary*, *Shrine*, *Seclusion*, and *Ascension*, which allude to spiritual life. For Albers, even seemingly impersonal abstractions could contain intimations of transcendence.

In 1944, organic forms resurfaced in an intriguing group of woodcuts. *Adapted*, *Adapted B*, and *Adjusted* are an index of the distance that Albers had travelled from the drawings and lithographs of rabbits in 1916 to a 'revelation and evocation of vision'. Far from copying, or even interpreting nature, Albers appropriated soft, smooth, wormlike creatures, transforming their protean bodies into pictorial elements, arranging them in sensuous pairs that allow multiple possibilities of combination and treatment.

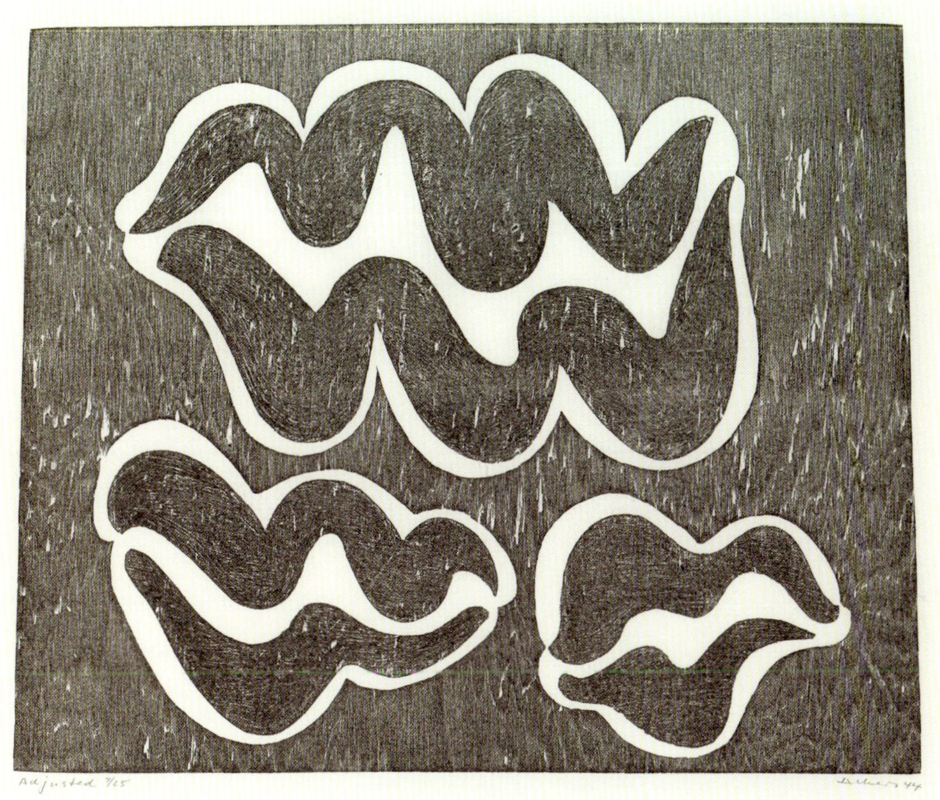

Adjusted, 1944,
woodcut, paper 34.6 × 40.6 cm,
image 23.8 × 29.8 cm. Josef and Anni
Albers Foundation, 1976.4.111

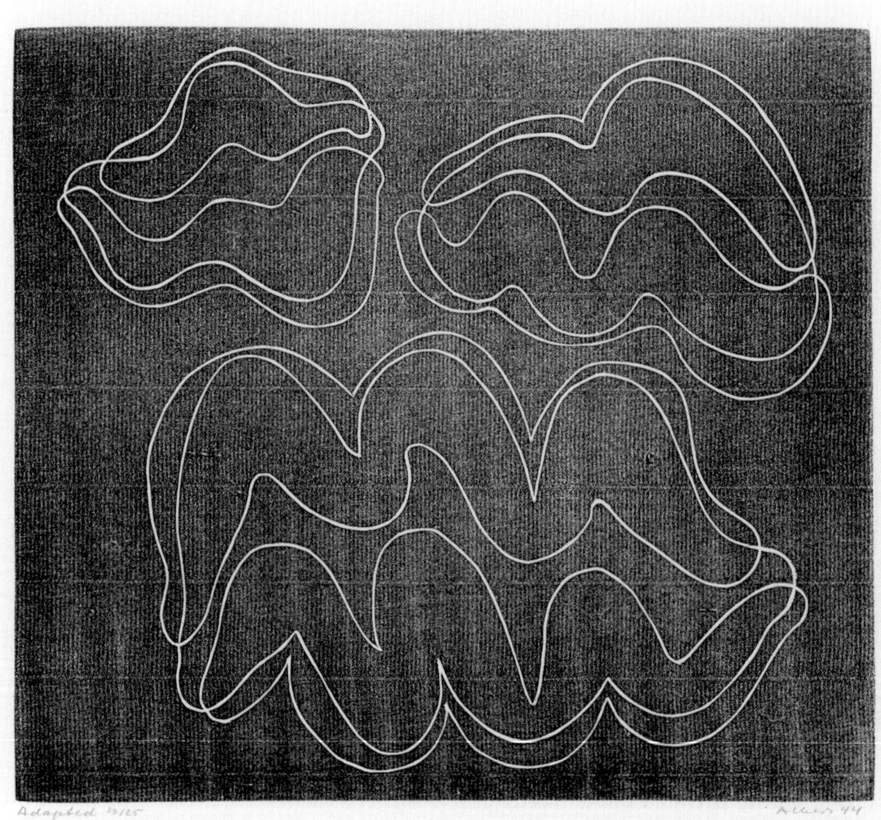

Adapted, 1944,
woodcut, paper 31.8 × 40.3 cm,
image 21.6 × 24.4 cm. Josef and Anni Albers Foundation, 1976.4.109

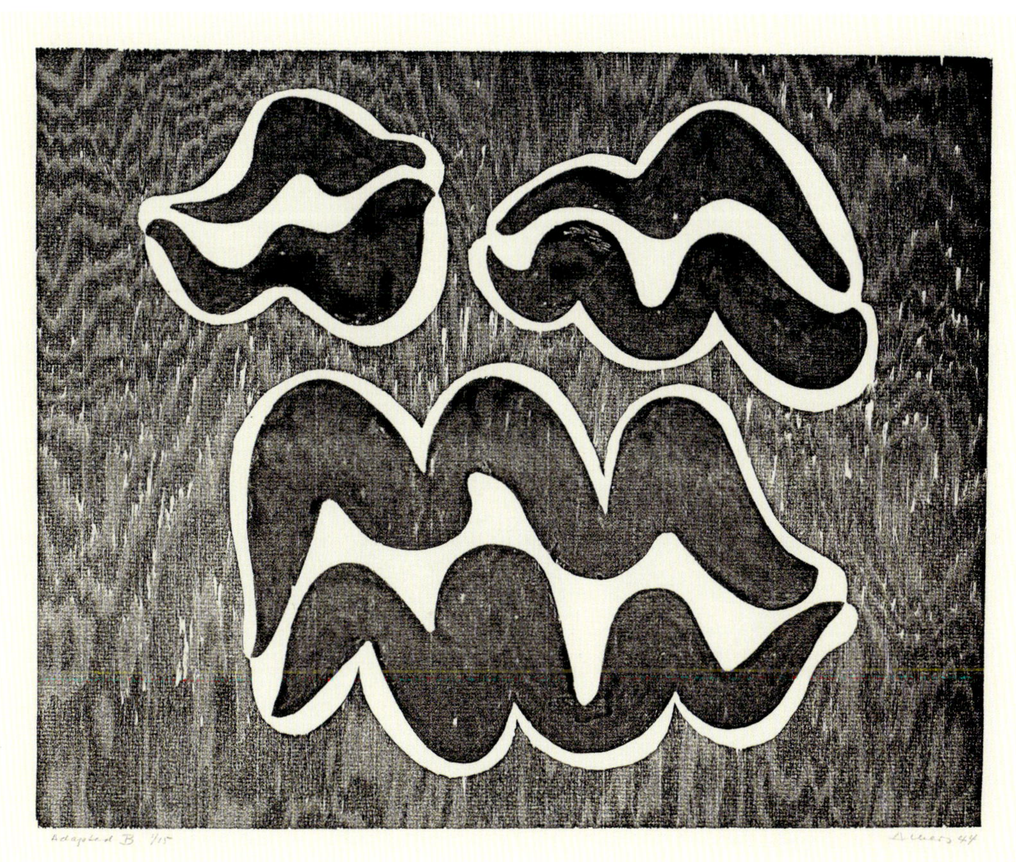

Adapted B, 1944,
woodcut, paper 33 × 38 cm,
image 23.8 × 29.8 cm. Josef and Anni
Albers Foundation, 1976.4.110

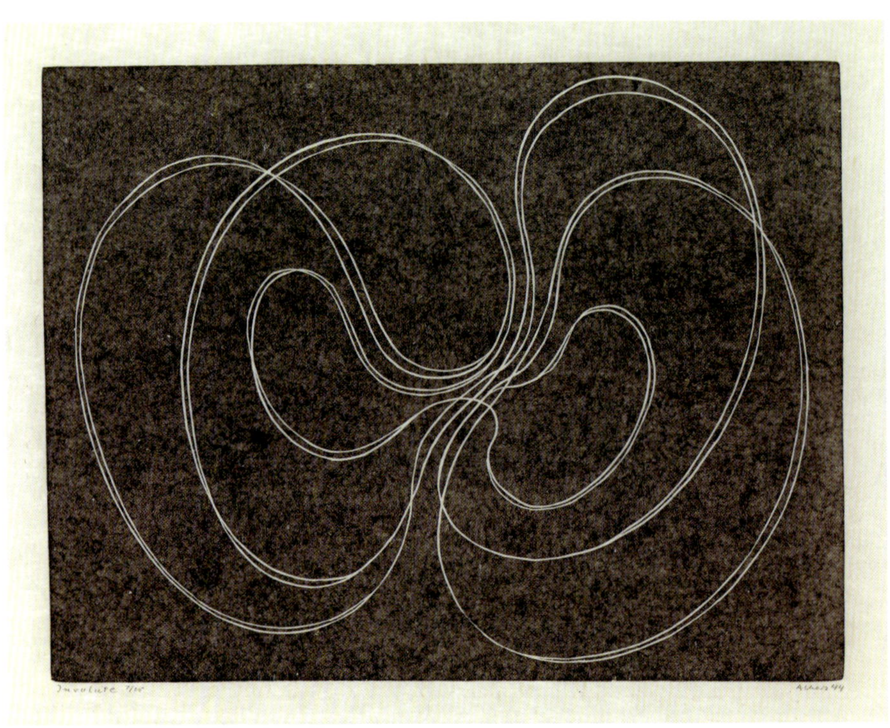

Involute, 1944,
cork relief, paper 28.9 × 45.1 cm,
image 24.1 × 31.8 cm. Josef and Anni
Albers Foundation, 1976.4.115

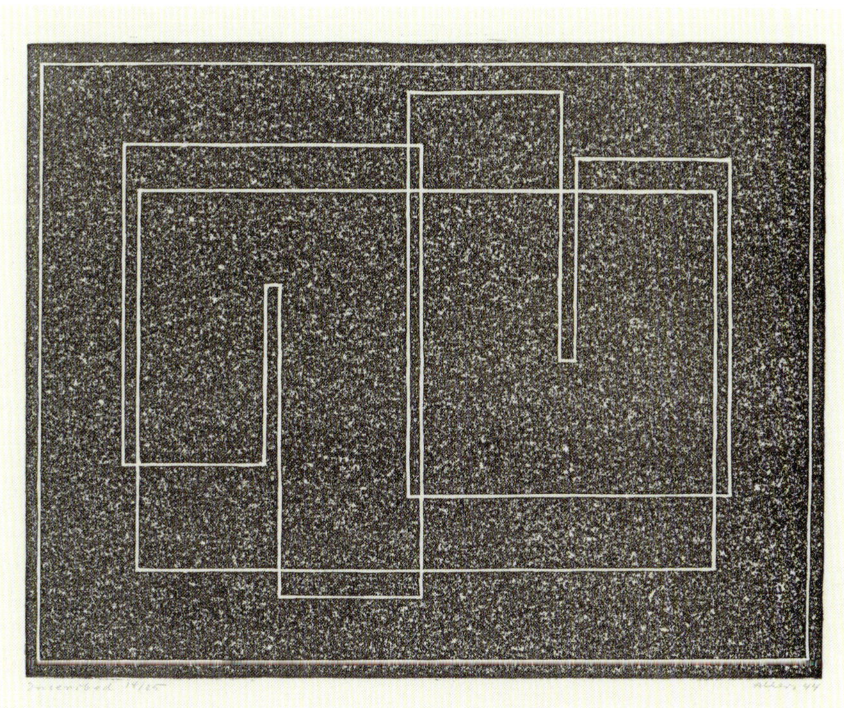

Inscribed, 1944,
cork relief, paper 30.5 × 39.4 cm,
image 22.2 × 28.6 cm. Josef and Anni
Albers Foundation, 1976.4.114

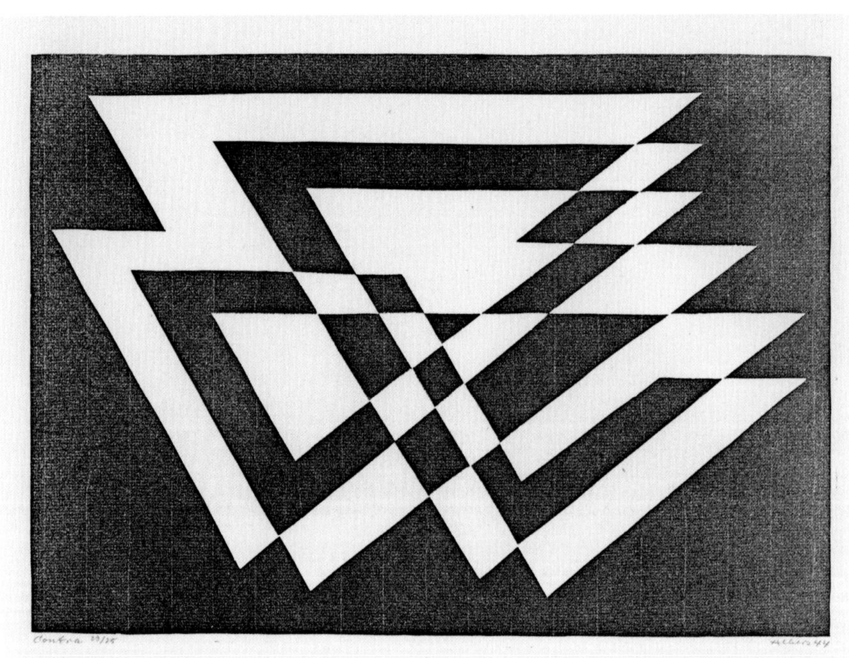

Contra, 1944,
linoleum cut, paper 33 × 38 cm,
image 23.5 × 33.3 cm. Josef and Anni
Albers Foundation, 1976.4.112

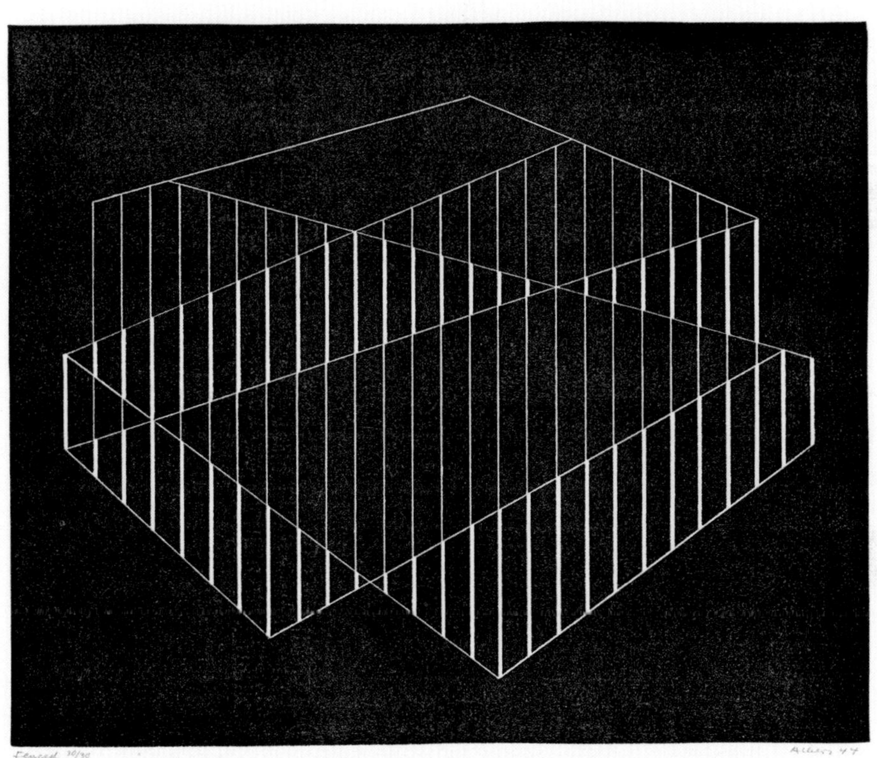

Fenced, 1944,
woodcut, paper 31.8 × 40.6 cm,
image 25.4 × 31.1 cm. Josef and Anni
Albers Foundation, 1976.4.113

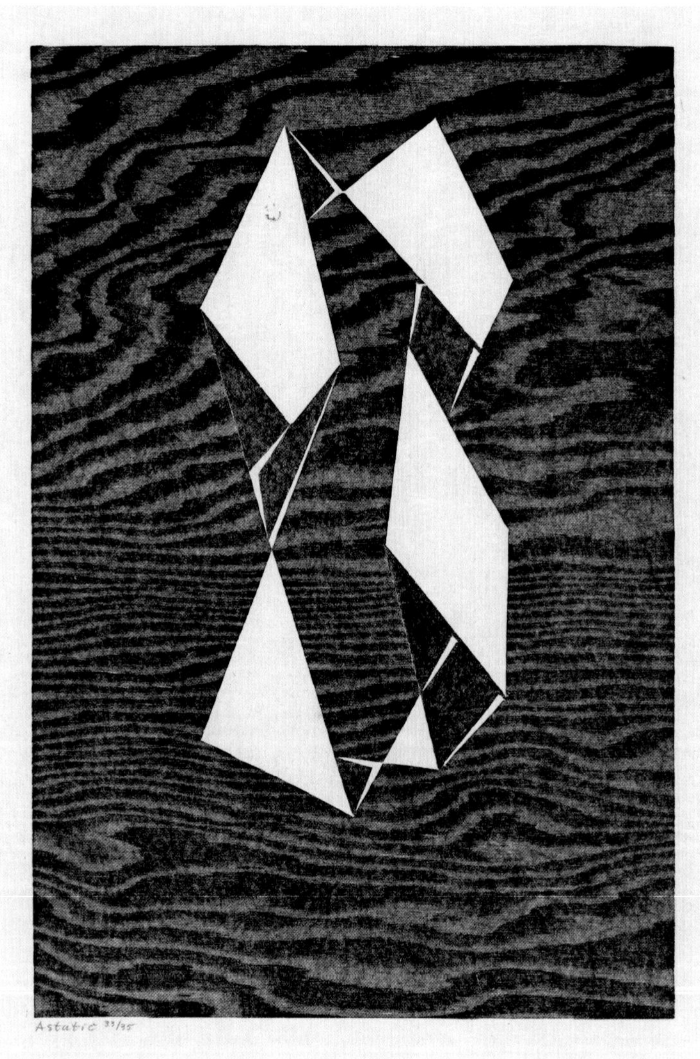

Astatic, 1944,
woodcut from plywood,
paper 44.5 × 28.3 cm,
image 33.6 × 22.9 cm. Josef and Anni
Albers Foundation, 1976.4.116

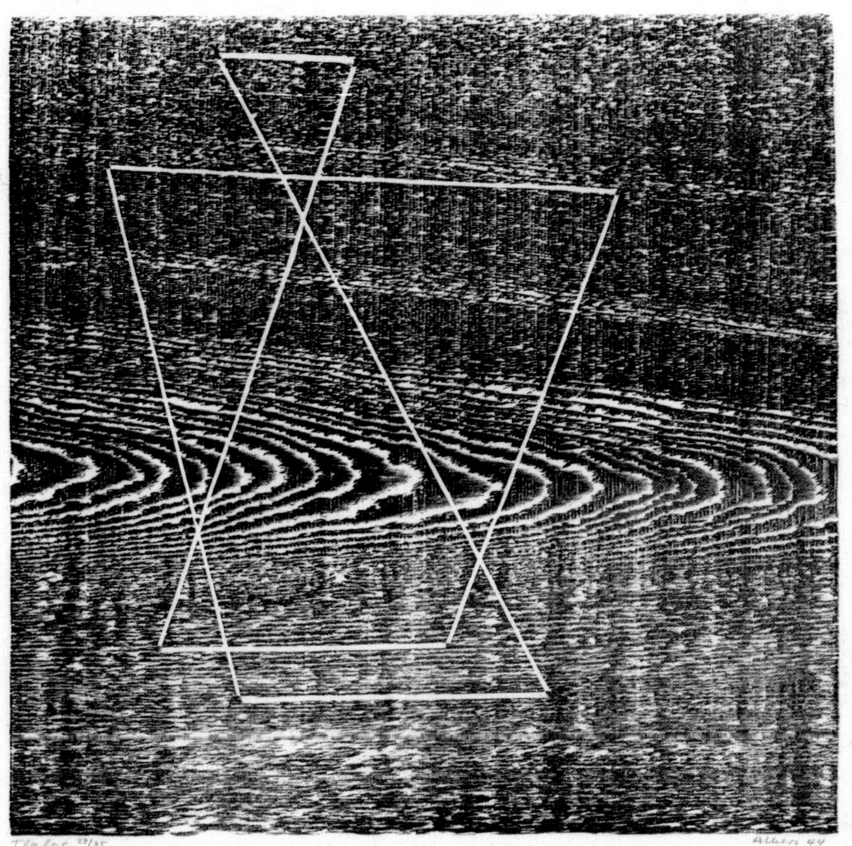

Tlaloc, 1044,
woodcut in rough pine board,
paper 38.1 × 36.8 cm,
image 30.5 × 31.8 cm. Josef and Anni
Albers Foundation, 1976.4.118

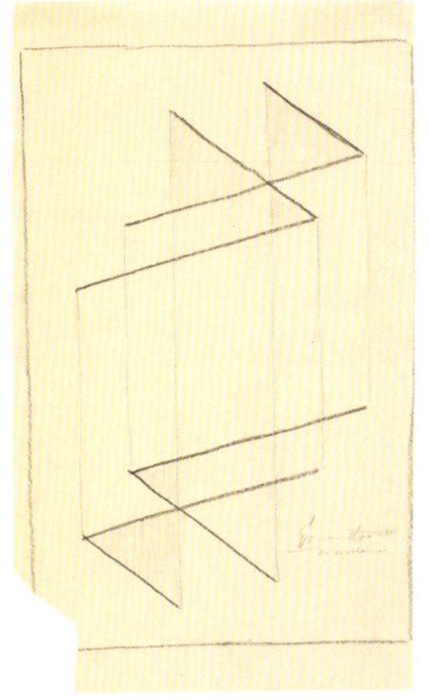

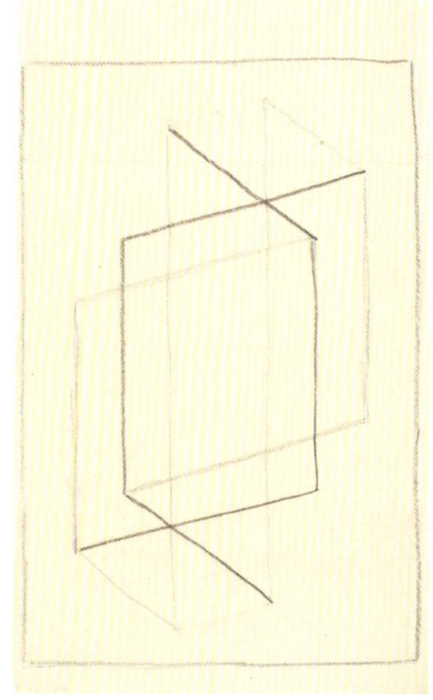

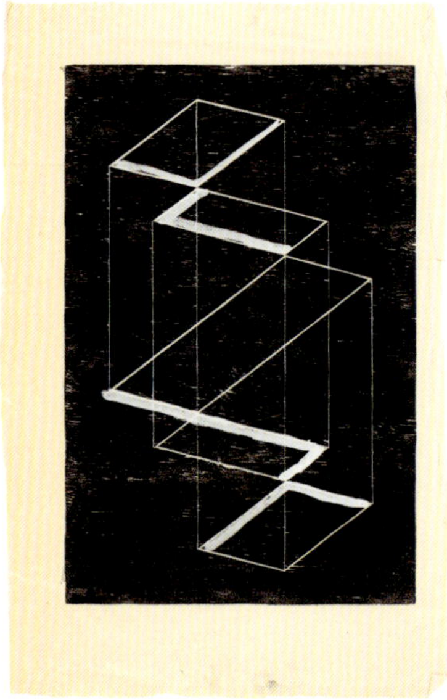

ABOVE LEFT Study for *Multiplex C*, *c.* 1948, pencil on tracing paper, 35 × 21.1 cm. Josef and Anni Albers Foundation, 1976.3.514

ABOVE MIDDLE Study for *Multiplex C*, *c.* 1948, pencil on paper, 35.2 × 21.3 cm. Josef and Anni Albers Foundation, 1976.3.673

ABOVE RIGHT Study for *Multiplex C*, *c.* 1948, gouache over proof of woodblock print, 39.1 × 25.7 cm. Josef and Anni Albers Foundation, 1976.3.702

At the same time, in *Astatic*, *Above the Water*, and *Tlaloc*, the organic structure of inked woodgrain surface plays off against the straight lines of the engraved figures so that the woodgrain becomes a vital pictorial element. These effects became more restrained in the *Multiplex* series of 1947 and 1948, where the large number of drawings that precede the final prints allow us to follow Albers's hand and his mind collaborating to attain just the right balance in the relationship of thick to thin, light to dark, line to surface. The result was an encyclopedia of invented form that, starting in 1949, invaded the picture plane and sustained Albers for the last four decades of his life in works he came to refer to as *Structural Constellations*. The largest of these were sculptural translations, made in stainless steel and other metals and commissioned from Albers as architectural sculptures; the smallest were drawn in a series of notebooks – some with pages measuring a mere 6.6 × 10.6 centimetres.

Early in 1949, the Alberses resigned from Black Mountain College and departed at the semester's end in May. Between then and August 1950, when, aged sixty-two, Josef took up a new position as chair of the Department of Design at Yale University

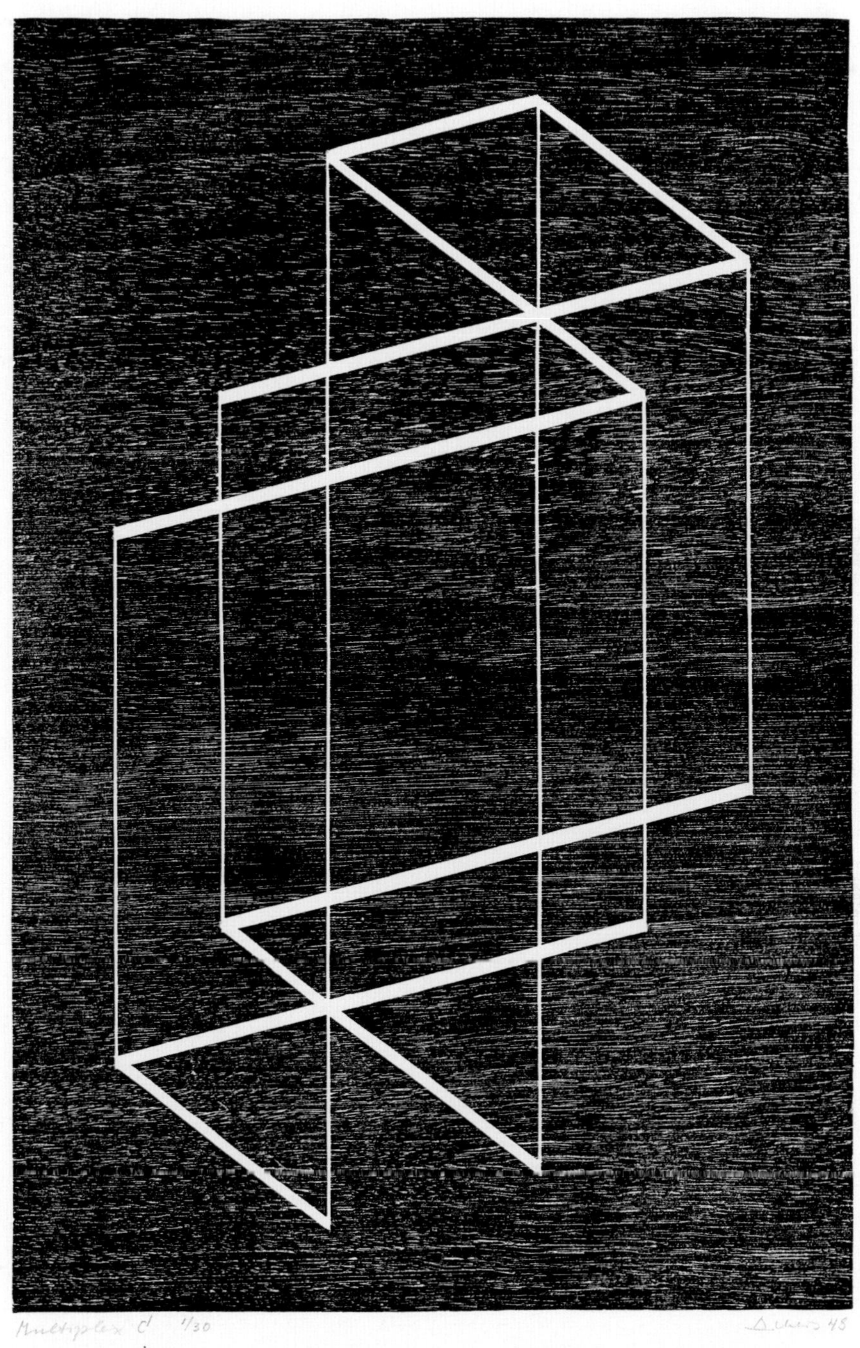

Multiplex C, 1948,
woodcut, paper 40.6 × 29.2 cm,
image 30.5 × 20.3 cm. Josef and Anni
Albers Foundation, 1976.4.122

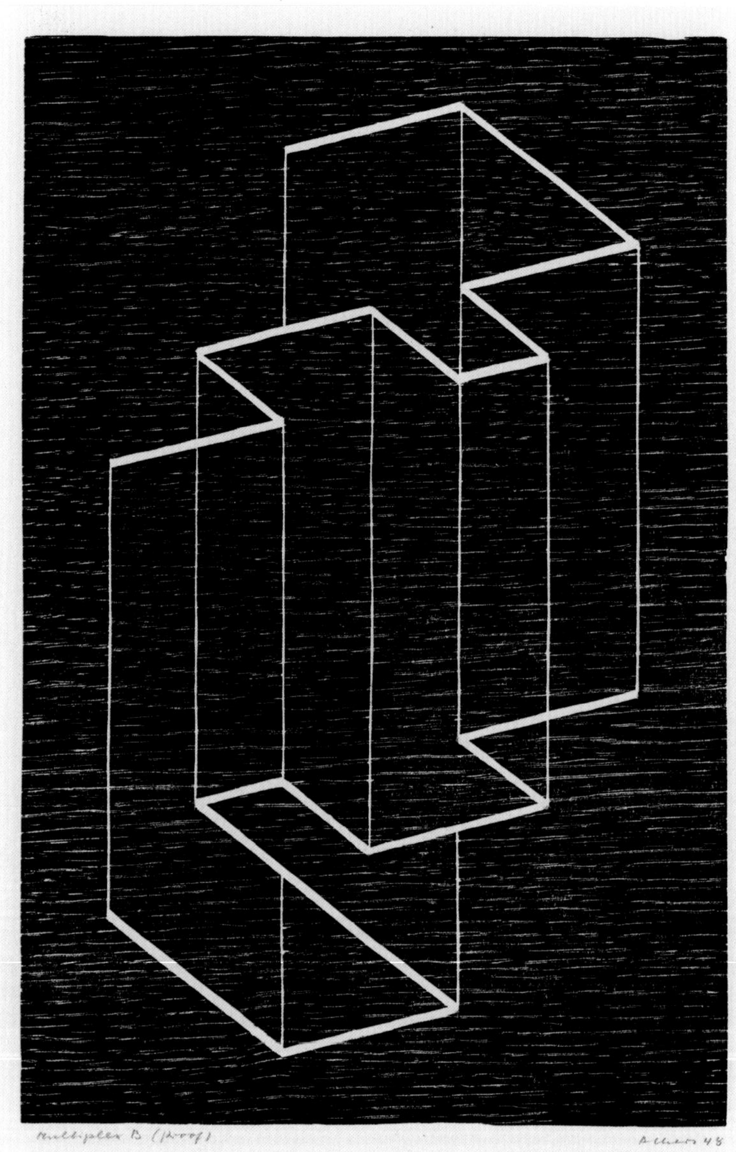

Multiplex B, 1948,
woodcut, paper 41.9 × 31.8 cm,
image 30.5 × 20.3 cm. Josef and Anni
Albers Foundation, 1976.4.121

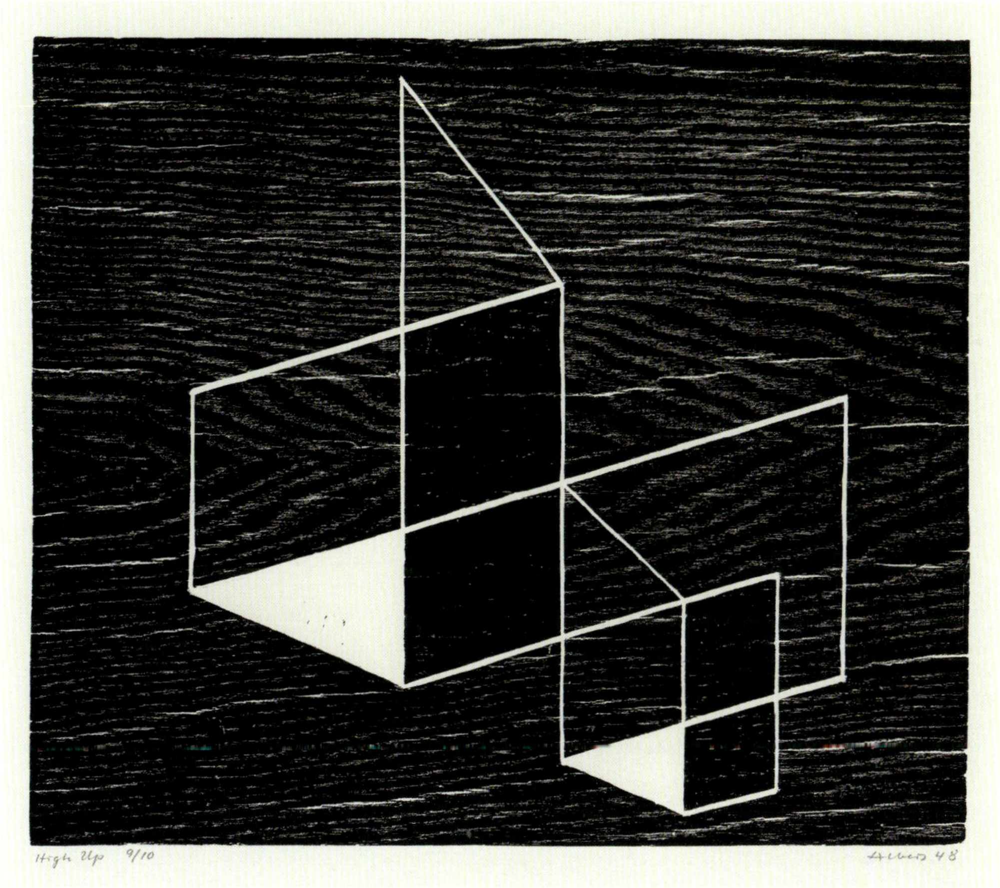

High Up, 1948,
woodcut, paper 27.9 × 39.4 cm,
image 20.3 × 24.1 cm. Josef and Anni
Albers Foundation, 1976.4.124

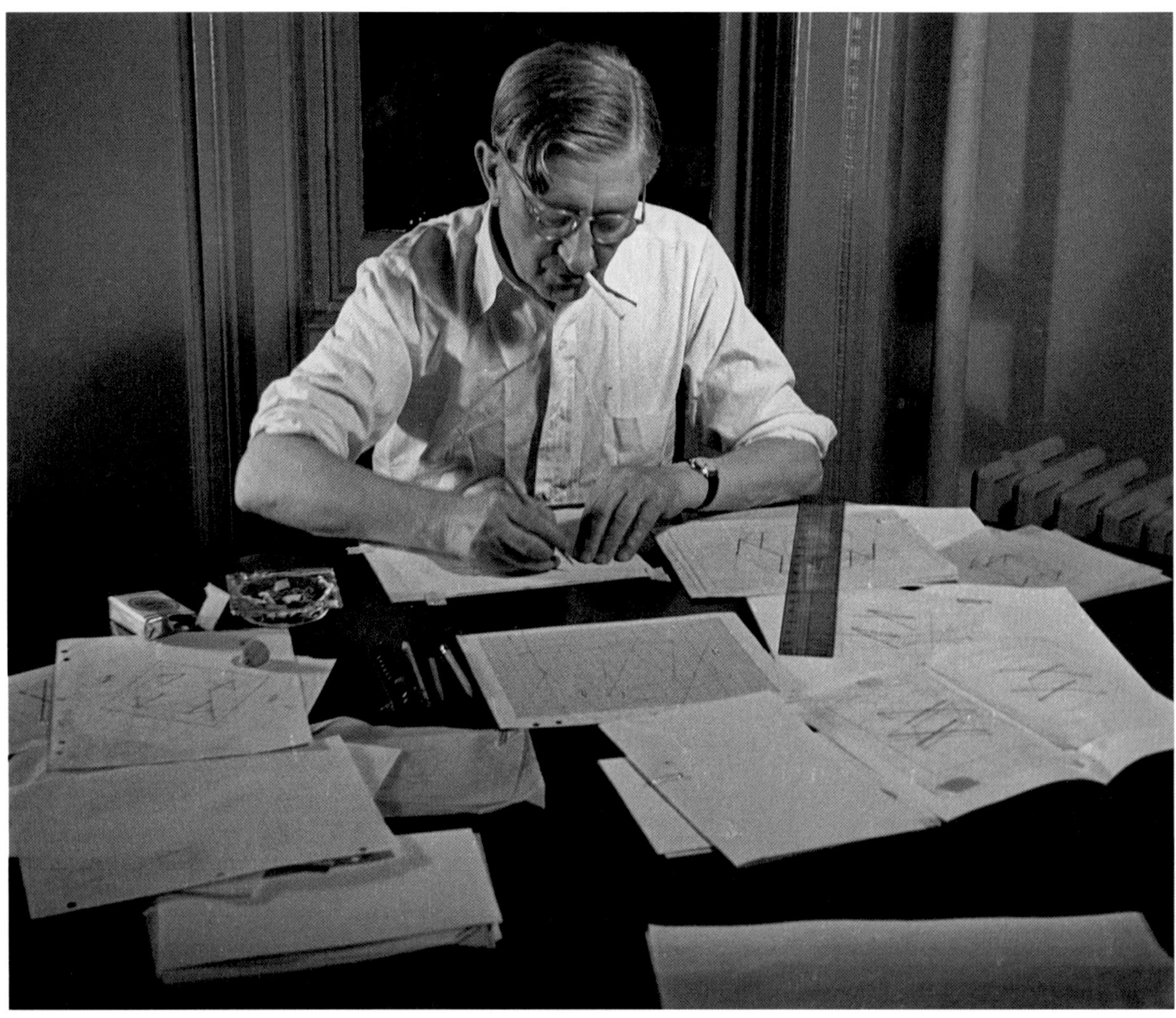

Josef Albers drawing some of the *Structural Constellations*, New York, 1950, photographed by Rudy Burckhardt

in New Haven, Connecticut, the Alberses lived between Mexico and New York City. By that time, he had given up his experiments with organic lines to concentrate on the dual manipulation of precise rectilinear form and of colour. His belief in the machine-made image, demonstrated in the *Graphic Tectonics*, is patent in the *Transformation* series, printed in 1950 at The Composing Room in New York City. The line drawings for these engravings were cut by machine into brass plates, enabling very fine yet absolutely clean lines in the velvety black-inked surfaces.

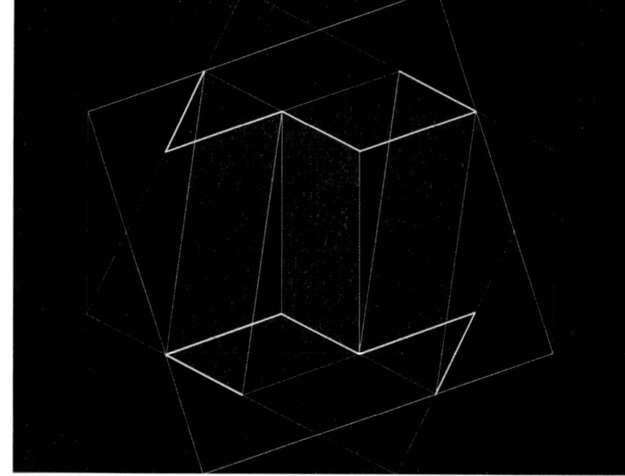

Structural Constellation: Transformation of a Scheme No. 10, 1950–1, machine-engraved and sandblasted black plastic laminate mounted on wood, 43.1 × 57.2 cm. Josef and Anni Albers Foundation, 1976.8.1704

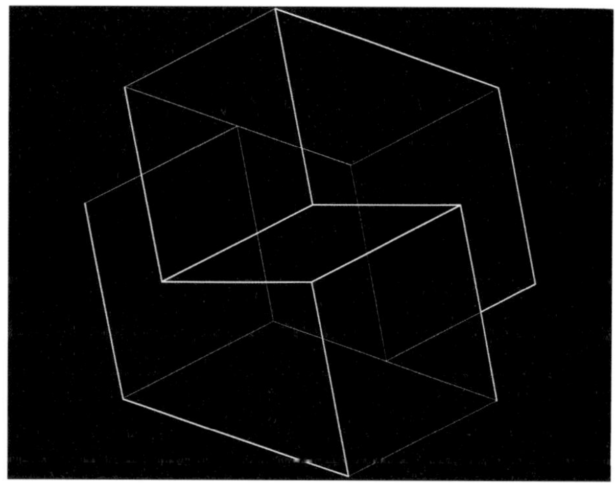

Structural Constellation, undated, machine-engraved black plastic laminate mounted on wood, 43.2 × 57.2 cm. Josef and Anni Albers Foundation, 1976.8.1716

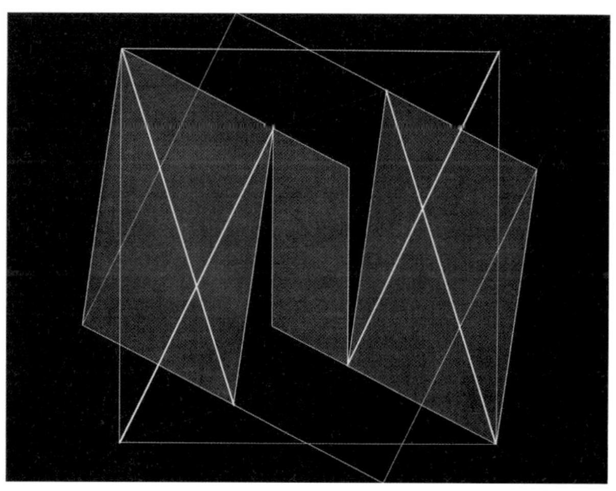

Structural Constellation: Transformation of a Scheme No. 19, 1950, machine-engraved and sandblasted brown plastic laminate mounted on wood, 43.2 × 57.2 cm. Josef and Anni Albers Foundation, 1976.8.1725

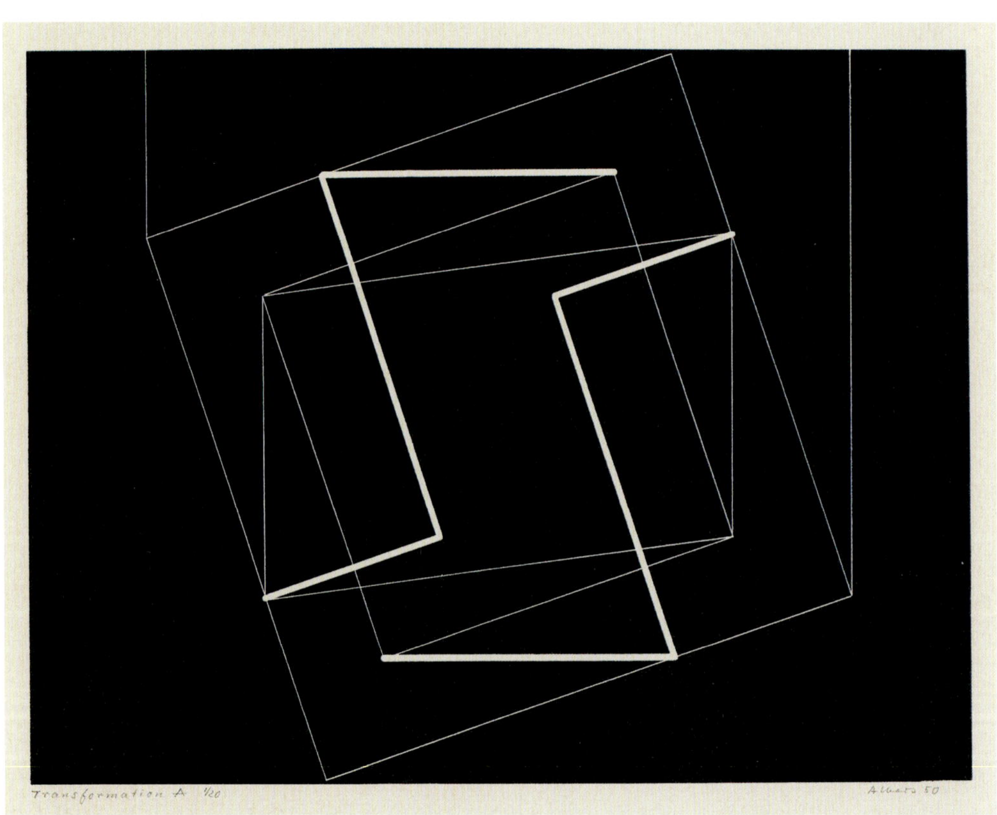

Transformation A, 1950,
Engraving from machine-engraved brass plate, paper 27.9 × 39.4 cm, image 18.1 × 24 cm. Josef and Anni Albers Foundation, 1976.4.125

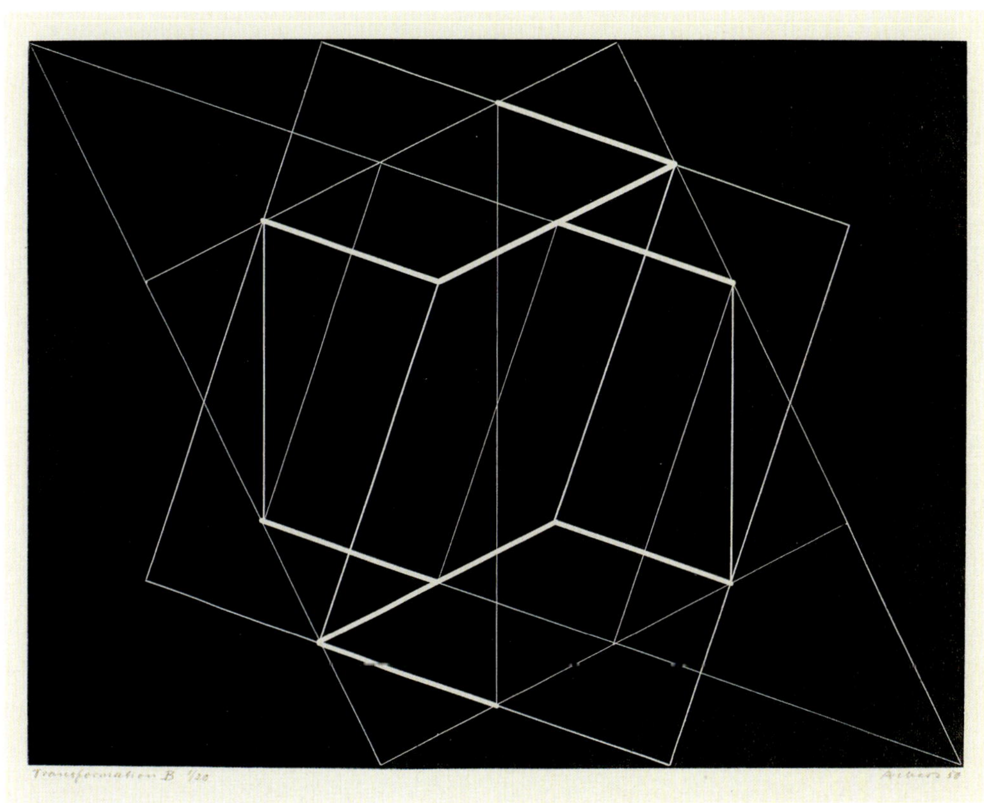

Transformation D, 1950,
Engraving from machine-engraved brass plate, paper 30.5 × 39.4 cm, image 18.1 × 24 cm. Josef and Anni Albers Foundation, 1976.4.126

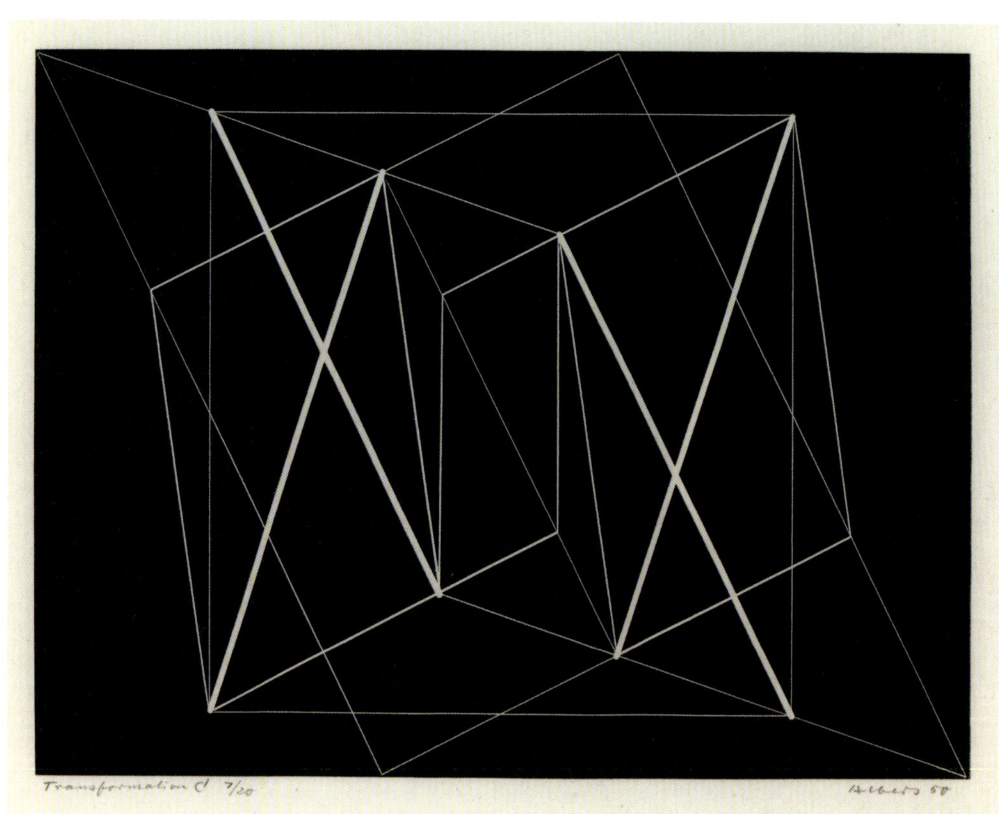

Transformation C, 1950,
Engraving from machine-engraved brass plate, paper 30.5 × 39.4 cm, image 18.1 × 24 cm. Josef and Anni Albers Foundation, 1976.4.127

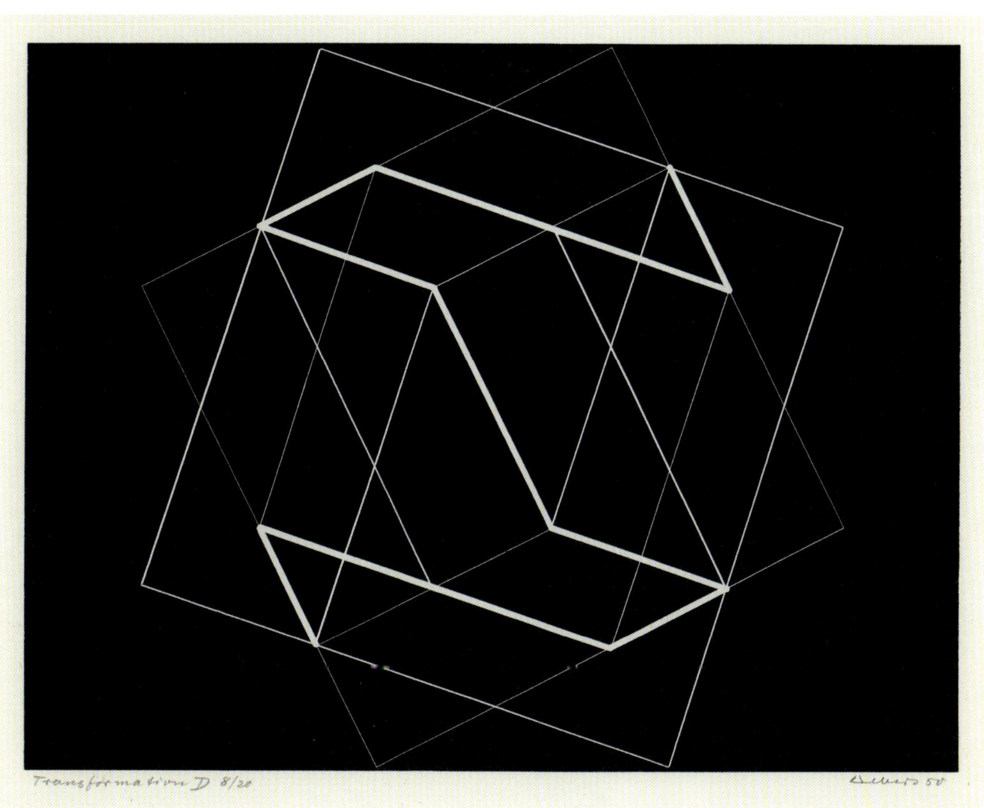

Transformation D, 1950,
Engraving from machine-engraved brass plate, paper 27.9 × 39.4 cm, image 18.1 × 24 cm. Josef and Anni Albers Foundation, 1976.4.128

FOLLOWING PAGES *Transformation C*, 1950 (detail)

Whether it came about by intention or by chance, Albers's method of engaging the 'HOW' of art was to separate his investigations in line from his fascination with colour. Since at least the fifteenth century in Europe, the relative status of *disegno* and *colore* in painting had been a topic of fervent discussion and dispute. *Disegno* usually won out – at least until the nineteenth century. Albers treated design and colour as separate but equal elements of form, and shifted back and forth between them from the late 1940s until the end of his life. As he put it in a letter to Franz Perdekamp in 1947, 'What interests me most now is how colors change one another according to the proportions and quantities [I use].... I'm especially proud when [I can make] colors lose their identity and become unrecognizable. Greens become blue, neutral grays become red-violet and so on. Dark colors become light and vice versa.'[33]

With colour as with line, Albers selected his materials with infinite care and engaged in the process with corporeal vitality. In hundreds of colour studies, both large and small, he tested the juxtaposition, placement, quantity, and quality of oil colours in preparation for screenprints, and then demanded an exact matching in printers' inks. These studies, which were the artist's private toolbox, are now prized for their immediacy. They generate an intense visual experience that brings the viewer into an intimate communication with the artist and his process. That experience confirms the power of the 'HOW' of art.

33. Josef Albers letter to Franz Perdekamp, 7 September 1947. Private collection. Copy at the Josef and Anni Albers Foundation. English translation by Jessica Csoma.

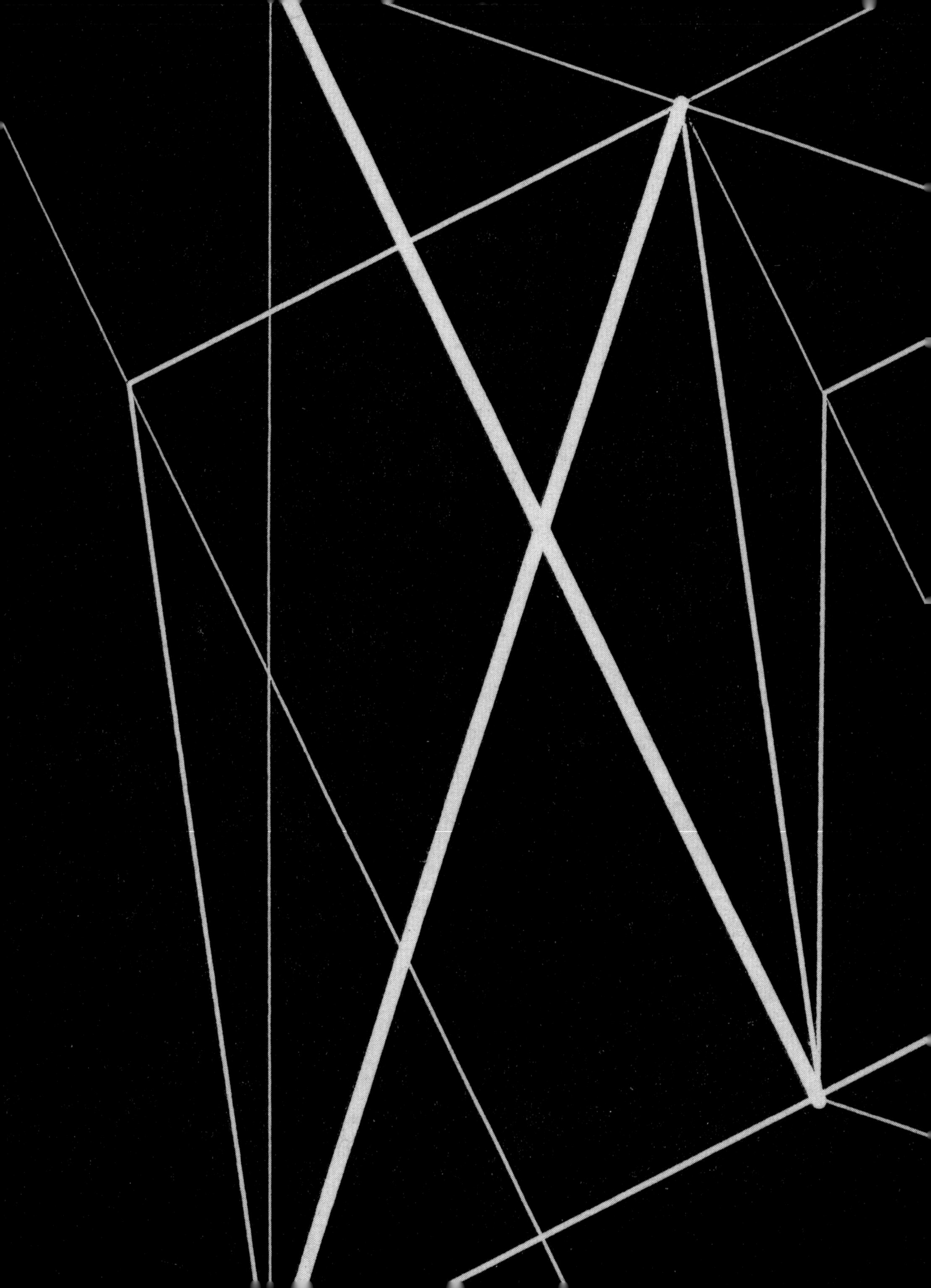

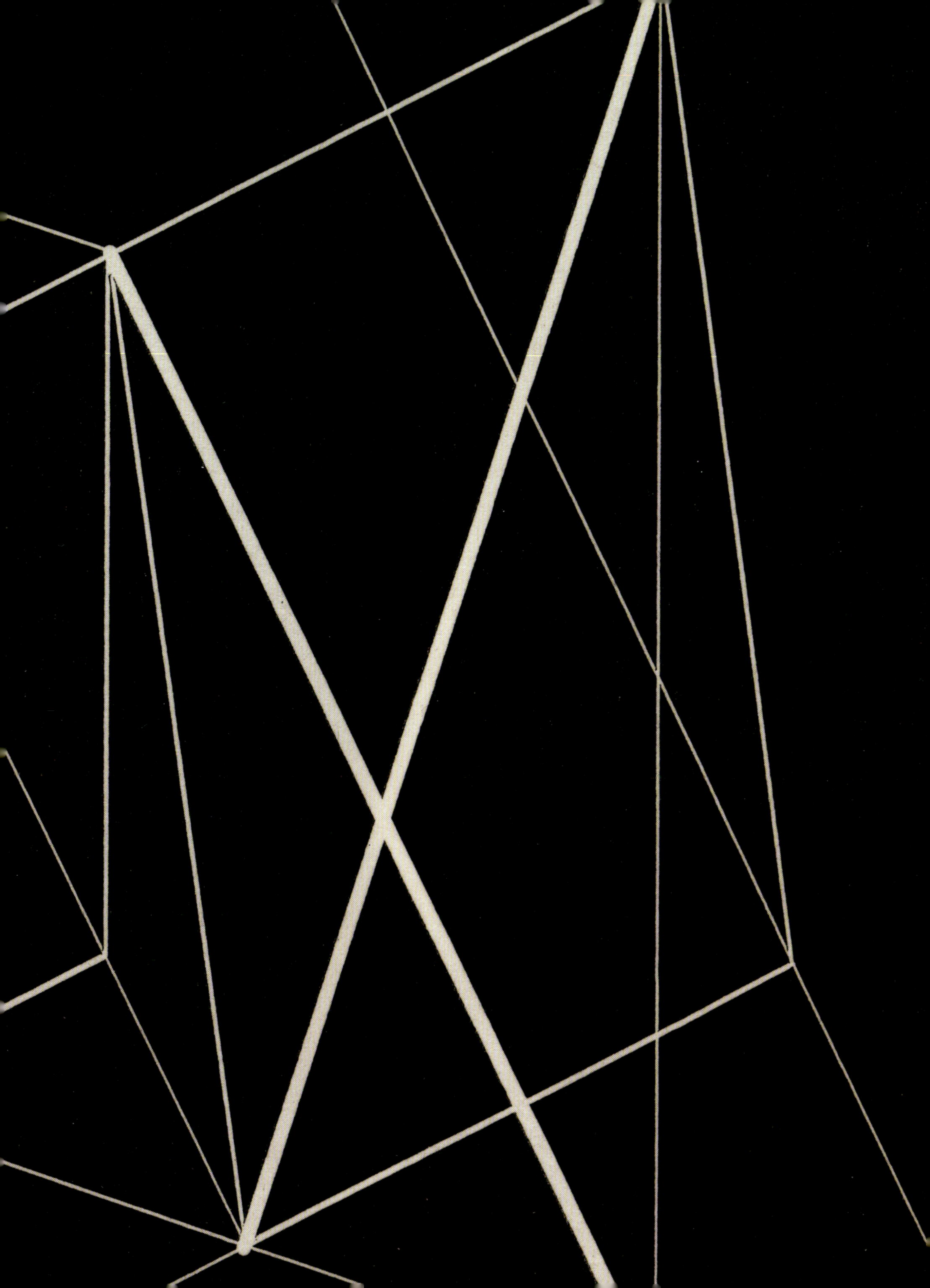

Artist's chronology

1888
On 19 March, Josef Albers is born in Bottrop in the industrializing Ruhr region of north-west Germany. His father, master craftsman Lorenz Albers, and his mother Magdalena, the daughter of a blacksmith, came from farming families in the forested hills of the Westphalian Sauerland.

1902–5
At the age of fourteen, Albers is enrolled in a preparatory school in nearby Langenhorst to begin training for a career as a schoolteacher.

1905–8
He continues his education at the Lehrerseminar in Büren and becomes certified as an elementary-school teacher.

1908–13
Albers teaches in rural and small-town schools in Dülmen and Stadtlohn, before returning to Bottrop to teach in the Josef Schule. He visits the Folkwang Museum in nearby Hagen and travels farther afield to museums in Munich. He encounters the works of Vincent van Gogh, Paul Gauguin, Edvard Munch, Henri Matisse, and Paul Cézanne, whom he especially admires. Albers sketches portraits of family and friends, and views of the Westphalian towns and countryside. A few of the latter are published in regional almanacs.

1913–15
Exempted from military service as a teacher, Albers enrolls at the Königliche Kunstschule (Royal School of Art) in Berlin, where he studies with Philipp Franck, and obtains his qualification as a high-school art teacher. Through visits to the museums and galleries of Berlin, he widens his knowledge of recent art and artists. He paints a series of brightly coloured still lifes in watercolour and tempera.

1916–18
Albers returns to the Ruhr region and elementary-school teaching. He attends evening printmaking classes with Wilhelm Pötter at the Handwerker und Kunstgewerbeschule (School of Crafts and Applied Arts) in Essen, and journeys to Düsseldorf and Duisburg to attend the theatre. He is especially inspired by Hugo von Hofmannsthal's operetta *The Green Flute* performed by a travelling company of the Deutsches Theater Berlin. In 1917, he is commissioned to create a window to commemorate fallen soldiers for St Michael Church in Bottrop, producing his first work in stained glass, *Rosa Mystica Ora Pro Nobis*.

1919
Albers moves to Munich to continue his artistic training at the Royal Bavarian Academy of Fine Arts. He studies with Franz von Stuck and creates numerous sketches in life-drawing sessions. As the denouement of the First World War leads to the economic disruptions of the German Revolution and short-lived Munich Soviet Republic, Albers's financial situation remains precarious.

1920
From a pamphlet announcing its founding, Albers learns of the Staatliches Bauhaus in Weimar, an art and design school founded by Walter Gropius in 1919 to create a synthesis of art and architecture. He moves to Weimar and enrolls in the Bauhaus, whose teachers include Paul Klee, Wassily Kandinsky, Lyonel Feininger, Johannes Itten, and Oskar Schlemmer.

1922–4
Albers rapidly graduates to working in the Bauhaus glass workshop and, with his previous experience as a teacher, is tapped by Gropius to teach the *Vorkurs*, or preliminary course, which he shares with László Moholy-Nagy. He receives major commissions for architectural stained glass.

1925
The Bauhaus moves from Weimar to the industrial city of Dessau. On 9 May, Albers marries Anneliese Fleischmann, a student in the Bauhaus weaving workshop. She adopts the name Anni Albers. Although the Bauhaus Dessau has no glass studio, Albers continues to produce flashed and sandblasted glass paintings with the Berlin firm of Puhl & Wagner, Gottfried Heinersdorff.

1926–7
While continuing his teaching, Albers designs large-scale windows for the newly built Grassi Museum of Applied Art in Leipzig and the Ullsteinhaus publishing works in Berlin. Using ready-made laboratory glass, he creates household tableware and designs a glass display typeface.

1928–9
Walter Gropius resigns from the Bauhaus, followed by Marcel Breuer and Moholy-Nagy. Josef and Anni Albers occupy one of the new Masters' Houses designed by Gropius in 1926. Swiss architect Hannes Meyer is appointed to head the school. In addition to his preliminary-course teaching, Albers heads the furniture workshop and, for a while, the wallpaper workshop. His work is included in a travelling exhibition organized by Hannes Meyer. He acquires his first camera – a Leica – and begins to photograph his surroundings and his colleagues.

1930–3
Hannes Meyer departs the Bauhaus and is replaced by Ludwig Mies van der Rohe. Albers exhibits his small-scale glass works at the Bauhaus, and in travelling exhibitions throughout Germany and Switzerland. The Nazi Party attains the majority in the local Dessau government and cuts off funding to the Bauhaus, which relocates to Berlin as a private school. In January 1933, Adolf Hitler is elected chancellor of Germany. Harassed by the Nazis, Mies van der Rohe and his colleagues decide to close the Bauhaus. In Berlin, Albers resumes his pre-Bauhaus printmaking, now with a new emphasis on formal elements. Anni works as a freelance textile designer.

On the recommendation of Philip Johnson, curator of architecture at the Museum of Modern Art in New York, Josef is invited to head the Art Department at Black Mountain College, a new liberal arts college in rural western North Carolina. Josef and Anni Albers accept the offer and arrive in New York on the SS *Europa* on 24 November 1933.

1934
Albers carries a full load of teaching at Black Mountain College and continues working on printmaking, primarily woodcuts and linoleum cuts. At the same time, he begins painting in oils. Anni, who had brought her loom from Berlin to the United States, organizes a new weaving workshop at the college. In December, invited by Cuban designer Clara Porset, the Alberses travel to Havana, where Josef's woodcuts are exhibited and where he gives three public lectures. An exhibition of his woodcuts, arranged by his Bauhaus student Xanti Schawinsky, opens at Galleria Il Milione in Milan, Italy.

1935
In December, the Alberses make the first of fourteen visits to Mexico, travelling first to Mexico City. After visiting the pre-Hispanic sites of Teotihuacán and Tenayuca, they travel on to Oaxaca, where they visit Mitla and Monte Albán.

1936
The Alberses spend the summer months in Mexico. Josef's prints are shown in an exhibition in the headquarters of the newspaper *El Nacional*. He begins a series of abstract line drawings and paintings that reflect the influence of pre-Hispanic architecture on his work. His first studies for *Tenayuca* develop into a series of drawings and paintings. Inspired by their travels to Mexico, Anni produces two large weavings, *Ancient Writing* and *Monte Alban*.

1937
Josef's paintings are included in the first exhibition of the American Abstract Artists group at Squibb Galleries in New York City. In February, Anni meets their former Bauhaus colleagues Walter and Ise Gropius, who are emigrating to the United States, at the docks in New York City. Josef and Anni again spend the summer in Mexico.

1938
Josef and Anni help the Gropiuses and Herbert Bayer assemble material for the Museum of Modern Art exhibition *Bauhaus 1919–1928*.

1939
Josef and Anni become American citizens. They again spend the summer months in Mexico. Josef produces a series of large lithographs *Alpha, Beta, Gamma, Delta* at Mexico City's legendary Taller de Gráfica Popular. As the political situation in Germany worsens, Anni's parents flee only a few months before the outbreak of the Second World War. They take a ship to Veracruz, Mexico, where they arrive on 22 June. Josef and Anni meet them at the port.

1940–1
The Alberses take a sabbatical leave from Black Mountain College and spend the summer in La Luz, New Mexico. In the autumn, they continue on to Mexico. In the spring of 1941, while teaching at Harvard University, Josef begins drawing studies for abstract geometrical compositions influenced by pre-Mexico's Hispanic architecture. He titles them *Graphic Tectonics*.

1942
Albers's *Graphic Tectonics* are printed as zinc-plate lithographs in Hickory, North Carolina, by Reinhard Schumann.

1943
Albers starts work on the *Biconjugate* and *Kinetic* series.

1944–5
Black Mountain College holds its first summer sessions that concentrate on both visual art and music. Visiting teachers invited include Robert Motherwell, Willem de Kooning, John Cage, Merce Cunningham, and R. Buckminster Fuller.

1946–7
In October, the Alberses embark on a year-long sabbatical from Black Mountain College. They travel by car across the United States before continuing on to Mexico. This is their first car journey since the start of the Second World War, when strict petrol rationing prevented long road trips. In New Mexico, Josef paints his first *Variants*, which evoke the domestic adobe architecture of Mexico.

1948
Albers is invited to serve on the Advisory Council of the School of the Arts, Yale University. His first postwar exhibition in Germany is held at the Galerie Herbert Herrmann in

Stuttgart, where his work is shown alongside that of Hans Arp and Max Bill. He makes his first engravings on plastic laminate.

1949
The Alberses resign from Black Mountain College in February and leave at the end of the school year in May. They travel to Mexico, where Josef teaches at the University of Mexico during the summer. On their return to the United States, he teaches at the Cincinnati Art Institute and at Pratt Institute in New York. In Cincinnati, he makes his first *Structural Constellations* engraving, using the new plastic laminate material Formica.

1950
Albers starts his *Homage to the Square* series of oil paintings in New York City. In January and February, he is visiting critic at the Yale University Art School and visiting professor at Harvard University's Graduate School of Design in the summer. In the autumn, he is appointed chair of the newly created Department of Design at Yale, and the Alberses move to New Haven. Josef designs the brick wall *America* above the fireplace in the new Harvard University Graduate Commons, designed by Walter Gropius. Anni designs textiles for the student dormitories.

1952
In February, Josef teaches in the architecture department of the University of Havana, Cuba. In the summer, the Alberses travel to Mexico, where they visit the Maya ruins in the Yucatán for the first time.

1953
Josef teaches a six-week course in the architecture department of the Pontificia Universidad Católica in Santiago, Chile, and lectures at the Institute of Technology in Lima, Peru. The Alberses travel widely in the two countries, which they are visiting for the first time. In December, Josef travels to Ulm, Germany, where he is visiting professor at the new Hochschule für Gestaltung.

1954
The Alberses travel to Hawaii in the summer. Josef teaches at the University of Honolulu. The exhibition *Josef and Anni Albers: Painting and Weaving* is held from 1 July to 2 August 1954 at the Honolulu Art Academy, where Josef gives the lecture 'Color: A Magic Power'.

1955
Albers returns to the Hochschule für Gestaltung in Ulm as visiting professor for the summer.

1956
The Yale University Art Gallery holds a retrospective exhibition of Albers's work curated by art historian George Heard Hamilton. Small screenprints of two *Homage to the Square* paintings, the first examples of Albers's use of this graphic medium, illustrate the catalogue.

1957
Albers has his first exhibition at Galerie Denise René in Paris.

1958
Albers, whose original six-year contract at Yale University was extended by two years in 1956, retires as head of the Department of Design at Yale but remains on as a visiting critic until 1960.

1959
Albers is awarded a Ford Foundation fellowship. His mural *Two Structural Constellations* is engraved in the lobby of the Corning Glass Building in Manhattan.

1961
Albers designs the mural *Two Portals* for the lobby of the Time and Life Building in Manhattan and a brick altar wall for St Patrick's Church, Oklahoma City.

1962
Albers is awarded a Graham Foundation fellowship and an honorary doctorate in fine arts from Yale University, one of the first of numerous honorary degrees he will receive over the next fourteen years. He is invited as visiting artist to the Tamarind Lithography Workshop in Los Angeles, where he creates the *Interlinear* stone lithograph series.

1963
Albers's monumental mural *Manhattan* is installed in the Pan Am Building in New York. *Repeat and Reverse,* a structural constellation sculpture in stainless steel, is installed over the entryway of Yale's newly completed Art and Architecture building, designed by the architect Paul Rudolph. The portfolio *Interaction of Color*, with text by Albers and eighty screenprinted plates, mostly by his students and based on his colour course, is published by Yale University Press.

1964
Albers is invited back to Tamarind as a fellow. He creates a series of eight colour lithographs, for the portfolio *Midnight and Noon*. The International Council of the Museum of Modern Art in New York organizes the exhibition *Josef Albers: Homage to the Square*. The exhibition opens in Caracas, Venezuela, in March 1964 and travels to museums throughout the Americas until January 1967.

1965
Albers gives a series of guest lectures at Trinity College, Hartford, Connecticut. The lectures are published as *Search Versus Re-Search* in 1969.

1967
Albers receives the Carnegie Institute award for painting at the Pittsburgh International Exhibition. His painted mural *Growth* and brick mural loggia wall are installed on the campus of the Rochester Institute of Technology.

1968
Albers receives the Grand Prix at the third Print Biennial (Bienal Americana de Grabado), Santiago, Chile, and the Grand Prix for painting from the State of Nordrhein-Westfalen, Germany. He is elected a member of the National Institute of Arts and Letters. The travelling exhibition *Albers*, organized by the Westfälisches Landesmuseum für Kunst und Kulturgeschichte in Münster, opens in April 1968 and travels in Europe until January 1970.

1970
The Alberses move from 8 North Forest Circle, New Haven, to 808 Birchwood Drive, Orange, Connecticut, a distance of three miles, so that Josef can have larger workspace. He is made an honorary citizen of his birthplace, Bottrop.

1971
Albers is the first living artist to have a retrospective exhibition at the Metropolitan Museum of Art, New York.

1972
Albers designs a steel structural constellation sculpture *Two Supraportas* for the facade of the Westfälisches Landesmuseum für Kunst and Kulturgeschichte. Other architectural works for this year are *Gemini*, a stainless-steel structural constellation relief for the lobby of the Grand Avenue National Bank in Kansas City, Missouri, and *Reclining Figure*, a mosaic mural for the Celanese Building at the Rockefeller Center, Manhattan (destroyed in 1980). *Formulation: Articulation*, a screenprint portfolio that reprises Josef's life's work, is published.

1973
Albers designs a free-standing outdoor sculptural wall for the campus of Stanford University. He receives the College Art Association's Distinguished Teaching Award.

1975
Albers receives the Fine Arts Medal of the American Institute of Architects.

1976
At the invitation of a former student, the architect Harry Seidler, Josef designs the structural constellation sculpture *Wrestling* for the outside elevation of Seidler's Mutual Life Center in Sydney, Australia.

Josef Albers dies on 25 March in New Haven, Connecticut. He is buried in Orange, Connecticut.

Works in the exhibition

p. 8
Self-Portrait 'Mephisto', 1916,
lithograph, monogrammed
in the plate and signed 'albers',
paper 34.9 × 26.7 cm (13¾ × 10½ in.),
image 21.3 × 5.1 cm (8⅜ × 2 in.).
Printed in a small edition,
exact size unknown. CR 1976.4.20

p. 46
Self-portrait, 1916,
linoleum cut, printed by the
artist and signed 'albers',
paper 46 × 29.5 cm (18⅛ × 11⅝ in.),
image 21.6 × 16.5 cm (8½ × 6½ in.).
Printed in a small edition,
exact size unknown. CR 1976.4.13a

p. 47
Self-portrait, 1916,
linoleum cut, printed by the
artist and signed 'albers',
paper 32.4 × 25.1 cm (12¾ × 9⅞ in.),
image 18.4 × 10.8 cm (7¼ × 4¼ in.).
Printed in a small edition,
exact size unknown. CR 1976.4.17b

p. 48
Eigentum von Aloys Wegener
(Property of Aloys Wegener), 1916,
lithograph on stone on
various wove and laid sheets,
monogrammed in the stone,
paper 20 × 14 cm (7⅞ × 5½ in.),
image 13.3 × 9.5 cm (5¼ × 3¾ in.).
Printed in a small edition,
exact size unknown. CR 1976.4.2

p. 49
In the Cathedral:
Small Middle Nave, 1916,
linoleum cut, signed 'albers',
paper 47 × 29.5 cm (18½ × 11⅝ in.),
image 16.8 × 14.3 cm (6⅝ × 5⅝ in.).
Printed in a small edition,
exact size unknown. CR 1976.4.9b

p. 54
Sandgrube I (Sandmine I), 1916,
linoleum cut, printed by the
artist and signed 'albers' and titled,
paper 35.2 × 30.2 cm (13⅞ × 11⅞ in.),
image 30.2 × 23.8 cm (11⅞ × 9⅜ in.).
Printed in a small edition,
exact size unknown. CR 1976.4.4

p. 55
Sandgrube III (Sandmine III), 1916,
linoleum cut, printed by the
artist and signed 'albers' and titled,
paper 45.1 × 33.7 cm (17¾ × 13¼ in.),
image 26.7 × 21 cm (10½ × 8¼ in.).
Printed in a small edition,
exact size unknown. CR 1976.4.6

p. 56
Sandgrube II (Sandmine II), state I, 1916,
linoleum cut, printed by the
artist and signed 'albers' and titled,
paper 26.4 × 28.6 cm (10⅜ × 11¼ in.),
image 23.5 × 26 cm (9¼ × 10¼ in.).
Printed in a small edition,
exact size unknown. CR 1976.4.5a

p. 57
Sandgrube II (Sandmine II), state II, 1916,
linoleum cut, printed by the
artist and signed 'albers' and titled,
paper 26.4 × 28.6 cm (10⅜ × 11¼ in.),
image 23.5 × 26 cm (9¼ × 10¼ in.).
Printed in a small edition,
exact size unknown. CR 1976.4.5b

p. 58
Girl, 1916,
lithograph on stone
with crayon and tusche,
monogrammed in the
stone and signed 'albers',
paper 42.5 × 30.5 cm (16¾ × 12 in.),
image 24.8 × 23.2 cm (9¾ × 9⅛ in.).
Printed in a small edition,
exact size unknown. CR 1976.4.28

p. 59
Portrait of Aloys Bürger, 1916,
transfer lithograph, monogrammed
and signed 'albers', paper
33.7 × 32.7 cm (13¼ × 12⅞ in.),
image 29.5 × 27.6 cm (11⅝ × 10⅞ in.).
Printed in a small edition,
exact size unknown. CR 1976.4.29

p. 61 top
Rabbit, 1916,
transfer lithograph, monogrammed
in the plate and signed 'albers',
paper 27.3 × 33 cm (10¾ × 13 in.),
image 13.3 × 21 cm (5¼ × 8¼ in.).
Printed in a small edition,
exact size unknown. CR 1976.4.24

p. 61 bottom
Rabbit, 1916,
transfer lithograph, monogrammed
in the plate and signed 'albers',
paper 26.4 × 31.4 cm (10⅜ × 12⅜ in.),
image 14 × 20.3 cm (5½ × 8 in.).
Printed in a small edition,
exact size unknown. CR 1976.4.25

p. 63 top
Frightened Pair from a Fairy Tale II, 1917,
lithograph and tusche, monogrammed
and signed 'albers', paper
34.8 × 49.5 cm (13¹¹⁄₁₆ × 19½ in.),
image 19 × 25.4 cm (7½ × 10 in.).
Printed in a small edition,
exact size unknown. CR 1976.4.39

p. 63 bottom
Standing figure, 1917,
transfer lithograph, signed 'albers',
paper 31.8 × 21.6 cm (12½ × 8½ in.),
image 15.6 × 7.6 cm (6⅛ × 3 in.).
Printed in a small edition,
exact size unknown. CR 1976.4.32

p. 70
Schwarzer Kreis (Black Circle), 1933,
woodcut, signed and dated 'Albers 33' and titled 'Schwarzer Kreis',
paper 35.6 × 50.2 cm (14 × 19¾ in.),
image 25.9 × 35.6 cm (10³⁄₁₆ × 14 in.).
Unnumbered, probably edition of 20.
CR 1976.4.59

p. 71
Weisser Kreis (White Circle), 1933,
woodcut, printed under the supervision of the artist, signed and dated 'Albers 33' and titled 'Weisser Kreis',
paper 35.6 × 50.2 cm (14 × 19¾ in.),
image 27.9 × 35.6 cm (11 × 14 in.).
Unnumbered, edition of 20 or 25.
CR 1976.4.60

p. 72
Östlich (Easterly), 1933,
cork relief, printed under the supervision of the artist, signed and dated 'Albers 33' and titled 'Östlich',
paper 35.6 × 50.5 cm (14 × 19⅞ in.),
image 21.6 × 31.1 cm (8½ × 12¼ in.).
Unnumbered, probably edition of 20.
CR 1976.4.66

p. 73
Umgeben (Surrounded), 1933,
linoleum cut, signed and dated 'Albers 33' and titled 'Umgeben',
paper 35.6 × 50.6 cm (14 × 20 in.),
image 19 × 25 cm (7½ × 9⅞ in.).
Unnumbered, probably edition of 20.
CR 1976.4.67

p. 74
Meer (Sea), 1933,
woodcut, printed under the supervision of the artist, signed and dated 'Albers 33' and titled 'Meer',
paper 35.6 × 44.8 cm (14 × 17⅝ in.),
image 19.7 × 32.4 cm (7¾ × 12¾ in.).
Unnumbered, edition of 20 or 25.
CR 1976.4.61

p. 75
Umschlüngen (Encircled), 1933,
woodcut, printed under the supervision of the artist, signed and dated 'Albers 33' and titled 'Umschlüngen',
paper 34.9 × 50.9 cm (13¾ × 20¹⁄₁₆ in.),
image 24.1 × 34.3 cm (9½ × 13½ in.).
Unnumbered, probably edition of 20.
CR 1976.4.62

p. 78
Oper (Opera), 1933,
woodcut, printed under the supervision of the artist, signed and dated 'Albers 33' and titled 'Oper',
paper 32.4 × 44.8 cm (12¾ × 17⅝ in.),
image 24.1 × 29.2 cm (9½ × 11½ in.).
Unnumbered, probably edition of 20.
CR 1976.4.64

p. 79
Zelte (Tents), 1933,
woodcut, printed under the supervision of the artist, signed and dated 'Albers 33' and titled 'Zelte',
paper 35.6 × 49.2 cm (14 × 19⅜ in.),
image 23 × 25.5 cm (9¹⁄₁₆ × 10¹⁄₁₆ in.).
Unnumbered, probably edition of 20.
CR 1976.4.65

p. 80
Ründe (Circle), 1933,
woodcut, signed and dated 'Albers 33' and titled 'Ründe',
paper 34.9 × 46.4 cm (13¾ × 18¼ in.),
image 26 × 27.9 cm (10¼ × 11 in.).
Unnumbered, probably edition of 20.
CR 1976.4.68

p. 81
Elefant (Elephant), 1933,
linoleum cut, signed 'Albers' and titled 'Elefant',
paper 35.6 × 50.5 cm (14 × 19⅞ in.),
image 20.3 × 20.3 cm (8 × 8 in.).
Edition of 10. CR 1976.4.69

p. 82
Gegenüber (Opposite), 1933,
linoleum cut, signed and dated 'Albers 33' and titled 'Gegenüber',
paper 34.9 × 44.5 cm (13¾ × 17⁹⁄₁₆ in.),
image 25.4 × 25.4 cm (10 × 10 in.).
Unnumbered, probably edition of 20.
CR 1976.4.70

p. 83
Zusammen (Together), 1933,
linoleum cut, signed and dated 'Albers 33' and titled 'Zusammen',
paper 33.6 × 43.2 cm (13¾ × 17 in.),
image 21.6 × 22.5 cm (8½ × 8⅞ in.).
Unnumbered, probably edition of 20.
CR 1976.4.71

p. 85
Placards, 1934,
linoleum cut, signed and dated 'Albers 34' and titled 'Placards' and numbered,
paper 40.6 × 26.7 cm (16 × 10½ in.),
image 29.2 × 22.2 cm (11½ × 8¾ in.).
Edition of 20. CR 1976.4.78

p. 86
Edged I, 1934,
woodcut, signed and dated 'Albers 34' and titled 'Edged I',
paper 26.7 × 41.3 cm (10½ × 16¼ in.),
image 22.2 × 31.8 cm (8¾ × 12½ in.).
Edition of 14. CR 1976.4.75

p. 87
Edged II, 1934,
woodcut, signed and dated 'Albers 34' and titled 'Edged II',
paper 26.7 × 41.3 cm (10½ × 16¼ in.),
image 22.2 × 31.8 cm (8¾ × 12½ in.).
Edition of 12. CR 1976.4.76

p. 88
i, 1934,
linoleum cut on laid and Hazelbourne Deckle Edge Book paper, signed and dated 'Albers 34', titled and numbered,
paper 35.3 × 38.1 cm (13⅞ × 15 in.),
image 20.3 × 27.9 cm (8 × 11 in.).
Edition of 20. CR 1976.4.77b

p. 89
Wings, 1934,
woodcut, signed and dated 'Albers 34', titled and numbered,
paper 26.7 × 41.6 cm (10½ × 16⅜ in.),
image 18.4 × 31.1 cm (7¼ × 12¼ in.).
Edition of 25. CR 1976.4.81

p. 90
Show Case, 1934,
linoleum cut, signed and dated 'Albers 34', titled and numbered,
paper 38.1 × 35.6 cm (15 × 14 in.),
image 27.3 × 23.8 cm (10¾ × 9⅜ in.).
Edition of 20. CR 1976.4.82

p. 91
Segments, 1934,
linoleum cut, signed and dated 'Albers 34', titled and numbered,
paper 35.2 × 40.6 cm (13⅞ × 16 in.),
image 24.1 × 28.3 cm (9½ × 11⅛ in.).
Edition of 20 and an edition of 25.
CR 1976.4.79

p. 98
Alpha, from *Mexican Lithographs*, 1939, lithograph on heavy wove Marquesa paper, signed and dated 'Albers 39', titled and numbered, paper 64.8 × 50.2 cm (25½ × 19¾ in.), image 36.2 × 30.5 cm (14¼ × 12 in.). Edition of 25. CR 1976.4.83

p. 99
Beta, from *Mexican Lithographs*, 1939, lithograph on heavy wove Marquesa paper, signed and dated 'Albers 39', titled and numbered, paper 50.2 × 64.8 cm (19¾ × 25½ in.), image 27.1 × 38.7 cm (10¾ × 15¼ in.). Edition of 25. CR 1976.4.84

p. 100
Gamma, from *Mexican Lithographs*, 1939, lithograph on heavy wove Marquesa paper, signed and dated 'Albers 39', titled and numbered, paper 50.2 × 64.8 cm (19¾ × 25½ in.), image 31.1 × 35.6 cm (12¼ × 14 in.). Edition of 25. CR 1976.4.85

p. 101
Delta, from *Mexican Lithographs*, 1939, lithograph on heavy wove Marquesa paper, signed and dated 'Albers 39', titled and numbered, paper 64.8 × 50.2 cm (25½ × 19¾ in.), image 35.6 × 34.5 cm (14 × 13½ in.). Edition of 30. CR 1976.4.86

p. 103
Eh-De, 1940, drypoint on heavy wove, signed and dated 'Albers 40', titled and numbered, paper 22.9 × 27.9 cm (9 × 11 in.), image 14 × 20.3 cm (5½ × 8 in.). Edition of 20. CR 1976.4.88

p. 104
Concerned, 1940, drypoint on heavy wove, signed and dated 'Albers 40', titled and numbered, paper 27.9 × 22.5 cm (11 × 8⅞ in.), image 20.3 × 14 cm (8 × 5½ in.). Edition of 20. CR 1976.4.87

p. 105
Rondo, 1942, drypoint, signed and dated 'Albers 42', titled and numbered, paper 28.6 × 22.2 cm (11¼ × 8¾ in.), image 20.3 × 14 cm (8 × 5½ in.). Edition of 20. CR 1976.4.97

p. 106
Nippon A, 1942, drypoint, signed and dated 'Albers 42', titled and numbered, paper 22 × 29.5 cm (8⅝ × 11⅝ in.), image 14 × 20.3 cm (5½ × 8 in.). Unnumbered proof from an edition of 20. CR 1976.4.98

p. 107
Nippon B, 1942, drypoint, signed and dated 'Albers 42', titled and numbered, paper 22 × 29.5 cm (8⅝ × 11⅝ in.), image 14 × 20.3 cm (5½ × 8 in.). Edition of 20. CR 1976.4.99

p. 110
Escape, 1942, drypoint on heavy wove, signed and dated 'Albers 42', titled and numbered, paper 20 × 26 cm (7⅞ × 10¼ in.), image 14 × 20.3 cm (5½ × 8 in.). Edition of 20. CR 1976.4.92

p. 111
Variants, 1942, drypoint, signed and dated 'Albers 42', titled and numbered, paper 21 × 27.3 cm (8¼ × 10¾ in.), image 15.3 × 22.5 cm (6 × 8⅞ in.). Edition of 20. CR 1976.4.93

p. 113
Introitus (unnumbered proof), 1942, zinc-plate lithograph, signed and dated 'Albers 42', titled, paper 61 × 48.3 cm (24 × 19 in.), image 35.6 × 17.8 cm (14 × 7 in.). Unnumbered proof from an edition of 30. CR 1976.4.102

p. 114
Introitus, 1942, zinc-plate lithograph, signed and dated 'Albers 42', titled and numbered, paper 61 × 48.3 cm (24 × 19 in.), image 35.6 × 17.8 cm (14 × 7 in.). Edition of 30. CR 1976.4.102

p. 116
Prefatio, 1942, zinc-plate lithograph, signed and dated 'Albers 42', titled and numbered, paper 48.3 × 61 cm (19 × 24 in.), image 29.8 × 40 cm (11¾ × 15¾ in.). Edition of 30. CR 1976.4.103

p. 117
Shrine, 1942, zinc-plate lithograph, signed and dated 'Albers 42', titled and numbered, paper 61 × 48.3 cm (24 × 19 in.), image 33 × 31.4 cm (13 × 12⅜ in.). Edition of 30. CR 1976.4.106

p. 118
Seclusion (unnumbered proof), 1942, zinc-plate lithograph, signed and dated 'Albers 42', titled and numbered, paper 48.3 × 61 cm (19 × 24 in.), image 30.5 × 31.7 cm (12 × 12½ in.). Unnumbered proof from an edition of 30. CR 1976.4.105

p. 119
Seclusion, 1942, zinc-plate lithograph, signed and dated 'Albers 42', titled and numbered, paper 48.3 × 61 cm (19 × 24 in.), image 30.5 × 31.7 cm (12 × 12½ in.). Edition of 30. CR 1976.4.105

p. 120
Interim, 1942, zinc-plate lithograph, signed and dated 'Albers 42', titled and numbered, paper 48.3 × 61 cm (19 × 24 in.), image 19.4 × 38.7 cm (7⅝ × 15¼ in.). Edition of 30. CR 1976.4.101

p. 121
Sanctuary, 1942, zinc-plate lithograph, signed and dated 'Albers 42', titled and numbered, paper 48.3 × 61 cm (19 × 24 in.), image 22 × 40 cm (8⅝ × 15¾ in.). Edition of 30. CR 1976.4.104

p. 122
To Monte Alban, 1942, zinc-plate lithograph, signed and dated 'Albers 42', titled and numbered, paper 61 × 48.3 cm (24 × 19 in.), image 33.7 × 26.7 cm (13¼ × 10½ in.). Edition of 30. CR 1976.4.107

p. 125
Adjusted, 1944,
woodcut, signed and dated
'Albers 44', titled and numbered,
paper 34.6 × 40.6 cm (13⅝ × 16 in.),
image 23.8 × 29.8 cm (9⅜ × 11¾ in.).
Edition of 25. CR 1976.4.111

p. 126
Adapted, 1944,
woodcut, signed and dated
'Albers 44', titled and numbered,
paper 31.8 × 40.3 cm (12½ × 15⅞ in.),
image 21.6 × 24.4 cm (8½ × 9⅝ in.).
Edition of 25. CR 1976.4.109

p. 127
Adapted B, 1944,
woodcut, signed and dated
'Albers 44', titled and numbered,
paper 33 × 38 cm (13 × 15 in.),
image 23.8 × 29.8 cm (9⅜ × 11¾ in.).
Edition of 15. CR 1976.4.110

p. 128
Involute, 1944,
cork relief, signed and dated
'Albers 44', titled and numbered,
paper 28.9 × 45.1 cm (11⅜ × 17¾ in.),
image 24.1 × 31.8 cm (9½ × 12½ in.).
Edition of 25. CR 1976.4.115

p. 129
Inscribed, 1944,
cork relief, signed and dated
'Albers 44', titled and numbered,
paper 30.5 × 39.4 cm (12 × 15½ in.),
image 22.2 × 28.6 cm (8¾ × 11¼ in.).
Edition of 25. CR 1976.4.114

p. 130
Contra, 1944,
linoleum cut, signed and dated
'Albers 44', titled and numbered,
paper 33 × 38 cm (13 × 15 in.),
image 23.5 × 33.3 cm (9¼ × 13⅛ in.).
Edition of 25. CR 1976.4.112

p. 131
Fenced, 1944,
woodcut, signed and dated
'Albers 44', titled and numbered,
paper 31.8 × 40.6 cm (12½ × 16 in.),
image 25.4 × 31.1 cm (10 × 12¼ in.).
Edition of 30. CR 1976.4.113

p. 132
Astatic, 1944,
woodcut from plywood,
signed and dated 'Albers 44',
titled and numbered,
paper 44.5 × 28.3 cm (17½ × 11⅛ in.),
image 33.6 × 22.9 cm (13¼ × 9 in.).
Edition of 35. CR 1976.4.116

p. 133
Tlaloc, 1944,
woodcut in rough pine board,
signed and dated 'Albers 44',
titled and numbered,
paper 38.1 × 36.8 cm (15 × 14½ in.),
image 30.5 × 31.8 cm (12 × 12½ in.).
Edition of 35. CR 1976.4.118

p. 135
Multiplex C, 1948,
woodcut, signed and dated
'Albers 48', titled and numbered,
paper 40.6 × 29.2 cm (16 × 11½ in.),
image 30.5 × 20.3 cm (12 × 8 in.).
Edition of 30. CR 1976.4.122

p. 136
Multiplex B, 1948,
woodcut, signed and dated
'Albers 48', titled and numbered,
paper 41.9 × 31.8 cm (16½ × 12½ in.),
image 30.5 × 20.3 cm (12 × 8 in.).
Edition of 30. CR 1976.4.121

p. 137
High Up, 1948,
woodcut, signed and dated
'Albers 48', titled and numbered,
paper 27.9 × 39.4 cm (11 × 15½ in.),
image 20.3 × 24.1 cm (8 × 9½ in.).
Edition of 10. CR 1976.4.124

p. 140
Transformation A, 1950,
engraving from machine-engraved
brass plate, signed and dated
'Albers 50', titled and numbered,
paper 27.9 × 39.4 cm (11 × 15½ in.),
image 18.1 × 24 cm (7⅛ × 9⁷⁄₁₆ in.).
Edition of 20. CR 1976.4.125

p. 141
Transformation B, 1950,
engraving from machine-engraved
brass plate, signed and dated
'Albers 50', titled and numbered,
paper 30.5 × 39.4 cm (12 × 15½ in.),
image 18.1 × 24 cm (7⅛ × 9⁷⁄₁₆ in.).
Edition of 20. CR 1976.4.126

p. 142
Transformation C, 1950,
engraving from machine-engraved
brass plate, signed and dated
'Albers 50', titled and numbered,
paper 30.5 × 39.4 cm (12 × 15½ in.),
image 18.1 × 24 cm (7⅛ × 9⁷⁄₁₆ in.).
Edition of 20. CR 1976.4.127

p. 143
Transformation D, 1950,
engraving from machine-engraved
brass plate, signed and dated
'Albers 50', titled and numbered,
paper 27.9 × 39.4 cm (11 × 15½ in.),
image 18.1 × 24 cm (7⅛ × 9⁷⁄₁₆ in.).
Edition of 20. CR 1976.4.128

Acknowledgments and credits

Cristea Roberts Gallery would like to thank the Josef and Anni Albers Foundation for its assistance and collaboration on the publication, particularly Nicholas Fox Weber, Brenda Danilowitz, Jeannette Redensek, Amy Jean Porter, and Samuel McCune.

All photography of artworks by Josef Albers by Tim Nighswander/Imaging4Art except:

Anna Arca
pp. 8, 10–11, 46, 47, 49, 56, 57, 58, 59, 61, 63, 70, 71, 72, 73, 74, 75, 78, 79, 80, 81, 82, 83, 86, 87, 89, 90, 99, 103, 104, 105, 110, 111, 113, 117, 118, 119, 120, 121, 122, 129, 130, 131, 132, 133, 137

Pete Braithwaite, Todd-White Art Photography
pp. 36–7, 50, 55, 88, 100, 101, 116, 125, 126, 128, 136, 142, 146–7